PVF

Miranda Innes is a rolli
inconvenient curiosity about

She and her long-suffering
Pearce, have lived for seven   years among the
olive and almond trees on a rocky hillside in Andalucia.
But other lives, other places beckon . . .

Getting to Mañana, the account of Miranda's life-
changing move to Spain, is also available as a Black Swan
paperback.

You can visit Miranda and Dan on their website:
<u>www.marocandalucia.co.uk</u>

www.**booksattransworld**.co.uk

Also by Miranda Innes

GETTING TO MAÑANA

and published by Black Swan

Miranda Innes

CINNAMON CITY

BLACK SWAN

CINNAMON CITY
A BLACK SWAN BOOK : 0 552 77286 0

PRINTING HISTORY
Originally published in Great Britain by Bantam Press,
a division of Transworld Publishers

PRINTING HISTORY
Bantam Press edition published 2005
Black Swan edition published 2005

1 3 5 7 9 10 8 6 4 2

Set in 11/14pt Melior by
Falcon Oast Graphic Art Ltd.

Black Swan Books are published by Transworld Publishers,
61–63 Uxbridge Road, London W5 5SA,
a division of The Random House Group Ltd,
in Australia by Random House Australia (Pty) Ltd,
20 Alfred Street, Milsons Point, Sydney, NSW 2061, Australia,
in New Zealand by Random House New Zealand Ltd,
18 Poland Road, Glenfield, Auckland 10, New Zealand
and in South Africa by Random House (Pty) Ltd,
Isle of Houghton, Corner Boundary Road & Carse O'Gowrie,
Houghton 2198, South Africa.

Printed and bound in Great Britain by
Cox & Wyman Ltd, Reading, Berkshire

Papers used by Transworld Publishers are natural, recyclable
products made from wood grown in sustainable forests. The
manufacturing processes conform to the environmental
regulations of the country of origin

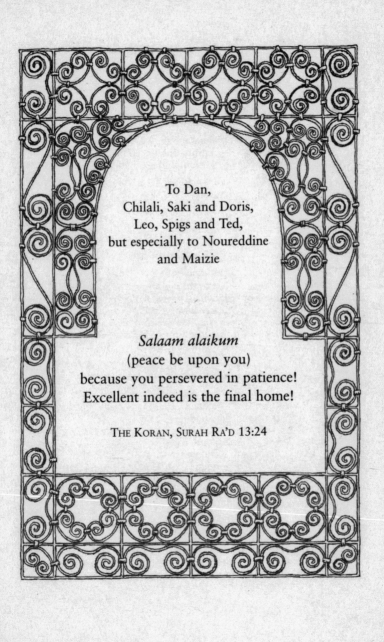

To Dan,
Chilali, Saki and Doris,
Leo, Spigs and Ted,
but especially to Noureddine
and Maizie

Salaam alaikum
(peace be upon you)
because you persevered in patience!
Excellent indeed is the final home!

THE KORAN, SURAH RA'D 13:24

1

INTO AFRICA

When I was just the wrong side of fifty and my two sons grown up, I awoke one day from a twenty-year slumber, stopped being a responsible single parent, ditched my London job and skipped the country. I moved to Spain, and took up residence in a decomposing Andalusian finca in the mountains with a brave and impecunious painter whom I hardly knew, Dan Pearce, whose main attraction was a talent for Scrabble. I have never regretted it, though I can see that it might have gone badly wrong.

Because life is so unspeakably random, I am always pleased when something happens neatly. When everything seemed scarily unpredictable, I derived superstitious comfort from the fact that it was the portentous year 2000 which slammed the door on whole chunks of my life and found me surfing the crest of newness, skimming unfamiliar waters with a smile on my face. The tired, passé, so last-millennium things that I jettisoned were journalism, Islington house, parental responsibilities and the UK.

The brave new things that took their place were Dan; the decision to survive by writing what I wanted to write as opposed to more books about cushions; two hundred newly planted olive trees and a readiness for adventure. Parts of our Spanish house were sort of habitable after three years of sporadic restoration – dependent on rare gobbets of money – still involving public private functions, unpredictable water and electricity, and cohabiting chummily with never fewer than four builders. By April 2000 a long cold winter had just drizzled to its end.

April in the south of Spain is like the Hallmark birthday card you send your granny – roadside and knobbly hilltops are washed with pink, mauve, purple and blue flowers: sweet sultan, columbine, morning glory, scruffy and fragrant wild mignonette, rock roses, lavender, phlomis, gladioli, the whole ensemble sequinned with white daisies and scarlet poppies. You couldn't do it better if you tried. The skies settle to forget-me-not blue; sun caresses pale skin; warm evenings thick with lemon blossom invite a dreamy stupor, sitting with glass in hand by the fountain to watch the moon roll huge and solemn up the contours of the hill.

So there had to be a strong inducement to prise us away from Spain in April. In 2000 it was Maggie. I had known Maggie and her photographer husband for many years – he was my trump card when I was Garden Editor at *Country Living*, with an astounding ability to make a turnip patch look gorgeous, and gorgeous gardens look like Paradise.

She rang one lunchtime with an idea that sent Dan into a fizz of excitement – she wanted to explore Marrakech with a view to buying a property, and she thought we might like to accompany her. Well, drive her, in fact, as she did not drive.

Our trip happened to coincide with Dan's birthday. His is the youngest star sign, Aries: bored in a blink, with a craving for novelty. By 2000 we had survived three years on our building site in the south of Spain together – intermittently, since I had been commuting to work in London every month – and it did seem like a good time to celebrate with an adventure. We had nothing serious in mind, just an Easter whim engendered by Maggie's conviction that there could be nothing we'd rather do. Maggie had decided to buy a riad, she needed a driver and a bodyguard, and we just wanted to have a laugh, a change of scene, a short absence from dogs and builders.

Maggie had fallen under the spell of Marrakech as

a young woman, staying at a riad owned by a sophisticated friend who had introduced her to the seductions of the city – languorous evenings on sun-warmed rooftops listening to the muezzin, eating gargantuan feasts of intriguingly spicy, unexpectedly sweet combinations of meat and fruit; shuffling bemused along dark alleys gleaming with polished-brass and jewelled merchandise; riding across the shimmering desert with the blue men whose indigo turbans sent dark rivulets down their faces; summoning Berber musicians like magic, with a snap of the fingers, to sing their rapture to the jasmine-scented night air. Several decades earlier she had wandered into this exotic world, and the tiny seed of an idea had settled, one day to find a corner in which to put down roots.

Now, on a drizzly day three decades later, Maggie arrived in a taxi, and was extremely good-humoured about the frieze of muddy footprints with which our convivial boxers, Oscar and Minnie, decorated her chic city black suit. We spent the evening giggling and packing – she had precise instructions for suitable clothing which involved being covered from head to toe at all times. I did what I could, though I have always had an aversion to the nun-like.

The next morning we scrambled – Maggie with a flicker of last-minute reluctance – into Dan's ancient, sticky Citroën van, and set off for Africa,

12

dropping the dogs off at the kennels on the way.

Three hours and a dizzying mixture of diesel and tobacco smoke later — Maggie was an extreme smoker — we were in Algeciras. Two and a half hours on a rusting ferry and we were in Africa. It was just like Channel crossings of yore, but sunny, and cost a mere £160 to transport the three of us and the old Citroën C15 van to another world altogether.

I was born in Africa (Pisces, the oldest star sign, and I felt it) – in Cairo, and had returned there on a visit with my mother and sister ten years earlier. I loved Egypt; it felt like home, familiar, even the hot dust and sand smelled right. I'm convinced that your very first breaths imprint an indelible memory of how things should be, upon which all subsequent experience is layered. I loved the Egyptians, their canniness, the way they danced rings round bemused tourists, their wit and humour and cleverness, their gentleness and warmth. I loved the heat, the sand, the dryness of the air. I was thrilled by deserts and riding camels.

Listening to melodic keening by a camel-dung fire beneath a spatter of stars was my idea of heaven. I had done that one autumn in the sand dunes of the Thar desert in northwest India. The shuffle of the camels' feet in the sand returning home by moonlight, their passion for eating very prickly things and dragging their unwilling riders through them, the lurching mechanics of mounting and dismounting

13

– I loved all that. So I felt I was slightly familiar with the world we were about to enter.

Actually, to be uncomfortably honest, I had come to Morocco before. Aged thirty-four I had come on a Club 18–30 holiday with a colleague, because it was so cheap. She had promised that we would peel off from the drinkers and fornicators and dredge our way through cultural things. She fibbed, and I ended up sharing our hotel room with both Barbara and an Essex central-heating engineer called Justin. Barbara also talked to me very loudly and slowly as though I was deaf and senile, in order to demonstrate – in the unlikely event that anyone was interested – that I was well past my bonk-by date. The experience had not led to a love-match between me and Morocco. I wasn't quite so matey with Barbara afterwards either.

But Dan had never been further south than Malaga and was beside himself with excitement. 'We're going to Africa. Africa. Africa on my birthday,' he kept saying, awed, his eyes sparkling. From time to time just 'Africa,' with a blissful sigh. It made up for his half-century birthday the previous year, spent in a stifling office next to a motorway, trying to fathom the Internet at my behest to apply for a job that I didn't get.

The Romans made their way to Morocco in AD 39, and, denigrating the indigenous population as barbarians – eventually corrupted to Berbers, though they prefer to be called Amazigh, free men – set about building colonies and pillaging the place for medicinal herbs, slaves, elephants, ivory, deer, horses and grain, which they continued to do until the Vandals and Goths took over in the fifth century and the Arabs in the seventh.

Let me tell you that if you come to Africa via the docks in Tangier, you may want to turn right round and head home. You will have a baptism by baksheesh that will make your head spin, empty your pockets of currency and fill you with indignation. First there is the passport baksheesh man, who snatches those vital documents and disappears. Then there is the car-papers-and-green-card baksheesh man, who takes all your car papers and makes off somewhere different. Finally there are the men who chivvy the other two. Having divested you of everything that identifies you in the world and taken their time, all of them require payment before they will return your documents. It is a bad start, and apt to instil panic in the unwary.

Dan was unwilling to tackle the many-headed money-grabbing hydra. Rescuing papers and getting free of the port and all the baksheesh boys came to something like three hundred dirhams, which of course we did not have since you cannot obtain dirhams abroad. So we handed over all our pesetas and pounds, thereby leaving ourselves with nothing. But I have to say that this is the nadir. From here on it gets better. And if you travel by plane, there is no problem at all.

Having extricated ourselves, we plunged into the seedy hinterland of Tangier. The city looked like jetsam washed up on a beach after a storm, encrusted with bleak office buildings and punctuated by spindly palms. *Priorité à droite* took a bit of getting used to, as did the suicidal tactics of pedestrians, and extended families piled on to mopeds like Chinese acrobats. Despite the air of life-threatening busyness, however, there were herds of goats grazing peacefully among the begonias in a public park. We ate leathery kebabs in a seafront restaurant, watching boys and camels playing on the huge wide beach, with a tasteful Rothko background of a faded denim sea blending into a forget-me-not sky.

After lunch we headed for Rabat, our stop for the night. Rabat El Fatah – Camp of Victory – was built to celebrate the defeat in 1195 of three Christian kings in Spain by El Mansour the Victorious, a mate of Saladin and an ally against Richard Coeur de Lion. He made his mark with the proceeds, building the Hassan tower in Rabat, the Giralda in Seville and the Koutoubia, towards which we were eventually heading, in Marrakech. You might make the mistake of thinking, as I did, that El Mansour had a startling life span of four hundred years – by extraordinary coincidence there was El Mansour

(Yacoub) the Victorious in the twelfth century, followed by El Mansour (Ahmed) aka El Dehbi the Victorious and Golden in the sixteenth century, who was also victorious at a battle of three kings, was a friend of Queen Elizabeth the First, and embarked on an audacious building programme which included the El Badi palace, whose construction took sixteen years and of which more later. There appears to be very little choice of names among Muslims – nicknames are essential to differentiate between the twelve Mohammeds and eight Fatimas of close acquaintance.

We drove southwest, parallel to the coast, on straight roads through miles of gently undulating open fields, bordered to the north by sand dunes. Occasionally there would be a cluster of roadside stalls selling brilliant painted bowls; boys at regular intervals proffered bead necklaces; knots of men waved huge carp caught in the lagoons by the sea; or handsome roosters strung bemused but un-complaining by their feet, swinging like feathered handbags. Men in hooded kaftans, women swathed in jangly bright salwar kameez were points of brilliance in a dun landscape. The houses we passed were two-room boxes, distinguished by fear-less colour – mauve and turquoise, saxe blue and pink.

The north gets rain, and we splattered through a short thunderburst, past thick plantations of eucalyptus, mimosa and pine. The sky cleared, and we occupied ourselves by naming the flowers at the roadside: flashes of magenta bougainvillea and mesembryanthemum clashing with scarlet saucers of hibiscus.

The landscape emptied as we went further south-west, the sand dunes becoming more sculptural. By Casablanca the sun was blasting away at full throttle, and we passed a mud-built compound bristling with towers and palm trees facing an aquamarine sea with sparkling breakers.

In Rabat we found a hotel that offered curiously communal rooms and hot water to slough the fine facial pebbledash we had acquired en route. 'Tomorrow I've booked us into the Tazi. I've often stayed there – you'll like it. It's very down to earth, but good. And right on Djemaa El Fna, the square where everything happens.' Sorely tempted, we resisted hot baths as it was getting dark, and skipped off in search of food. The wide boulevards of Rabat were flanked by giant palm trees lagged in ivy. We were the sole pedestrians. Having trawled for twenty minutes or so, we found the Café Français, where we were the only diners. The chicken livers with parsley and garlic were fine, though we were a little put out to find ourselves in a Café Français without wine. 'Don't worry,' Maggie said, 'you can get wine at the Tazi.'

The grey waiter loitered spectrally in his overcoat,

occasionally piling chairs on tables, until we capitulated and left. It could not have been much later than nine p.m. – as night-life goes, it was healthfully sober. But Dan's eyes were still sparkling with the thrill of the Maghreb El Aksa, the land of the setting sun, as our heads hit the rigid bolster on our tiny bed.

2

A PLACE OF SMOKE
AND MIRRORS

The next morning the car was still in the market cum car park, surrounded by people selling plastic buckets, and it appeared to be complete. This, in the town that had a College of Piracy on its northern bank in the fifteenth century, came as a relief: wealthy European Christians returning from the Indies laden with treasure used to be their favoured target, and though we did not entirely fit the bill, having a vehicle, albeit a geriatric C15, might well have denoted wealth here. Early in his career Robinson Crusoe suffered at the hands of the college alumni, known affectionately as the Salli Rovers, and did a spell as their slave. Fortunately for sea-faring travellers, the Salli half of Rabat was reduced to a mere husk by the thoughtless renunciation of piracy by Moulay Slimane in 1818, but the city burgeoned when the French made it the seat of their Moroccan residency. Today, Rabat is still the administrative and political capital of the country and the official royal residence, though the young king Mohammed VI, fondly dubbed M6 by his adoring fans, prefers to spend time in his relatively humble home in Marrakech, where he can be seen from time to time drinking coffee in the old city.

We wandered among the scribes leaning disconsolately on their elderly Adlers, the knicker and pyjama vendors, the plastic-shoe and tin-pot sellers, wondering what had become of the opulence – the gold and ivory, the honey, the wild animal skins and the fine Merino wool of the eponymous Merinides that were traded here on these high sunset-red cliffs, where the once navigable river debouches into the Atlantic. We spent an extortionate amount on dates, almonds, figs and pistachios to eat en route to Marrakech and clambered into the van. Maggie lit her fourth of the day as we negotiated narrow roads cluttered with bikes, mopeds, horse-drawn calèches and carts.

We eschewed the Bab El Had, the Sunday Gate, once decorated with the salted and preserved heads of malefactors, left the city of the sacred eels and headed south, past little pink shanty towns whose roofs mushroomed satellite dishes, and mosques

with green glazed tiles and filigree towers, pale
turquoise and white against an azure sky,
carbuncled with loudspeakers to call the scattered
faithful to prayer. Cows and goats grazed by the
roadside, donkey carts meandered along the verges
that were still green with eucalyptus and feathery
false pepper trees, though the further south we went
the fewer there were. The low terracotta buildings
were hardly visible against the bare flat earth
from which they were built. Startled, we flashed
past compounds emblazoned with logos – Daewoo,
or Johnson and Johnson – ugly pockets of industry
in cocoa-brown desert, with sudden eruptions of
public gardens and hideous pretentious architecture. We shot past *koubbas*, little square
buildings commemorating a holy man or marabout,
and drifted from the flatlands into low hills where
adobe courtyard compounds glowed pink, plum,
pale green, turquoise, ice blue.

We had an omelette by the roadside at Ben Guerir,
with cheese and lots of cumin, big round crusty
baps, mineral water and good coffee, during the
endless televised drone of the muezzin. The bill
came to £2.50 for the three of us. Maggie paid. 'This
is very good food.' She leaned forward and
whispered, 'But look at his teeth!' It was true. The
proprietor's teeth were apparently made from Mars
Bars.

During the course of the long drive, many police

22

with flash motorbikes loitered at the roadside, to whom Moroccan drivers appeared to be giving money. The cops ignored us completely, and were very embarrassed on the one occasion when they inadvertently stopped us, asking merely where we were going and did we like Morocco, looking all of a sudden like fancily dressed tour guides bearing pistols instead of umbrellas.

As we approached Marrakech we passed a huge military enclosure in the desert, guarded from the perimeter watchtowers by hot uniformed men, a distant relic of the city's belligerent beginnings. At the crossroads between North and South, the city was endlessly fought over by Berbers and Muslims, vying for the caravan route bearing oranges, spices, nuts, dates, grains, animal skins and precious metals. The military compound was to become one of the familiar landmarks of this journey, since there is only one road from Tangier to Marrakech: right at Tangier, left at Casablanca, past the compound and there – many hours later – you are.

The road snaked around low cinnamon-coloured hills dotted with verdigris eucalyptus. Rounding a gentle bend, we suddenly saw the low sprawl of Marrakech shimmering in its vast palm-filled oasis, still irrigated by the original *khettara* (wells and channels) of the eleventh century. The palms, known as the Palmeraie or millionaires' row, are a legacy of the staple diet of the soldiers who guarded this camp where gold and African slaves were once traded. Kidnapped from Guinea and the Sudan, four thousand slaves continued to be traded annually in the slave souk on Wednesday, Thursday and Friday evenings until 1912. You could buy a brace of standard slaves for the price of a camel.

As we approached the city, its encircling walls loomed: six miles of thirty-foot-high pink mud-and-lime *pise* fortifications, bristling with two hundred towers and punctuated by twenty gates of varying ingenuity and strength to hold off successive bands of raiders – and they had needed to. Berbers, Almoravids, Almohads, Merenids and Saadians had all laid siege to the city since its foundation as Almoravid Youssef Ben Tachfine's military garrison in 1062. Under threat from the Almohads, it took Sultan Ali Ben Youssef's labour force just one year to complete the fortifications in 1126, and they remain unchanged today, though their niches are fortunately empty of decomposing traitors' heads. I learned later that the Merenid Sultan Abu Thabit had excelled at this, decking the crenellations of the Bab er-Robb gate with some six hundred after a spot of repression in 1308. Nice work for the resident Jews, though, whose grizzly job it was to preserve the heads with salt. Such was the call for their services that the Jewish quarter of the city is called the Mellah – the Arabic word for salt. When not preserving heads, the Marakchi Jews ran the banks

24

and the sugar trade, made fantastically beautiful jewellery, forged metal and were tailors of distinction. Sultan Abdallah El Ghalib formally took them in when the Spanish Christians began to persecute them in 1558, and as a sign of his royal protection he gave them the forty-five acres in the shadow of the palace walls that their dwindling numbers still occupy. Today a mere ten thousand of the half-million Jews who once lived in Morocco remain. Though they seemed to co-exist peaceably with the Arabs, they decamped in droves to Israel in the 1950s, and there they stay.

At the city's heart gleams the shining minaret of Yacoub El Mansour's Koutoubia, the seventy-metre-high pivot around which the city revolves, named the Mosque of the Booksellers in honour of the manuscript merchants from whose souk it arose. It was designed by a Christian slave and built by thousands of Spanish captives during the second Crusade, when Saladin was rampaging around, having taken Jerusalem; it was finished in 1189, the year when Richard Coeur de Lion was crowned King of England. The gilded copper spheres at its pinnacle are rumoured to be the jewels of Mrs Yacoub El Mansour, melted down as self-inflicted punishment for the four grapes she ate during Ramadan, and now fiercely guarded by a genie.

We plunged into the navigational challenge of inner Marrakech and, thanks to Dan's remarkable orientation abilities, skirted the shoals of bikes spinning round the city walls, and drew up thirsty, dusty and tired outside the Grand Hôtel Tazi at around four, where total chaos greeted us. We seemed to number more than they were expecting, the rooms were not ready, our luggage disappeared immediately and could not be retrieved, there was no soap, no loo paper, we could not lay hands on a cup of tea, and we were in the tetchy panic that kicks in after an anxious drive.

We occupied ourselves, trying to look busy by making a list of essentials to bring in future: soap, teabags, backgammon or Scrabble, candles, bath plug, cigarette papers, tobacco and loo paper. As you leave Tangier, little boys tap on the car window, eager to press boxes of extortionate pink 'Iris' tissues upon you. Buy them. You will need them.

Our feathers finally settled, we recovered from the drive, were allotted rooms, Maggie changed into perfectly pressed black linen, and Dan was instantly spellbound by Marrakech. He rhapsodized about the light, the maze of buildings, the thousand subtle variations on Marrakech pink, the flatweave carpets of orange and blue draped casually over balconies, the cascading sparks and smell of flux in the metal-work souk. We wove our way unmolested through the monkey men and snake-charmers; the story-tellers surrounded by a mesmerized audience; the old men, guerrab, tricked up in scarlet and tinsel, selling water; the ostrich-egg and false-teeth vendors in the Djemaa El Fna. Africa surged at Dan, who capered to meet it with open arms.

Sourly I kept comparing it with northern India, with which it had an unnerving similarity, and finding it wanting. I was still crabby after the journey.

But there was one comparison where Marrakech was the unquestionable winner, even I had to admit it, and that was in the matter of smells. For a start, there were no green clouds of low-lying sewage. Maybe high summer would be a different matter, but in April one's nose could roam unfettered, searching out the clean smells of coriander, mint, rose geranium, artemisia and sage in abundance from the herb-sellers, all manner of citrus, wafts of hot cinnamon from the street-corner pastry-makers and occasional swoons of incense eerily familiar to anyone who has had a Catholic childhood. Old men wandered the streets swinging censers that wafted wisps of frankincense into the dusk.

The vast heart of Marrakech, Place Djemaa El Fna, is known as the Assembly of the Dead or the Sinners, after the heads of conspirators were routinely exhibited there by the reigning sultan – more work for the men of the Mellah. According to the cognoscenti it is three different squares depending on the time of day – just before dawn it awakes to a vegetable and spice market, though I must admit to never having been there early enough to

In the carpet souk

D.P.

see it in this guise. By mid afternoon it segues into a carnival, throbbing with the sound of drums, cymbals, bells and pipes, with groups of snake-charmers and monkey men, sword-swallowers, fire-eaters and storytellers, fantastically garbed water-sellers – members of a hereditary guild dating back several hundred years, with their bulging goatskins and brass cups – magicians and fortune-tellers, slender Gnawa dancers apparently made of rubber, spinning the tassels of their cowrie-shell-decorated skullcaps, and women offering to decorate the hands and feet of passers-by with intricate designs in henna. But it is at twilight that the full heady magic is released, when festoons of light bulbs and flickering acetylene lamps lend a festive air, smoky wafts of food seduce the senses, and the conspiratorial knots of men and women listening awestruck to polemics look like dramatically lit extras from a mad, intense Eisenstein film.

Any time is the right time to buy false teeth and ostrich eggs, not to mention nuts, dates and figs, orange juice. And all around, stretching way back into the souk, you can buy a wealth of blue plastic buckets and bowls, sequinned belly-dancing outfits, soft bags, hats and slippers made of rainbow leather, desirable chunky jewels, glorious glazed bowls in Balkan Sobranie cocktail-cigarette colours, daggers, absurd long-barrelled guns and a gleaming multitude of chased, engraved, polished and inlaid metalwork.

That evening Djemaa El Fna was full of the smell of cooking: meat being seared, spices sprinkled, fish fried to perfect crispness, hot bread, and snails smelling like, well, snails. There were ranks of open-air restaurants consisting simply of a heat source, food, a cook, and benches and tables for assembled diners. Kefta meat balls, lamb kebabs, briouats and bstilas, tagines, and threading through it all carts laden with twenty different kinds of sesame and honey halva. The food is very good, particularly if you like snails, sheep's head and entrails.

As evening fell a cloud of white egrets drifted home to their roosts, smoke plumes and dusty sun-set merged in a haze of purple and orange, the elegant tower of the Koutoubia donned its floodlit evening outfit of phosphorescent brilliance, and the million lights around the square added their sparkle to a scene charged to bursting with glamour. Huge palm trees swayed gently in the tiny park opposite the bank, and way over in the distance the ghostly white peak of the Toubkal, the highest in northern Africa at 4,165 metres, glimmered as delicately as a shred of white tissue.

Dan wanted to hug everything, everywhere. He wanted to eat all the food, be draped with all the snakes, josh with all the monkeys. He wanted to wade in up to his neck.

Maggie took us to eat in a place that was awash with romance. The Marakchi was up a discreet flight of stairs in a building overlooking Djemaa El Fna, whose magic carpet unrolled below, teasing the tourists, getting on with normal life, enacting a million dramas, with a constant background rhythm of muttering drums. Above, spangled indigo slowly drenched the sky from side to side. Within the restaurant, mirrors and windows reflected the light-show outside, the walls glinted with a kaleidoscope of tiny *zellig* tiles, lights flickered gently from brass lamps and candles, the oud player was as old as the surrounding mountains, and a fountain burbled through a floating pot pourri of garnet and pink rose petals. Maggie kissed everybody, and told us what to eat.

Halfway through dinner, a broad woman – descendant of the Wife of Bath – in a shapeless mackintosh erupted into the room. After a short altercation with the manager she proceeded to remove her mac, revealing voluminous red gauze harem pants and a sequinned bra, worn fetchingly over a rather grey third age vest. An ancient man, who had been sitting in the corner quietly burbling on the fretless strings of his intricately inlaid pear-shaped oud, changed his tune sorrowfully to something slightly less dirge-like and the big smiling woman gyrated, causing impressive ripples and slaps of flesh from twinkling bra to beaded panniers. Dan and I thought she was rather endearing, and when invited with a raunchy wink and an extra wobble, Dan tucked some paper money into the cleavage of her lagged and reinforced bra. She donned her mackintosh and disappeared into the night.

The oud player had a little trick of his own. Every time a cup of tea was poured, he would play a little descending octave to mimic the sound of liquid falling from a height. After maybe twenty-three repetitions, irritation definitely took the place of wonderment, and greed grappled with our need to escape. Greed won, and we topped off a gargantuan feast with plates full of little cakes. We paid, resisting tea and trickle music, and staggered out into the night.

Maggie had stayed at the Tazi when she first succumbed to Marrakech, and the staff now took on her house-hunting project with intelligence and generosity, with Samir, the manager, escorting her to just about every riad that was for sale in the city.

A riad is a house and garden turned inside out. Open the anonymous front door in a windowless wall, tread a narrow passage, holding your breath as you pass the hole-in-the-floor lavatory, turn a corner and you find yourself in a cool, quiet courtyard, its somnolent peace animated by the babble of a central fountain and a canary singing in one of the four orange trees. Around two, three or four sides are rooms that open straight out into this serene space, which is called the *wast ed-dar*, the heart of the house. A *dar* is the same thing but smaller and minus the trees.

Over the following few days Dan and I accompanied Maggie on some of her house-hunting forays. Otherwise we just wandered, happily falling prey to carpet-vendors and bowl-sellers. We bought each other Berber rugs for birthday presents: the Berber women stay at home – while their nomadic husbands do whatever they do – weaving rugs that function as multicoloured diaries to show their returning spouses how they have passed the time. Cooking pots, camels, flowers, candles and goblets tell who knows what tales of family reunions, babies being celebrated, wedding feasts and journeys. Dan's rug is blue and mine is pink. I also bought a fistful of rings, milky quartz, dark marbled malachite, and a pile of garnets, all with heavy silver settings.

We ate frequently in the Tazi, lounging on over-stuffed banquettes, wading through courses until we were like overstuffed bolsters ourselves, incapable of bending in the middle. We also frequented a scruffy caff, Chegrouni's, overlooking the Djemaa El Fna, where you write your order from the unchanging menu on the paper napkins, and eat excellent keftas and tagines from terracotta pyramids off paper tablecloths. Chegrouni's swiftly became our regular, surviving redecoration with menu and prices unchanged.

Mastering the cooking of a tagine is a delicate business – the food has to be stacked in the dish just so, with meat in the middle, surrounded by vegetables and a neat edging of potato slices. The sauce is very yellow and oily – I guess that turmeric and cumin feature heavily, maybe saffron in the posh places. The dish, covered by its conical lid, is cooked on a little terracotta barbecue with a few coals – you can buy the whole kit on every street – and a vigilant process takes place of coal-fanning, lid-lifting to observe contents, lid-stopping with a tomato blocking the vent on the apex, lid-balancing, with a spoon wedged in to allow a little more air to the food. Every restaurant will have a table where eight or so tagines all bubble away, and the cook stays close and busy fine-tuning his production line. The result is always good, though occasionally the meat takes some chewing and requires a vigorous finale with a toothpick. Couscous, the dish most usually connected with Morocco, can be somewhat dull to my mind: parsimonious stringy meat, over-cooked vegetables and tasteless semolina stuff – though there are times when soothingly dull is just what you want.

We also ate at the house of Ahmed, a young, provocatively rasta entrepreneur who became

Maggie's self-appointed guide in this labyrinthine city. 'Isn't he magnificent? He knows everybody. And he has promised to help with finding a riad.' He accompanied our house hunt and probably did us no good at all, since most Marakchis found him alarming, with his heavy sheaf of tightly plaited braids and his air of being out of it. He was constantly stopped by the police and accused of being an unofficial guide, which can elicit heavy penalties, including prison.

He invited us for dinner, and we felt very flattered and part of the swinging scene. He had two rooms, side by side, in a multi-occupied riad, with a window from one to the other. Dinner took place in a typical long narrow room, to which he had given a warm, slightly brothelesque atmosphere with brass lamps and pink light bulbs, swathes of pink and red velvet, and candles on low tables. We lounged on a divan and Ahmed plied us with red wine while he drank Coke – three opened bottles for us, he was obviously expecting an orgy – and played Morcheeba loudly for our benefit.

He abandoned us to the wine. There was a long wait while he disappeared somewhere. He brought us plates. More time passed. He came in with a flourish of cutlery. Then he left the house entirely. We weren't quite sure what to do, but continued to lounge and chatter, quite hungrily by now. When he returned twenty minutes later it was with a terrific tagine made by his sister – beef, peas, green olives, harissa, potatoes, lemon, cumin, garlic, all cooked together for forty minutes in a pressure cooker. This was a dinner party unlike any we had ever attended, and we did not know the protocol: we should have left as soon as we had eaten but as it was we stayed, to our mutual embarrassment, while Ahmed retired to the adjoining room to prepare for an evening on the town with his German girlfriend.

Maggie saw many riads, but nothing that seemed right. She knew exactly what she was looking for, having stayed in the perfect place belonging to a designer friend of hers decades previously. Dan and I continued to idle, spending money on trifles and a huge, monstrously heavy blue and terracotta mosaic tabletop, which we tied precariously to the luggage rack on Dan's old van. The inside of the van was stuffed with rugs and a gorgeous panoply of enormous bowls glazed in bright yellow, lime green, and blue and white concentric circles.

Had money been no object, we would have further crammed the space with appliquéd canvas Berber tents the size of a small house; finely painted sandalwood furniture; baskets of every capacity and style; heavy silver, turquoise and amber jewellery; embroidered rainbow-bright babouches; enormous wooden metal-studded doors; brass and iron lamps; exquisitely braided and buttoned burnouses and djellabas; carpets as plain or intricate as you could wish for; natural pigments in a dolly-mixture array of sugar pink, orange, saxe blue, verdigris, intense cochineal red and indigo; shiny oval hammered-brass and copper hand-basins, intricate lemonwood, cedar and thuya inlaid boxes, and tables with a clean resinous fragrance. We did in fact buy a backgammon set, and its sweet smell consoles me every time Dan trounces me.

After four days in Marrakech we squeezed our-selves into the van – by now full of heavy objects and low on its suspension – and took off for home. Despite myself, I had enjoyed dropping into such a different world, such a different century, but I was eager to return to the safe and predictable familiarity of southern Spain. Morocco, I thought, is *very* foreign for somewhere so close. Dan, for his part, was off in a dream world – picturing himself fearlessly wading like a pasha through those exotic alleys, greeting other djellaba-clad figures, sipping fierce bitter coffee as he watched the coruscating circus of Djemaa El Fna.

3

A STAR-SPANGLED SOIRÉE

In the late summer of 2001, after four years of living in the wrecking zone with a changing cast of builders, the completion of our Spanish house in the wild rocky hills behind Malaga was finally truly in sight. The thought may have flittered across the back of Dan's mind that once the house and his studio were finished he would have no convenient excuse not to paint. He is an artist, but a blank canvas has been known to make him wash up, cut down weeds or tackle his income tax. My workroom was finished and neatly organized too, there was nothing to stop me from writing The Novel. However, that too was strangely resistible – gathering wild gladiolus bulbs from the newly ploughed fields and planting them beneath the *datura*, sorting the washing, putting summer clothes away, even making lavender sachets and bagging up fallen leaves for next year's leaf-mould, for heaven's sake – there were many ways to avoid doing what we should.

We might even have been a tad bored. By way of excitement we went on a detox diet, inspired by the recently even more gorgeous than usual Doris (Dan's daughter), and became completely obsessed by it. We could have taken a masters degree in advanced metabolism, trace elements, locating your hara, chanting your mantra and the joys of water. I was thrilled to bits: Dan finally taking an interest in his own well-being was a miracle that could only bode well.

We boldly cold turkeyed – no cigarettes, no re-creational drugs, no tea, coffee, alcohol, and progressively less and less of anything at all as we slogged through the weeks, until we were down to a lentil and a glass of spring water. After a fortnight of homicidal rage, Dan became bouncy, he lost the small bolster that he had been carrying down the front of his T-shirt, he awoke without groaning, he did not slump away the morning at the breakfast table with his head in his hands. He ran twice daily with the dogs round the rocky, scraggly, uphill slither and slide that stands between us and a view of the sea. I cannot tell you what an amazing trans-formation that detox achieved. Not that he can have been very toxed in the first place, since, unlike me, he is moderate in all things, does not have an addictive personality, has never been known to binge on Bendicks Bittermints, get drunk, absent-mindedly absorb an entire packet of Hobnobs or eat every single chocolate in a box, including the strawberry creams. He would always rather have a nice cup of tea. I guess he just has a sensitive system – maybe coffee, maybe wheat had been the cause of his chronic insomnia. Whatever the cause, whether less of the bad things or more of the good, Eeyore suddenly became Superman, brimming with positive vibes and bristling with energy. Suddenly nothing was impossible. For me, by contrast, the diet had the effect of making all my clothes much tighter, particularly around the bottom.

Out of the blue, at exactly the most parsimonious nadir of this regime, we were invited to Marrakech to celebrate the opening of Maggie's hotel. She had been through every kind of tribulation en route. After our foray together she had returned to Morocco solo and trawled Marrakech, visiting about a hundred riads on foot in the blazing August sun the previous summer before she found one that was big enough, cheap enough, and pretty enough. A builder had absconded with her money in the way that builders have been known to do since man first created hod, it had all taken months longer than scheduled, and there was an expensive problem with the drains. In order to get the job done at all, she had had to live in the eviscerated building for three months over the summer when there was no privacy, loo or bath and the temperature nudged 50 degrees. Completing the building had taken more than a year. But in October 2001, she invited us to come and celebrate the inauguration of Riad Magi.

It was exactly the diversion that Dan and I wanted, and we booked our tickets instantly – Malaga to Casablanca, Casablanca to Marrakech – arriving at midnight on Monday. Everyone was edgy in the aftermath of the recent Twin Towers tragedy, most flights were almost empty, and we were not surprised when ours were cancelled. It wasn't a serious problem, we simply rebooked. But I felt a little shiver of apprehension.

The plane for the first half of our journey was tiny, had propellers (not good), and we were almost the sole passengers. It was as confidence-inspiring as the Russian plane in which I had been an unwilling passenger in Guatemala, which had grey canvas and tubular metal seats like the ones in the old Citroën Dyanes; also an oval of dotted lines painted on the outside at the back with the legend in English, 'Cut here in case of emergency.' Somebody had nicked the tin-opener.

However, Dan was soothingly unfazed by bouncing above the tawny patchwork of northern Morocco in a quaintly outmoded flying machine, and thrilled with the soggy white torpedo roll with a slab of damp white meatish substance that we were given by way of airline food. Me, I like all the fidget: 'What would you like to drink?', 'Would you like ice and lemon with your Valium?' and 'Could you get your elbow out of my left breast while I wrestle with this plastic container and shower us both with gravy and carrot cubes?' It takes my mind off death. However, for this purpose on this journey I had had the foresight to bring the Spanish equivalent of the great *Celebrity Bodies*, along with *Hola!*, an interior-decorating mag, an archaeological journal and a literary magazine, all in Spanish, the idea being to improve my mind and broaden my vocabulary as we dodged death. I just looked at the pictures and swigged Dr Bach's Rescue Remedy. Dan held my hand for the scary bits, and read his book. The spindly little propellers did their job, and we arrived alive at Casablanca.

We settled down to a little light fretting in Casablanca airport while we awaited our connection. I was nervous and Dan was hungry, and it was with a little squeak of excitement that I remembered some dirhams – about sixteen pounds' worth – stashed in my wallet from our previous visit. I went to the airport shop and bought four packets of nuts and a small bag of dates from the unspeakably sleek woman in the nut and gewgaw shop. This came to the equivalent of twenty-five pounds.

Winded with incredulity, instead of putting the ridiculously overpriced hoard back on the shelves, I feebly made up the shortfall with my last pesetas. We chomped priceless almonds while waiting for our plane to announce boarding. In the end righteous indignation got the better of me, and I returned to the shop determined to be assertive. Glossy hair and brown lips patiently went through the addition all over again, and yes, that was how much our snackette had set us back. I was just glad that I hadn't idly picked up a decorative bottle of argan oil along with my other purchases.

The flight was uneventful, and on landing we walked through the velvety midnight warmth of the airport runway to Maggie, who was waiting just beyond the formalities with her right-hand man, Abdeltif.

She was delighted to see us, and astounded by the new improved, slender Dan. 'Well, look at you both. Dan, you look like George Clooney. What have you been doing? Cabbage-soup diet?' She linked her arms through ours, frowning momentarily at the unsuitability of my garb. 'Miranda, you *must* cover up. You must *never* flaunt your body in front of Arab men, it makes their blood boil.' I looked about with interest, hoping to spot an incandescent Arab, but the assembled airport officials appeared unmoved by my bare arms. There wasn't a hint of anything torrid.

Despite my sartorial blunders she allowed herself to be kissed on both cheeks, we shook hands with Abdeltif – briefly clocking that he was darkly handsome, with long thick eyelashes – and clambered into one of the ubiquitous Mercedes taxis. We drove past the phalanx of palm trees that line the airport road and the kaleidoscope planting of the Bab Jdid, through the ramparts into the twinkling city, past the haughty grandeur of the Mamounia, past the Koutoubia as slender and glamorous as Marlene Dietrich despite its 850 years, past the smoke and swirl of Djemaa El Fna, and into an impossibly narrow and busy side street, which seemed to become ever narrower. I was convinced that we were going to get inextricably wedged, trapped in the car and unable to open the doors.

At last the taxi stopped and we tumbled out to be greeted by a waft of cinnamon – Maggie's alleyway had a pastry stall on the corner, where spirals of dough emerged crisp and sizzling from hot fat, to be sprinkled with spices and sesame seeds. I could probably find my way to Maggie's by nose. Citrus and fish and cumin from Djemaa El Fna, coriander from the vegetable stand, cinnamon from the corner stall.

We were led away from the vehicular thoroughfare down a pedestrian sidewalk. It was well lit in patches, inky black in others. At the street end, someone had taken oil drums, painted them blue and planted them with a little garden: oleander, perennial morning glory, palms, French beans and jasmine. We walked in the spice-coloured canyon between windowless buildings, sometimes ducking into unlit tunnels, passing clots of boys who wished us 'bonne nuit' and mangy cats with orange eyes. Occasionally Maggie took the odd moment out of queenly wafting to greet one of the more attractive and well-scrubbed boys.

The cobbled path followed a ziggurat route – right and left and right and left – past tributary tracks under arches and adjacent alleys. Within seconds the frantic turmoil of the vehicle street had dwindled to a memory, and we were in a shadowed and silent world. I had a brief panic about ever finding my way out of this maze – it was as unmemorable as a computer circuit board. A trail of crumbs or tiny pebbles would help. String, even. There were just high pinkish-brown walls unbroken by windows, and doors.

We stopped outside a handsome front door with a little carved wooden canopy and a spherical punched-brass lamp casting scintillas of light.

Abdeltif produced keys with a magician's flourish, and we stepped over the threshold into a dream refuge for the heartsore and overstressed. Candlelight flickered everywhere from large metal and glass lanterns, through little windows with twinkling dark-blue and green glass and behind wooden fretwork fanlights. Beyond the entrance lobby with its impressive painted desk was a courtyard canopied by four orange trees. In the middle stood a fountain, which plashed irregularly, depending on whether or not it was blocked by rose petals.

There was another fountain against one wall, a lion's head in brass, spitting or dribbling according to the water pressure, embedded in dark-green *zellig* tiles. Above the trees we saw a fathomless diamond-studded indigo sky; in the branches, two chameleons impersonating leaves. Abelard and Eloïse, Maggie had christened them, with tragic prescience. They had been brought from the High Atlas and their role was to look cute and catch flies. There were problems on both counts: they were invisibly camouflaged most of the time, except when very indignant – when they met each other, for example – which instantly transformed them into fresh tarmac with lime-green spots. And there were no flies. Marrakech is strangely fly-free: even the open-air meat stalls appear to have no flies, and to be ignored by the many cats.

Maggie introduced us to her other Moroccan accomplice, Mohammed, who looked like a pixie and spoke no English, just Arabic and an alarmingly emphatic kind of French. More frighteningly contemptuous than a native-born Parisian, he would say, 'Non!' furiously in answer to almost anything. This impression of fury was a mistake, the result of concentration and incomprehension, because he was actually a very kind, gentle and endlessly help-ful young man. He took care of the chameleons –

trying to tempt them with minced snail when there were no fresh flies to be had – arranged constellations of candles at nightfall, fiddled with the recalcitrant fountain, cooked and shopped and generally cared for people.

Maggie invited us to have a vodka and orange juice with her, but we were still being tiresomely goody-goody and sipped a nice glass of water instead, while listening to Mozart being strangled by her execrable second-hand Marakchi tape player. We sat beneath the stars and drank to her hotel and her courage and good taste, and shivered with the swash-buckle of it all. The Riad Magi was enchanting.

She had found an old house with lots of interest-ing original quirks and carving, and with the help of two architect friends had turned it into the perfect mixture of quaintly ancient and contemporary comfortable. All the rooms were furnished with heavy divans littered with cushions and low hexagonal tables in the Marakchi style, which does not make pernickety distinctions between different room functions. Each of Maggie's six bedrooms had its own en suite *tadelakt* bathroom with coloured walls as smooth as marble in the traditional finish of hammams. She had scrutinized the old house for traces of the original paint colours, and reproduced a fresh and breezy scheme, a swatch of pale ivory, rich clotted cream, turquoise, sage green and Virgin Mary blue. The courtyard was cream, with the intricate old wooden screens and shutters painted the odd chalky green of verdigris. All the rooms had floors of smooth glazed tiles, wonderfully cool to the bare foot, and the walls gleamed with *tadelakt* to dado height. The courtyard was tiled with little terracotta tiles, a neat herringbone pattern around the edge.

Maggie put a stunningly cool and urbane face on what I now know to have been complete chaos. The problem with the plumbing was that it did not exist: the loos discharged straight into the ground beneath the courtyard and the orange trees. The building had been nowhere near finished when promised, the foreman had bolted taking the last of the money with him, and yet here she was looking relaxed, soignée and only marginally chain-smoking.

She had been rescued at the nadir of her building

disaster by Abdeltif, who had crossed her path at just the right moment, and flexing his formidable managerial muscle had assembled a gang of efficient workmen, volunteers from his mosque, to complete the building in record time. He had provided her with staff and appointed himself as the manager of the Riad Magi.

Abdeltif was young and handsome, given to wearing dramatic costumes – a typical working outfit would be a voluminous black salwar kameez in self-patterned silk with exquisite braid and button details, a large black turban, and a pair of repellent Nike trainers on his enormous feet. He had a stocky kick-boxer's build, having once been a national champion, but had to give up because he broke too many arms and legs, most of them his own. Maggie had made an incredibly fortunate choice – as well as radiating the physical splendour of a slightly rotund panther in the prime of pantherhood, Abdeltif was attentive, listened gravely to instructions, usually said the magic words 'no problem' and meant them, spoke French, Arabic and English fluently, German and Japanese appallingly, and had extraordinary charisma and competence. He had been judicious with his bribes, so that all paths were smoothed, and, best of all, he had a wonderful sense of humour.

We sat there enviously for a bit. But as I travel more I find that any journey, however easy, causes geriatric senility on arrival. When Dan did one of his cavernous yawns, giving us an eyeful of all his dental aberrations, Abdeltif suggested that we might like to go up to our room. Actually, we would have preferred to be carried, but we did manage the stairs, and fell gratefully into bed.

The hour-of-the-wolf muezzin, the dawn chorus in the multi-storey orange tree outside our bedroom window, the pathetic little bleeps from my Psion organizer, all passed unheard. We eventually stumbled down to a morning of brilliant sunshine and a courtyard full of activity. Maggie was sitting regally at one of the *zellig*-tiled tables, engulfed by a heavy wrought-iron throne, dressed in a vaguely medieval long black crepe dressing-gown edged with hand-woven cream silk braid, directing the thumping of the divan mattresses and the polishing of the *tadelakt*, arduous tasks which took place regularly. The mattresses were so dead-weight heavy that I could not lift a corner of mine to tuck my sheet back in place, but Mohammed and Fatima, the third member of Maggie's trio of staff, seemed to have no problem with wrestling them into the open and beating them senseless. Fatima was a large, strong-armed, capable woman with a wide, flat face and glittery eyes, wearing a nylon overall and pyjama bottoms, every hair on her head scraped back invisibly into a tightly tied cotton scarf.

She eyed us with interest, and shook hands shyly.

She paused briefly in her domestic violence to bring us breakfast, including delicious vanilla yoghurt that I could happily live on. Like most Arab women, she spoke nothing but Arabic and body language – vigorous arm-flapping and squawking meant 'Would you like a boiled egg?', plucking, sniffing, pouring from a great height and drinking with much lip-smacking meant ditto a cup of mint tea. We kept our dietary needs simple, consistently choosing yoghurt, and eggs, which might be hard-boiled or raw, according to Fatima's mood.

We did have some moderately arcane requests, though, in other areas – we wanted to buy some Marrakech-pink pigment for a friend of ours. I also wanted some henna, since the Indian henna with a very fetching picture of Ganesh on its box, bought from the herb shop in Malaga, was about as effective as a mixture of mushroom soup and Vim in terms of colour and conditioning. Henna was used by Mohammed as a symbol of peace, and I was eager to do my bit for peace. On the Egyptian trip with my mother, I had had the most brilliant henna experience in our hotel on the Red Sea, from which I emerged with a thick, lustrous scarlet mane. Brilliant but for the surprising wandering hands of Abdul the hairdresser.

Moulay Omar ('Moulay', normally a term of respect, is here used ironically), a friend of Abdeltif, was charged with this detail, since he had worked in the magic souk for fifteen years. This was where he had bought Abelard and Eloïse – without checking their pedigrees – and he was supposed to know his way around powders and pigments, dried iguanas, aphrodisiacs, essential oils and alarming cosmetics. He was gone for several hours, and bustled back at lunchtime in a state of shoppers' hysteria, with myriad little bags of ground pigment in turquoise, Schiaparelli pink, bright emerald, two kinds of indigo, poppy scarlet, chrome yellow, plus vials of the essential oils of frankincense, jasmine and sandalwood. We were surprised and thrilled with this cargo of mixed blessings, but searched in vain for the Marrakech pink. He dismissed our concern with a shrug of the shoulders, and produced a triumphant newspaper twist of henna which contained a tiny tissue packet of cochineal, which, he assured me, was the essential secret ingredient for any self-respecting fake redhead.

Fatima offered to do the henna when Moulay Omar finally did return, and he, Mohammed and Abdeltif watched with interest as she mixed water with the powders to make an earthy-smelling brown paste, and smothered the resulting cool cowpat on to my hair, wrapped my head in a plastic carrier bag fastened with Sellotape and topped it all off with a flourish, making a rather natty turban from a couple of dishtowels and a scarf.

This novelty headgear limited my options for adventure, so I spent my first day in Marrakech at Maggie's while Dan plunged greedily into the souk in search of the elusive Marrakech-pink pigment. The enclosed tranquillity of the riad was the perfect antidote to my previous agoraphobia, and gradually the world outside her walls began to seem less daunting. Inviting, even, particularly when Dan returned, beaming from ear to ear, with a couple of blue glass candlesticks and no pigment. What was it with Marrakech pink?

Having marinated for five hours, I was relieved when Fatima indicated that the time had come to wash the stuff off my hair. Anyone who has had dealings with henna will know that this is an opportunity to get a hypothermic shrunken head and redecorate your bathroom à la Jackson Pollock with splatters of dun-coloured residue. It always takes ages, and when I managed to get free of Fatima's alarmingly strong fingers I had an unnerving flash preview in a passing mirror of a person with a fluorescent marigold-orange head. In fact it dried a magnificent rich deep gorgeous red, and so *shiny*. I couldn't believe it. What had she put in the mixture? Some magic or other, but her body language left me none the wiser. It probably involved dried iguanas.

Maggie suggested that since we were having guests for dinner, we might like to change into something a little more formal, and we trundled obediently up the stairs. Dan did a bit of elementary grooming and I gazed with dismay at the curious motley jumble of clothes that I had considered right for Marrakech in October when I was packing:

1. An amusing 1950s full cotton skirt with a pattern of pagodas. Should be worn with a tiny waist and lots of net petticoats, neither of which I had. Its presence on this occasion was a complete mystery – it had lurked inoffensively in a trunk, unworn, unmourned for thirty years. Why had I decided to liberate it now?

2. A minuscule black lace cardie, which was neither warm nor decent by Marrakech standards.

3. A sleeveless pink linen trouser suit that had given me an uncommon resemblance to long pig when it was crisp and newly ironed. Now that it was as crumpled as W. H. Auden's face it was like nothing so much as that old pink J-cloth that has been quietly ponging in the cupboard under the sink for the last two years.

4. About a dozen sleeveless bodies, which are never suitable in Marrakech.

5. A shocking-pink pashmina, whose potential as a rather fetching sari I briefly pondered. Unsuccessfully. If all else failed, however, it could perhaps be brought into service as an all-concealing tent.

6. I had also brought a collection of unwearable shoes that did not go with any of the above.

After I had spent about half an hour trying to put together a decent unpeculiar outfit from these uncooperative elements, Maggie appeared. 'My God, what are you doing? Having a jumble sale?' Gingerly she picked up the pagoda skirt. 'Miranda, you're not a teenager any more. This thing is ridiculous.' She looked at the sorry pile of clothing on the bed. 'Is this all you have? What on earth were you thinking of?'

She pattered downstairs in her embroidered babouches, and returned with an armful of black linen. She is always elegant, in any colour as long as it's black. So, funereally decent, thanks entirely to Maggie, whose wardrobe I continued to plunder throughout our stay, with my flaming hair pinned in a ladylike knot, I descended to the candlelit courtyard where Dan was already sipping an exploratory gin and tonic.

Flakes of golden light were sprinkled on the walls from the brass lamps, above was the leaf canopy with spheres of ripening oranges against the vibrant blue sky, and the fountains had risen to the occasion and were plashing quite respectably, despite their cargo of rose petals.

As the sky darkened to scintillating indigo, a handsome Gnawa singer, Manu, with enormous glittering teeth and the eyes of a child loped into the courtyard, trailing his French lover – Mireille, an interior decorator by profession, dressed stylishly in black, cream and bamboo colours. I could picture her back in France, very much in control, wearing coordinating designer clothes, shopping, cooking, choosing the perfect marriage of entrée with hors d'oeuvre.

Like Dan, I thought the prospect of a celebratory evening drinking water was just too prissy to contemplate, and succumbed immediately to Abdeltif's suggestion of a gin and tonic. Maggie's bank manager Hassam, a small dapper moustachioed man with twinkling black eyes and a penchant for orange Fanta, was the next to arrive, followed by a tall, etiolated man with obtrusively knobbled knuckles and knees: Morten, a Norwegian neighbour. He had the pallor of a cave creature, a consequence perhaps of being a true intellectual, having spent most of his life in the half-light of dusty libraries, researching the ways of the Berbers and learning to converse fluently in four of their many dialects, not to mention classical and colloquial Arabic, French, English, Swedish and no doubt a smattering of romance languages. On this and subsequent occasions he reduced me to awed silence. In his company I felt as inconsequential as a fluffy pink rabbit won and abandoned at a fairground.

As we sat sipping, Manu would burst into soulful

song at unpredictable intervals, gazing up at the stars, to the accompaniment of his crudely constructed *gimbri* – a musical instrument very like a shoebox with a few strings. He yodelled with wrenching passion of the desert, slavery, heartbreak and defiant joy, while Mireille talked in a small desolate monotone of her loneliness and of missing her family, whom she had left for this big, vague, erratic man from the Sahara. For the time being she had taken Manu in hand, as stylish French women do: his dark unfathomably yearning eyes, his blinding smile, his skin like polished and patinated ebony were set off to perfection by a searing-orange cotton shirt with a mandarin collar. He was resplendent.

Their relationship, I learned later, was a microcosm of that between France and Morocco. From 1911 until 1956 Morocco was a French protectorate. This meant that the French bequeathed brilliant roads and railways, a sense of gaiety, and suburbs with an air of being loved, sophisticated, gardened, tended – of being choice places to live, rather than the usual scummy tidemark of the city. They instituted cafés where you can still get good strong coffee and tiny delectable cakes. They set up good flower and cheese markets, everything clean and tidy and well run. French became the lawyer's language, and held the wobbling bureaucracy together. They contributed much more, including their continuing passion for the place. The Moroccans brought their magic to the mixture, attempting to ignore their erstwhile colonizers, resenting their arrogant parsimony, enjoying the best and leaving the rest. Both nationalities seemed to get along surprisingly well, I reflected, for people from different planets.

One of the many wonderful things about this enchanted place is that most people speak French, and that night I made a startling discovery. Lurking in the dusty repository of my mind were two boxes, grimy and cobwebbed. One was black wood with heavy iron bolts and padlocks, and in Gothic letters had 𝕲𝖊𝖗𝖒𝖆𝖓 carved on its side. That one always had been and will always remain locked shut. The other was soft brown leather, with gilt studs and a shiny gold lock which, to my astonishment, sprang open at first touch. This one was labelled in delicate copperplate *French*. My ancient A-level French was sitting in there, neatly filed and ready to use.

I had been coerced into learning German – though I loathed it – because I was considered unacademic, and the Ursuline nuns who masterminded my education decided that I should do needlework and cookery in order to facilitate finding a husband. Plainly the only career possibility open to me. Husband-finding clashed with history, Spanish and Italian – all of which I really wanted to learn, but fitted in nicely with German. So there it was, that reviled black box, still using up precious mind-space. Along with advanced buttonholes and beef stew with dumplings.

But finding my French in good working order after four decades of disuse was amazing.

That evening, candles glimmered on every horizontal surface and reflected mistily from every vertical one, the lion's head tinkled discreetly and the central fountain attempted to overcome its spout problems, sending a tiny trickle crookedly into the carpet of deep magenta rose petals floating upon its bowl. I chatted politely, if somewhat languidly, to Maggie's guests, vaunting my new-found fluency in French and rather wishing that Dan and I were alone to enjoy the balmy night, the jasmine and the stars winking above the orange trees, not to mention the pastila, a festive Big Occasion pie made with crisp millefeuille pastry wrapped around a filling of pigeon, egg sauce and almonds, dredged with icing sugar and apt to explode in a confetti of tiny sticky flakes all over the front of the emergency black garment Maggie had lent me.

She observed, she frowned, she relented, and we clinked glasses in honour of her triumphant achievement.

4

CLUELESS IN MARRAKECH

The following morning we breakfasted in the sun beneath Maggie's orange trees on yoghurt and pain au chocolat. I was eager to explore the city, and after a bemused attempt at appropriate clothing we plunged into the maelstrom. Perhaps Fatima had mixed a benign spell into the cowpat, but there was no vestige of my previous diffidence about Marrakech. Titian-haired and dizzily joyful, I just *loved* this place. I don't remember exactly what our excuse for the foray was – maybe the Marrakech pink was preying on my mind – but our toes were itching with a passion to be out among the motley, chancing our luck with the canny bargainers, buying the wrong thing at the wrong price from the wrong place.

Since we'd be travelling home by plane, we had in mind small portable things, gorgeous presents for our families that we could transport in a carrier bag. Pennywise trinkets. Amusing ethnic gewgaws. Small and charming prayer mats, candlesticks, tiny hand-carved thuya-wood chess sets. What we did not really intend buying, the thing that appeared nowhere on our must-have list, was a *house*. I sometimes think I have a bit of a shopping problem. Wherever I go, for whatever purpose, I seem to come back with huge carrier bags.

But as an impulse buy, a house was taking things a bit far.

What happened was that Maggie and Abdeltif accompanied us. They knew Marrakech, after all, and we thought they would prevent us from doing anything too stupid. Up to a point they did. We first visited the djellaba-maker to Moroccan royalty and Yves St Laurent, where I spent twice as much as I have ever spent on a garment, any garment, including the black outfit I got married in, to obtain a blue woollen suit. There was a very good reason for this – I was going to meet my publisher the following week and had a mind to look elegant and memorable. I was dubious about the price, but convinced by the reasoning: I was not vaingloriously buying an outfit, I was making a canny investment. It was a pity in retrospect that it had trousers cut like rompers and two centimetres too short. Memorable, possibly, but elegant only for Andy Pandy fanciers. Where Maggie saved the day was in persuading us with a discreet twitch of the left eyebrow that an exquisitely tailored and pricey white linen suit was not the thing for Dan. Whatever he wears looks like a paint-rag after a few minutes.

He bought a flowing black gandora, which was a sensible price due, I think, to the fact that it seemed to be made from recycled carrier bags and became revealingly adhesive with static and covered with bobbles on its first outing. Dan was cheerfully unconcerned and strutted about like a Nigerian potentate in his clinging pebble-dashed robe. And I just had to buy a dark-blue djellaba as well as the suit, because Maggie said it would be perfect for sitting by the fire in the long cold Spanish winter – something I have since never done, because I feel as though I am impersonating the Reverend Mother Joseph – the bane of my juvenile years – wearing the voluminous tent, and keep expecting to find a clanking crucifix attached to my middle and a coif and wimple to materialize along with an air of comprehensive disapproval of all forms of life. Having made our garment purchases, however, I heaved a sigh of satisfaction and looked forward to resisting all further temptation.

Which we did, for several hours. I resisted the sapphire and ruby silk and woollen shawls. I resisted all jewellery (falls apart on first wearing),

embroidered slippers (only for shufflers) and plaited leather sandals (too lentilly). Dan resisted another *zellig* table (too heavy), leather briefcases (too serious), metal lamps (too spiky), and tortoises (too much responsibility).

We were feeling pretty pleased with ourselves: we had trawled the souks (overflowing shopaholic paradise bazaars) from La Maison de Tissage in Znikhet Rahba to Maître de la Céramique in Souk Sebbaghine. We had not succumbed to dried fruit in Souk Kchacha, Spanish fly in Place Rabha Kdima, rugs in Souk Joutia Zrabi, scarlet shoes in Souk Smata, hideous pouffes in Souk Cherratine, iron candlesticks in Souk Haddadine, saddles in Souk Serrajine, teapots in Souk Attarine, or *gimbris* in Souk Kimakhine. We were doing well. What else could there be to resist?

We stopped and had a mint tea, in order to restore the virtuous spring to our step, and commented on the Swede who slithered past in transparent brown linen, then a couple in unprepossessing matching turquoise nylon tops and shorts, who just had to be English.

Emptying their glasses, Maggie and Abdeltif rose to their feet, and beckoned us to continue with our Lenten renunciation of all things material.

It was too good to last.

We were walking along a small, relatively chichi stretch of Derb Doukkala (where we resisted tiles as fine as cloisonné and fountains as richly decorated as the Crown Jewels) when Maggie announced casually that the inconspicuous building on our left was the estate agency she had mentioned in the *Evening Standard* article she had written with a journalist friend about buying property in Marrakech, to publicize her riad.

'Let's go and have a look. They are very charming in there; they know me well. It is always interesting to look at property prices, don't you think?'

'Why not?' I answered enthusiastically. Dan may have rolled his eyes to the heavens. We heaved open the door to a *dar* with one side in the form of an open cloister, furnished with twenty feet of continuous divan and a handful of small tables. A jazzy stretch of multicoloured appliqué lined the wall behind the cushion-strewn seating.

A beautiful woman with high cheekbones and perfect almond-shaped eyes introduced herself as Khadija, and motioned us to take a seat among the cushions. Her junior partner, Djendahl, joined us, and before we were able to gather our resistance or formulate the words 'No, thank you,' we were drinking mint tea and looking at house details.

How did this happen? Why? Having been through the purgatory of rebuilding one old house, having reached the point at which we could just live in it without needing to line up buckets under the leaks or to climb over a rattling slag-heap of cement bags and iron rods to enter or leave, what was I thinking of, even considering another? Who did I think I was: J. K. Rowling?

We looked at the pictures of sumptuous *dars* and intricately detailed, opulent riads, and swiftly realized that the only folders of interest to us were the green ones – bottom of the heap. No chance that we could afford the ones in the pink folders, let alone the blue and cream. We flicked through the tiny, the dilapidated, the hideous, the disastrous. We pored over pictures of fifty different houses, showing fifty variations on overcrowded neglect. Our enthusiasm waned; with a sense of madness averted, we began to feel that this was not only lunacy, but very depressing as well. Half-heartedly we allowed Djendahl to persuade us to visit three. As we congratulated ourselves on a narrow escape, he set up appointments for the next day.

'It can't do any harm to have a look. It'll be fascinating,' I said to Dan. 'How else are we going to see what Marrakech houses are really like, since all you can see from the outside is a locked door?'

In the eleventh century, Abu Bakr the Wise started a settlement in the great wide bowl of the Haouz, which he named Marrakech, for which one translation is 'leave quickly'. Had we but heeded the sage words of the city's founder, life would have been so different.

Khadija came over to see how we were getting on,

and handed Djendahl another folder that had been sitting on her desk. He put it on top of our rejects and ambled off to find a map. Curiosity was too much for me, and I opened the last folder. Within were terrible pictures of a gorgeous house. It had huge arched doorways with massive doors, painted ceilings, wonderful curly wrought-iron work and a wide shady balcony, all in a long-abandoned state of dilapidation. Both Dan and I gasped. We wanted that house. We adored that house. Maggie signalled 'Cool it' to us, but when Djendahl returned we were babbling with enthusiasm about Number 95, Derb Al Qadi.

The only Marrakech interiors we had actually seen were Maggie's and, during our first visit, her Norwegian friend Morten's. His house is restrained, with all the attention to detail and discreet palette of a Ben Nicholson painting. Moroccan houses being invisible to the passing observer, we had little to guide us. But Number 95, with its carved hexes and, surprisingly, six-pointed stars on the shutters, its old patterned wall tiles weathered to a soft multi-coloured patina rather like Harris tweed, exerted a strange pull to the heart. Looking at the stamp-sized shaky photos, we knew we had stumbled upon a house with a spell, a place of enchantment.

The next day Djendahl gave Dan and me the full tour of the medina, the 600-hectare old city within the walls. This extraordinary maze of interlocking hidden buildings would probably still look familiar to Ali ibn Yusuf, who began the construction of the city walls in 1126, using a mixture of lime from the hills of Guéliz and the characteristic red mud, *tabia*, that tints the town pink.

Marrakech was the capital of Morocco until the turn of the seventeenth century, when Moulay Ismail the Bloodthirsty decided to up and off with his 500-strong harem and 888 children (his amatory labour was not in vain – he made it to the *Guinness Book of Records*) to his new capital, Meknès, around which he had twenty-five kilometres of ramparts built. Though he certainly did not lack ambition, he was not a lovable man: he liked to incorporate Christians in the walls, entertained by their slow deaths. It is safe to say that he had a short fuse, from which even his nearest and dearest suffered: one day, irritated by the way his concubines chattered, he had all their teeth pulled out. Of his subjects, he said: 'They are like rats in a basket. If I don't give the basket a good shake, they will gnaw their way out.'

It took his men thirteen years to dismantle the glorious El-Badi palace, pride of the medina, next to the Mellah and the present Royal Palace, built by the Saadian Sultan Ahmed El Mansour (aka, unsurprisingly, the Golden One) – just half the time it took to build it – and plunder the best of it for his new capital, Meknès. The ceilings of El-Badi 'the incomparable' had glimmered with gold. Onyx, mosaic, stucco, carved cedar and sandalwood embellished the interior, and huge pools lined with Carrara marble adorned the exterior. But for the music-and-dance festival that fills these ghost-patrolled courtyards with riotous life at the beginning of every June, the only living inhabitants of this sad, plundered shell are the storks which nest here, leaving, it is said, on July 17th annually.

As the centuries passed, Marrakech grew organic-ally, piece by piece, like a giant Lego construction, and nothing has changed – bar the grand buildings, of course, as each new sultan felt compelled to destroy everything wonderful built by his pre-decessors. However, if you take away the mobile phones, TV aerials, the cars and Mobylettes, you traverse almost a millennium as you step from the busy tarmac of Avenue des Nations Unies through the toll gate of the twelfth-century Bab Doukkala with its great towers into Avenue Fatima Zohra.

The old city is a fascinating window into history, the physical expression of Islamic values of hospitality, discretion, neighbourliness, mutual tolerance and harmony. It became a UNESCO universal heritage site in 1985, and there are laws governing restoration and building – for example, no building may be taller than the tallest palm tree, which in effect means two storeys high. The irregular skyline suggests that baksheesh may have bent the rules from time to time.

Djendahl was saving Number 95 until dusk. In the meantime, he kept us busy. House 351 had eight very narrow rooms, was close to the souks, and the courtyard was overshadowed by four enormous lemon trees. Number 349 had a *doueria* (a granny flat where redundant wives or mothers could moulder away their final years) and was more expensive, but negotiable. Two of the rooms were like prison cells. Another house had charming frilly edges around the roof of wooden barge-boarding painted sky blue, and small children who burst inquisitively out of every room to stare at us, paralysed by shock into stunned silence. We trespassed on many lives, blundered into one multi-occupied riad after another, never knowing whether we could stay shod or were being horribly rude by not wrestling with our laces and exposing reluctant feet to the icy floors. The houses of four, six or eight rooms seemed to be inhabited by entire villages of curious families: women and children emerged from every room to observe mutely. From time to time dignified spherical old men would indicate that we should partake of a glass of mint tea, shuffling their ample bottoms comfortably into sateen-covered divans and snapping fingers at some invisible woman.

But we had places to go, houses to see, and

continued to track Djendahl through the tangle of indistinguishable walkways. The secluded residences of Marrakech present a blank face to the outside world – long high featureless alleys punctuated only by doors, not a window to be seen. The places we saw all made me feel terribly sad, as has almost every house that I have ever been able to afford. Where would these people go? What did they live on? Who was selling their home? Why were all the women wearing pyjamas and slippers? The walls crowded in with a terrible oppression of claustrophobia. Some were tidy, some were empty of junk but clean and polished, some were like the musty emporiums of second-hand-furniture dealers, with tables teetering on mattresses, wardrobes shoved at dangerous angles into corners and propped up with bricks, televisions blaring into the faces of lounging viewers from perilous perches on boxes or chairs.

I was disheartened. My feet hurt, jostling among the crowds was making me paranoid, and I had forgotten the itch of curiosity, the momentary thrill of enchantment that had driven us out on this meandering quest. I just wanted to get back to Maggie's and have a cup of tea. Djendahl wavered, reading exhaustion on our faces, and then rallied.

He took us to a riad that did have something appealing – a sort of tiny dower house attached to but separated by a screen from the main building. It was bigger than most, with a fascinating, intricate layout. We climbed a rickety twig ladder to see the roof with its view of pink sky, black silhouetted palm and cypress trees, and the gleaming Koutoubia. Djendahl idly flirted with a frisky pyjama-clad young girl hanging up washing, while we muttered things like, 'Well, it's got lots of character,' 'This is the one to beat so far, then,' and 'That little separate bit could be like a flat for us to stay in when the rest is let.' He then recalled that Number 95 Derb Al Qadi was next door. In fact we could lean over the railing, so, and look down into its courtyard – an act that would be strictly forbidden if anyone lived there.

We peered into the clotted darkness and made out three pairs of high doors opening on to a serene tiled courtyard, white-painted wrought iron like lace shielding windows and edging the balcony, all of it composed of the same metal arabesques, but differently put together, in delicate theme and variation. It looked like an embroidered house, so finely and fastidiously assembled, each of its elements perfect yet slightly different. We gazed down in awe at a *dar* composed by Cartier, waiting for us like some sleeping princess. Was it possible that we might one day own something so beautiful?

Suddenly Dan and I were supercharged, and perfectly game to visit the house next door. We had not quite taken in the fact that next door in the medina meant walking almost a mile round winding and now dark pathways to circumnavigate an entire block and reach a place a couple of yards away from our starting point. It was really night by now, pitch dark in places, but Djendahl sauntered confidently to the end of an alley, scritched the key in a dusty, rusty lock, did a brief salsa to get the reluctant door to open, stepped into the house and out of sight. The three of us crowded into a cave-dark lobby, whose gloom was only slightly relieved by opening the door at the other end.

The house had long been empty, and there were no lights to guide us over the erupting floor tiles, lead us up the winding staircase with its high uneven risers and narrow treads, or help us avoid the hole-in-the-floor loo. There were unexpected steps between one room and another, which meant that we did a lot of lurching and apologizing. But as the obliterating indigo rolled overhead, we felt that this was a benign house, with a wonderful sense of space. The houses we had hitherto looked at were all composed of rooms round a central courtyard, a wonderfully private yet intimate way to live. But rooms like long narrow corridors, frequently dark even in broad daylight, marred all of them. These rooms seemed wider, the windows larger, the courtyard more open, and there was a completely unlit mystery bit at the back that had all kinds of possibilities. Upstairs there was a large veranda looking down into the courtyard.

By the time we allowed Djendahl to lead us back to the familiar smells and bustle of the Djemaa El Fna, night had fallen. Good-naturedly he agreed to take us back to Number 95 the next morning. We babbled our way back to Maggie's, delirious with plans and excitement. We had found our Arabian Nights Dream Palace.

The next morning the house was all we imagined and more. For a start it was empty – the only disturbance we caused was to decades of dust. The only tragic revelation was the lavatory. I had to admit that this was a bit of a problem for me that morning, as I had eaten something that had sent fireworks through my guts, but I clenched my cheeks and soldiered on.

The house had five big rooms, significantly wider, we thought, than the ones we had seen elsewhere. The front door led into a little corridor, and thence to the courtyard, which measured fifty-two square metres. There was nothing remarkable about it, no fountain, no trees, but it did have an open, friendly air. There was a large room to the right, a smaller room to the left with a shallow, battered Belfast sink minus plumbing, and a small dark north-facing room at the end. Behind this was another room of such impenetrable blackness that we fell over each other – though it was bright sunlight outside – and could not get the measure of it at all. It seemed to have many cupboards – at least that was what we assumed the doors that kept smacking our faces belonged to. To make matters more difficult, the floor was uneven, with many small steps, and loose shifting angled tiles laid on bare dust. A dark corridor joined this Stygian room to the courtyard, and off it there was a featureless black hole whose purpose was indicated by the lingering stench, and a flight of stairs with tiny treads and dangerous risers. There was a sort of light well at the end of the corridor, with a view of the underside of a room, which appeared to be suspended like a swallow's nest from the roof and to be made of twigs.

Cautiously we climbed the stairs and found a relatively recently constructed balcony on to which opened another large room, and a magnificent gallery overlooking the courtyard, with a high painted wooden ceiling – a large north-facing out-door space. Behind it was another room, with another delicious painted ceiling in rather better condition, and a niche whose curved roof was of carved and painted plaster in intricate arabesques. This wonderful area was the heart of the house: spacious, dignified, cool, connected to the rest and yet separate. All the courtyard rooms and this one had huge three-metre-high double doors, heavy and panelled, with bolts the size of oboes, containing smaller human-sized doors, all of which appeared to have been thickly painted with milky cocoa.

The walls to all the rooms were probably a metre thick, and the windows had low broad sills, carved wooden shutters, occasionally glass, and the lacy wrought-iron work we had glimpsed previously, through which you could see out clearly, but which conferred daylight invisibility to those within. I decided not to risk the suspended twig-floored room, which was a simple small square lit by a tiny window, but did brave the home-made ladder which was obviously a thrifty alternative use for kindling, and grunted and puffed my way through the tiny vertiginous hole at the very top to find myself on the roof.

Djendahl immediately cautioned us not to set foot upon this undulating area of what appeared to be plain beaten earth, which he discovered to have a disturbing bounciness to it. There were satellite dishes, washing and palm trees in every direction. Cats yowled as they sprang from one rooftop to the next, and a neighbouring dog, large by the sound of it, barked disapproval at our unexpected appearance. All the roofs of Marrakech interconnect, and I am sure that you can leap from one end to the other of the old city, bounding from one roof to the next over the narrow light wells below. There was a narrow uneven walkway around the unprotected edge, which Djendahl judged to be safe if vertigo was not your problem, since it had a ten-centimetre wall at convenient tripping height, and a seven-metre drop to the courtyard below.

We were both enchanted by the house, and it took only a very brief discussion to decide that we would buy it immediately. Yes, we thought, this would be a sensible investment for our dwindling capital – a place to let, from which we could make an income to subsidize our pauperish writing and painting. Having set the deal in motion we hardly noticed the flight back to Spain, happily diverted as we skimmed the arid landscape by envisaging the few changes – plumbing, electricity, sticking down those naughty tiles – that would restore our sleeping beauty to splendour.

How little we knew.

5

CAVEAT EMPTOR

If an airy whim ever crosses your mind to buy a riad, as you sit in Chegrouni's wrestling with your kebab in unaccustomed winter sunshine, you would do well to attend closely to this chapter.

Dan and I were embroiled in the acquisition of a *dar* (so-called since our courtyard as yet had no trees) whether we liked it or not, and were due to return to Marrakech a couple of weeks after our exploration with Djendahl to complete. This entailed many phone calls to my bank in the UK, transferring money from one account to another. I listened to Enya, punched in numbers, became hysterical as large sums of money wandered from my London bank to another in Madrid, holidayed there for a while, ambled to Casablanca, disappeared, and eventually fetched up in Marrakech. The secret was to do a lot of yoga and meditation, to cultivate a cosmic timescale. Banks have quite a different attitude to money you owe them and money they owe you. The former unleashes rabid dogs with medieval punishments and letters in red, the latter a languid casualness, mañana but without the sense of urgency.

Dan and I were punch-drunk and breathless with apprehension about the provocative thing we were doing. He was alternately pretty pleased with himself for being such a swashbuckling kind of guy, and pretty horrified at me for being so impetuous, so spendthrift, so alarming.

Remembering the simple route we had taken that very first time when we went with Maggie, we decided to drive back to finalize the paperwork. Right at Tangier, left at Casablanca. We planned to make the trip in one day, with military precision: get green card for journey in rattling Suzuki Samurai; drop dogs off at 8.15 a.m.; milometer registering 17,333 kilometres at our nearest village, Almogia; tank half full; 750 pesetas *péage*; crossing every hour from Algeciras; fill tank: 3,000 pesetas; five ticket booths en route; milometer says 17,393 kilometres at Algeciras; fill in landing card on board; boat crossing from 12 p.m. to 3.20 p.m., 2.20 p.m. Moroccan time.

We brought a hi-fi, presents for Abdeltif and Layla

his wife, and a petrol can – there were not many functioning garages. I sat primly taking notes as to what happened where, how long it took, and how much it cost.

Clever stuff, but as always we were confounded by the usual incomprehensible delay at Tangier – strutting policemen, clusters of querulous geriatrics, buzzing throngs of young and predatory men – passports and car papers came and went. A stern uniformed official wanted to know the car chassis number. One hundred and forty dirhams baksheesh had to be paid to the main tough guy and his ancient side-kick, and a thousand pesetas to a harasser of no discernible role in order to leave the dock. We finally escaped at four, Moroccan time.

Breathing a sigh of relief, we headed for Rabat, which we reached three hours later. We stuffed ourselves with dried apricots, nuts, and surprisingly edible rabbit-dropping-like things made of sesame seeds bought in the one garage we passed that did have petrol. At Berrechid we allowed ourselves a proper stop for supper. Just another two hundred kilometres to go, but Dan, heroically doing all the driving, was beginning to wilt. We sat at a pavement café gazing blankly at the car in exhaustion – you'd be surprised how tiring it is to passenge for any distance – and had the usual humble and delicious tagine, one of a row bubbling away under an awning at the pavement's edge: a queue of charcoal braziers watched over by a busy elderly man, whose job it was to regulate the amount of steam by occasionally removing the tomatoes that sealed the vents on the top of the earthenware cooking vessels, and to fan the embers whenever they seemed to need it. We rang Abdeltif with our estimated time of arrival – midnight – and he generously offered to wait for us in Djemaa El Fna.

The last two hours of the journey were a nightmare. Dan's eyes kept closing as he drove, though he insisted in a manly way that he was *fine*. It was not surprising that he was in a trance: the road past the dusty, scarred desolation of le Plateau des Phosphates is dead flat, dead straight, and has a strangely hypnotic quality even when the driver is as fresh as a newly plucked dew-sprinkled lettuce. We did not even register the familiar landmark Golf University at Settat, so tired were we; did not speculate about advanced tee management, caddy control, comparative swing technology or Fanta at the nineteenth hole. After hours of the endless unvarying ribbon of tarmac in the darkness we were almost relieved to be stopped in error by the police, who were embarrassed, and could only think of touristic questions to ask – Where were we going? Did we like Morocco? We nodded enthusiastically to everything, and were grateful for the surge of adrenalin that this little exchange elicited.

We were less grateful for the excitement that

followed. Dan asked me some innocuous question whose answer required a look in the wallet – probably how many dirhams we had. So I looked in my bag, and then in the glove compartment, and then in our suitcase, and concluded, dry-mouthed and heart pounding, that we had left our money and passports on the table in Berrechid. Dan squealed the Suzuki to an emergency stop in the darkness of mid nowhere, and for a moment we were paralysed, calculating the extent of the emergency. Total. We just had time for a short lacerating argument before it occurred to him to check out the back seat. YES – there was all our necessary stuff, where we had chucked it after the last garage stop.

For the final hour of the journey – why did I not just take over the wheel? God knows – I sang, chatted inanely, asked about the most painful episodes in Dan's life, played I Spy, babbled about my childhood, anything to keep him awake, resorting to pinching him hard when all else failed. Understandably he began to feel persecuted as well as very tired, and our exchanges became noticeably snappier as we approached Marrakech. The Suzuki behaved itself admirably in a Suzuki sort of way, but even for a short journey it is the sort of car that makes your teeth rattle and your ears go numb – noisy, bouncing, flapping, heavy to steer, slightly less comfortable than a church pew after a long sermon, needing as frequent feeds as a newborn kitten, thanks to its tiny tank. It was possibly not a wise choice for this pilgrimage.

We eventually made it quite some time after midnight: the square was shuttered and empty, and the solitary frozen figure of Abdeltif surged from the shadows of the Café France, too late to go home to his wife Layla, but disarmingly, effusively welcoming nonetheless.

Maggie was away, but had generously offered us a room at her riad. Gratefully we fell into one of the beds, and slept like sloths.

The next morning, after fresh orange juice, pain au chocolat and eggs that were whimsically liquid, we convened at the bank, where we extracted money through the good offices of Maggie's friend Hassam, a poet and dreamer with a surprising and endearing falsetto voice. He bullied and tutted and shoved me through the forms in French, exploding with indignant coloratura when my adjectives did not match my nouns in terms of gender and quantity.

Thence, clutching wads of dirhams, we crammed into a petit taxi and sped off to a meeting with a notary, Maître Yakub in the Guéliz, the French quarter. He was laid-back, affable, chain-smoking, and talked mostly to Abdeltif in Arabic. All three men seemed inordinately interested in a handsome sulky girl who appeared to be Maître Yakub's assistant and who stomped in and out of his office in her high-heeled boots bearing papers. Each time there was a lull in their discourse.

What with the incomprehensible language and the love-smitten longueurs, I had plenty of time to study Maître Yakub's extensive collection of paintings – lumpy landscapes of Pluto, possibly, or depictions of keyhole surgery on a bile duct; old men painted apparently in coloured porridge, reading the Koran by candlelight. There seemed to be a general weakness for Braille art – Abdeltif took us later to the atelier of his favourite painter, whose proudly exhibited oeuvre consisted of texts and squiggles executed on boards and clock frames in primary-bright wood glue.

The deposit was paid, papers were signed, Abdeltif commented approvingly on the sulky girl: 'She has a very nice Toyota,' we had a coffee in the sun in a pavement café and took a taxi back to Hassam at the bank to arrange a transfer of more cash to the notary. This done, we collected almond-eyed Khadija from the estate agent's, and with me on the back of her moped and Dan on the back of Abdeltif's, we survived the swirl of traffic – wandering donkeys, heavy-goods vehicles – and returned to the notary to sign more documents.

Back in the medina we wandered towards Maggie's. Abdeltif is not a native Marakchi – he was born and brought up in Larache, a seaside town in the north – but you would not guess so from the number of acquaintances he bumped into on every street. Progress was always slow as he ricocheted from one greeting to another, including on this occasion two blokes on a bike who literally rode into him; they then all threw their arms round each other in a tornado of kisses and hugs.

This drama over, I laughed and said, 'Is there anyone you don't know, Abdeltif?' Looking across the crowded alley at a dapper fellow clad in black and bearing an obviously very important briefcase, I said, 'I bet you know him.'

Abdeltif followed my gaze, and immediately broke into another flurry of effusive recognition. 'He is my brother-in-law, Khaled,' he said with a great proprietorial beam, his arm round his shoulder in a great bear-hug. Well, Abdeltif was one of eleven children, and his wife Layla was one of eleven children, so I suppose there were quite a few in-laws on any street at any given time. We were introduced to each other, and thus began a relationship of crucial importance.

As night fell we passed the discreetly grand entrance of a riad that had been converted into a hotel. The doorman clapped Abdeltif affectionately on the back, and ushered us all into an interior straight out of *Citizen Kane* via Hollywood – a huge mosaic fountain splashed in the entrance hall, giving birth to myriad small cascades and rivulets, embedded in a glade of small luxuriant trees.

Chandeliers the size of hot-air balloons scintillated some way over our heads, and our gaze was drawn out to a brilliantly lit courtyard thick with palms and frangipani at whose heart was a large glowing aquamarine swimming pool. We were led outside by a hotel manager who might well have modelled for Armani, and were introduced to a small, anxious and fairly elderly American, Chuck Walker IV, clad in turquoise nylon sportsgear, whose passion and labour this palatial riad had been for the last fifteen years, and who insisted hospitably that we drink a hypothermic gin and tonic beside the pool, beneath the palm trees.

Chuck was a brave example of the many Americans to fall in love with this very un-American country, to forge real relationships and invest heart, soul and dollar in this elusive, mysterious place. His hotel had multiple suites of opulent emperor-sized bedrooms whose bathrooms glittered with gold and mosaic-stepped plunge baths and saunas. The heavy curtains had gold hands of Fatima, clunky with emeralds and rubies, as tie-backs, the sitting-room had a baronial fire-place that was a conglomerate of Lutyens and Walter Scott, with a strong whiff of Disney; there were ante-rooms off which were more ante-rooms, all darkly panelled wood, and stuffed with fatly dimpled silk brocade banquettes from which to view a Seattle skyline of glittering bottles and glasses. It was grandly sumptuous, and as Chuck enthusiastically showed us round, Dan and I felt more and more like a pair of impoverished hicks, gormlessly open-mouthed, up from the country.

At the parting of the ways, Abdeltif, who seemed permanently attached to his mobile phone, melted into the night with Khaled the briefcase-bearing brother-in-law to measure up 95 Derb Al Qadi by torchlight, and thankfully we wound our way back through the increasingly familiar labyrinth to Maggie's.

It was the beginning of November, dark by seven, and there was no one else staying. After a quick kebab in the square, Dan and I were so cold we went to bed at the unusually early time of eight o'clock, fully clothed in my case, and clung tight to one another all night desperately seeking heat.

As usual, the morning dawned brilliantly sunny. We awoke for a breakfast meeting with Abdeltif to be introduced to the prospective workmen, grumbling about the earliness of the appointment – eight thirty. He did not arrive to pick us up until ten, and having fortified ourselves in an alleyside café with a glassful of homemade vanilla yoghurt, we negotiated the human and animal traffic, the mopeds and donkey-drawn *carrossas* of the main thoroughfares, down ever-diminishing bustling booth-lined walkways – past the pink nylon underwear and the black plastic shoes; past the ladies selling baskets and skullcaps in the square surrounded by the caged and bottled mysteries of the magic souk; we jogged past the spice shops and the tripe and fish vendors; past the lively heaps of wrinkles selling two cloves of garlic and a small pepper artfully arranged on a filthy green cloth; past the herb sellers, sitting behind aromatic clouds of coriander, artemisia, mint and rose geranium; past the cheeky fruit and veg vendors with mounds of tangerines, potatoes and mallow leaves, all being given a serious once-over by prospective buyers.

We trotted along after Abdeltif, and understood why his outfit is always impeccably smart, up-to-date, black, bar his shoes – he always wears wide leather shoes like squelching camel's feet fresh from a Hobbit shoemaker. The thing is that in these unpaved alleys, where manholes erupt and puddles lurk after the occasional but heavy downpour, you need a good wide footing. We pattered after him, emitting little shrieks at regular intervals as we twisted our ankles.

The bustle gradually diminished, and at a kitsch rooftop still-life of plastic flowers and tinsel star we turned left from Azbezt and into the comparatively quiet, mercifully paved residential maze of Derb Al Qadi, the Street of the Judge. Here there were only three difficulties. The first was the small, bent man with no teeth and one cloudy boiled-looking eye to

In The Souks   D.P.

whom Dan had given a cigarette in a moment of madness on our first visit and who was now his best friend, always beseeching more. The next was the local glue-sniffer, a tall, rather distinguished gentleman in a brown burnous, hood drawn up around his face, his nose deep in a paper bag. The third was the intricacy of the route along the Derb, the shadowed side alleys we avoided, the twists and turns, sudden bright openings and corners so dark that we had to feel our way, nervously scrunching over bags of rubbish which exploded with yowling cats. The streets were always alive with scavenging cats, surprisingly large and well-fed-looking thanks to the generous diet of chicken gizzards and sardines contributed by residents grateful for their rat-proofing prowess.

In addition we found that we accreted a shrieking, laughing gaggle of schoolchildren outriders, self-appointed bodyguards. Over time they became individually familiar, always gravely wishing us 'bonjour' as they watched us skirt the small square where they played football and chattered.

Enough of this aside – though asides become familiar to the visitor to Marrakech. We arrived at the house at ten thirty to find others ahead of us, most importantly Khaled, Abdeltif's brother-in-law and our newly appointed foreman in whose hands the whole operation now resided. Still clutching his briefcase, he had assembled ten workmen to meet us that morning, some of whom made a lasting impression. The plumber, whom they referred to with much jocularity as Bin Laden because of his feverish fanatic's eyes and solid black beard; an electrician; a mason; a structural engineer; a handsome, impeccably dressed *jibs* frieze expert, who did nothing but carve the extensive frieze that meandered round walls, doors and windows for the next six months while muddy and cementy chaos erupted around his shiny black shoes. There were builders and jobbers, handymen, carpenters, and a young man with shy black eyes, Rachid, who eventually painted all the furniture, ceilings and doors with fine interweaving parterres of intricate strapwork in sophisticated colour harmonies.

I tried to memorize every name and face. We paced the building, the respectful retinue shuffling after us; we measured rooms, made suggestions, listened with interest to their ideas, planned possible staircases, bathrooms and kitchens. We assembled cautiously on the rotten roof and looked down into the sad and dusty courtyard, while Khaled, his eyes shining with excitement, rhapsodized in French about fountains, and painted doors, galleries and greenery.

Khaled was a small, dapper man, with lustrous black eyes, tiny perfectly white teeth in a narrow fox-like jaw, and he listened with an air of grave attention at all times. He was quick on the uptake, and as we discovered had a great natural sense of style and innate good taste. Immediately likeable, he always seemed surprised when he laughed, which he did often, and exuded total trustworthiness. He was never without his briefcase, which contained business cards, colour swatches, fabric samples, notes, drawings, calculator, tape measure, paper and pencil, prototype taps and spouts. Everything we ever needed was to be found in Khaled's briefcase.

We conversed surprisingly effectively in French. Dan and I made a whole raft of major decisions, and then had to return precipitately to Maggie's because of my inconveniently outraged insides. Whether thrown off course by food, water or post-palace-acquisition panic I do not know, but I needed conveniences that our building site could not offer, and I needed them NOW. We bid a perfunctory farewell to the ten men who were about to change our lives, and speed-walked, stiffly in my case, the ten-minute winding maze to Maggie's.

The money for this unexpected venture was what remained after selling my London house. It had mouldered for a year in the bank earning progressively less 'high interest'. There was sufficient to buy Number 95, with enough left over for the restoration, we hoped. Abdeltif had been as vague as builders are when asked for estimates – 'Oh, it will not cost you much. You will have to pay maybe the same again for the work.' I could sense him estimating not the cost of the building work but the potential of my bank balance. I wish I could learn faith, because statements like this throw me into an agony of pointless calculation. The best thing is to just let be what will be, and not get ulcers trying to pin down the future.

As I saw it, my lunatic impulse buy was, in fact, incredibly sensible. It was, as I kept telling Dan – whose eye always grew dreamy with the thought of living in Marrakech – a business venture, pure and simple. Over and over again I reminded him that we were not going to *live* in Marrakech, we were just going to visit for the occasional treat, the point being to make an income from the riad. But Dan, I could see, had a secret dream of becoming a resident Marakchi – I thought I'd defer that battle for when we had a house that was habitable. He loved the city, it made him fizz with energy – he needed no excuse to stride around the souk in a flowing djellaba, getting up to who knows what boys' scams with his Marakchi mates.

Having spent the rest of the day planning and making drawings, we had an afternoon meeting with Khadija at the estate agency, after which, as I jogged back towards the hotel breathlessly, way behind Dan's energized Marakchi stride, I remarked that if he always walked on ahead I would never be able to find my way around this city. I was unreasonably certain that I could orientate us by the shop whose window permanently displayed the hideous djellaba fashioned, it appeared, from ex-London Underground upholstery moquette, and the tripe-vendor whose wares came in twenty fashionable shades of beige and brown.

Dan stopped. 'OK,' he said, 'you navigate.'

I struck off confidently in the direction of Maggie's and Djemaa El Fna, a leisurely ten-minute stroll.

A change of window display here, an early run on tripe futures there, and my confidence faltered. For well over an hour we meandered along the warren of identical narrow twilit alleys, unable to find navigational landmarks, without even the position of the sun to guide us. The streets grew dark, and in this sparsely lit unknown part of the medina deserted, but for sinister hooded figures lurking in the shadows. One of the Grim Reapers detached himself from his doorway and began to follow us. As his footsteps echoed ours, I got seriously frightened and my knees became wobbly. He was gaining on us; his rapid steps were the only sound in this vacant wasteland, apart from heavy breathing. Mine.

Our Spanish friends have always said that it was madness for us to go to Morocco. 'All Moroccans carry knives,' they warned, breathless with horror, every time we said we were off to Morocco, 'and they use them for the slightest thing.' Even Dan had remarked how many Moroccan men had facial scars, and had ruminated about knife fights.

When the Grim Reaper drew level with us, the shadow cast by his hood meant that I could not see the expression on his face. He ordered us to stop, and with pure adrenaline coursing in our veins, we did. He uttered a staccato imprecation, gutturally, an incomprehensible mixture of Arabic and French, and as we stood there miserably awaiting our fate, he signalled another Grim Reaper to leave his doorway, shuffle across the alley and join our group.

'He want to know if you are lost?' GR2 asked, and after one look at our travel-weary faces, gave us succinct directions for Djemaa El Fna. Shaking, we tottered off, following his directions, while the two of them watched us like kindly shepherds guarding their strays.

The thing is not to panic. Though it is likely that every newcomer will get lost in this city, because all the windowless alleys and anonymous front doors look identical, the fact to remember is that within the medina you are never more than walking distance from the epicentre, Djemaa El Fna – I'd guess a mile at most. Wherever you fetch up, any passing toddler can, and gleefully will, show you how to get there.

We turned a corner and found ourselves in a lighted street, where a café provided two vanilla yoghurts and a couple of sticky cakes, and suddenly everything was just fine again. Dan did not encourage me to do any more navigation.

We dined off takeaway cakes that night, too cold and tired to bother with a balanced diet – Marakchi cakes are sublime confections of almonds, honey, violent colouring and spices. Rejuvenated, Dan designed an elegant spiral staircase which he continued to refine and embellish until half past two, when he finally consented to be my hot-water bottle.

We woke up to sun, orange juice, croissants and Abdeltif with an estimate. He and Khaled had managed to account for everything in this complicated restoration. The vital document was composed of smudged pencil squiggles on the back of an old Christmas card, which became ever more blurred and squiggled as the months passed. I had no idea quite how much work was involved, but the estimate seemed reasonable to me, and we accompanied Abdeltif without demur to the bank to withdraw the initial payment. The bank was impressively closed, but Abdeltif is not a man to take a massive locked and barred steel door as any kind of deterrent, and he simply went round to the back where the shoe-cleaners and kebab-sellers congregate, and knocked loudly on the gate. The rather less magnificent back door was opened by a disgruntled minion who ushered us in with much tut-tutting, and there, frowning over his computer, was Hassam, delighted to see us and happy to drop whatever major transaction he was engaged in to attend to our needs.

A wad of money weightier, we wandered the souk and bought a simple carved stone fountain to take back to Spain in the Suzuki. We ambled into our estate agency and were invited to have tea with the owner, a passionate and urbane man whose mission it was to help conserve what was left of the original medina, and who agonized about the shady deals that resulted in historic traditional buildings being razed to make way for bland hotels. His grand-parents' riad, once the largest in the medina, had been flattened, he told us, and the site was in the process of becoming a hotel. As we left he handed us a photocopied sheet of guidelines for restoration of old buildings in the medina, and shuffled off to a shuttered office.

Like seasoned habitués we dropped into Chegrouni's to sit out in the sun and watch the world amble by while we ate a tagine with raisins and almonds. After our unpretentious lunch we had another meeting with Abdeltif – this time we were to visit the translator who was going to make all the paperwork we had signed comprehensible. I felt a surprising confidence in my French, but Abdeltif insisted that we should have all the documents in English as well, so thanks to the polyglot skills of

Samir, we bound ourselves into a trilingual agreement whereby Abdeltif promised to finish the building work by 12 June, six months away, and gave himself a penalty clause for late completion – all his idea, not ours. 'And if when everything is completed you are very happy, you will give me and Khaled five hundred pounds each?'

Yes, I cheerfully agreed. It seemed laughably little.

After our meeting with Samir the translator, we crossed the sun-baked expanse of Djemaa El Fna to the shambling police compound where we had the documents ratified and stamped. This involved a lot of hanging around in a bare room painted in functional cream and green gloss, while people shuffled up, bearing sheaves of papers, to one of two old wooden desks that would have been laughed out of school in Billy Bunter's day. Behind each desk sat a severe functionary, and upon each desk lay a pile of multi-columned ledgers into which every transaction was painstakingly entered and stamped. The equivalent of forty pence then changed hands.

The following day we returned to Spain in the Suzuki, with our fountain in the back and a large envelope containing the papers stating that we were the owners of a dar, 95 Derb Al Qadi, Azbezt, Marrakech.

6

SOLO

Morocco is all about trading, and it is alarmingly easy to buy just about anything. All you need is an Arab speaker whom you trust, a *notaire*, and a bag full of dirhams. A smattering of French is useful too, since all legal business takes place in French. Buying a house is a straightforward two-part process; in the end ours turned out to be a four-part process, but we were unaware of that then. A fortnight after our first meeting with Maître Yakub I had to return to arrange final payments and to sign a great raft of completion papers that Abdeltif had assembled in the meantime.

In Spain, Dan and I had not been idle – we had had our annual terminal row. As I boarded the balsa-wood plane for Casablanca, bidding him a curt goodbye – I had to get to the airport somehow – I wondered how I would get home on my return, since Dan was leaving, had had enough, and would most likely be ensconced in some rich, efficient, nice woman's flat in London by the time I got back. They are annual events, these rows, but at the time they always seem pretty final – the sun goes white, the sky goes grey and my brain turns to pulp. A slight advantage was that I didn't care that the pilot sounded like a hyperactive ten-year-old who'd had a Coke too many, or that the turbulence bounced my little polystyrene roll off my tray. It was all dust and ashes anyway.

So it was not in the perkiest frame of mind that I greeted Abdeltif several hours later at the Marrakech Menara airport. He assessed the situation within two minutes, asked no questions and just left me to get on with it. We sped in his giant new four-wheel-drive Pajero – which I was alarmed to notice had a DVD screen on the dashboard – to Maggie's, where once again I was the solitary guest.

'Madame Maggie does not like my car,' Abdeltif said in tones of astonished pain. 'She says it is uncomfortable and vulgar. You don't think so, do you?'

Difficult question. 'Well, Abdeltif, it is not exactly uncomfortable, though four doors would make life easier. But it is definitely vulgar. Surely you wouldn't have it any other way?'

He burst into a great guffaw, which made all his

wonderful and quite undeserved white teeth flash in the sun, shook a clunky stainless steel and gold watch down his wrist, and said, 'What do you think of my new Rolex Oyster?'

Abdeltif's idea of heaven was to be seen driving his mammoth car, gold Gucci sunglasses on the end of his nose, a mobile phone clapped to each ear, and a Bruce Lee film on the DVD. He was such a nice man, and during that miserable week he looked after me in the most gentle and sensitive way, never asking why I sat gloomily in my room all day, never mentioning Dan, just providing orange juice, mint tea, salads and occasional gusts of laughter.

Also terror. We had a date with Maître Yakub, and for some reason Abdeltif's vehicle was out of action – probably getting a new Coca-Cola dispenser, or a billiard table put in the back – so, having talked to Hassam to arrange the final cash transfer, and then to Khadija at the estate agency, Abdeltif asked if we could borrow Khadija's moped for the journey to the French quarter. She did not look overjoyed, but probably calculating that she was insured and that the company would pay for a new bike, she assented. As usual, I was smartly clad for this inter-view with the Maître – it didn't do to look like the normal Spanish tramp in this very fastidious city where even the glue-sniffer's brown polyester trousers are clean and pressed – and it was with trepidation that I swept my beautiful embroidered

Rajasthani coat about my knees and my perilously Isadora Duncan scarf about my neck, regretting the cavalier manner in which bike helmets are dispensed with in this giant accident of a city.

Abdeltif, in his car, is a considerate, sensible and remarkably middle-aged driver. Abdeltif on Khadija's moped is a testosteroneous madman. He slashed through the rush-hour traffic, scattering pedestrians left and right. He serpentined among tightly packed vehicles to be first at any lights and revved the engine in a fury to be gone until the first flicker of green, he skimmed pavements, roundabouts and traffic islands, missing road hardware, donkeys, horses and wing mirrors by a millimetre. I was absolutely terrified, hanging on to him with a sense of despair, knowing that when he did whack us straight into a wall there was nothing to stop us from becoming a pair of pizzas.

As we left the tightly packed circuitry of the old city and took off along the wide, busy boulevards of the French quarter beyond the walls, a new thrill presented itself to his crazed speed-maddened reflexes. A man, a surprisingly old and respectable man, attempted to challenge Abdeltif's role as King of the Road. In vain the old guy spurred his vehicle on, made fruitless attempts to catch up with us at the lights, failed utterly to draw up alongside us at roundabouts. Abdeltif merely revved and roared. Even the back of his head exuded mastery.

However, after a mile or so of this adrenaline-charged race there came a moment when the traffic was stopped by a very thorough policeman, and Abdeltif could do nothing legal to escape our grizzled challenger. He scowled as the old man drew up alongside us, and revved the engine as per usual. The old man merely tapped me gently on the shoulder, and pointed out that the hem of my coat was dangerously close to the bike chain – one flutter in the wrong direction and I would have been flipped under the next HGV without any help from Abdeltif. For me it was a sobering moment – as if I needed *more* sobriety – but it made not the slightest difference to Abdeltif, who continued to speed with euphoric mania.

As I stepped off the lethal beast I told him that there was no chance that I would be his passenger back to the medina on that thing. 'You are the worst driver in the whole of Marrakech. You very nearly killed us because of your ridiculous juvenile competitiveness.'

Completely unabashed, he grinned. 'But it was *fun*, wasn't it?'

After our meeting with the Maître, we tumbled down on to the pavement where Abdeltif's brother-in-law, Khaled, was mysteriously waiting for us, his magic briefcase at the ready. Marrakech is a small city, and its inhabitants think nothing of shooting from one end to the other several times a day on the slightest pretext – and Abdeltif had plainly calculated that this property acquisition could have major implications for both of them. We had a coffee while we inspected the new batch of papers. They signalled complete and final ownership of the *dar*. Bravely Khaled volunteered to be Abdeltif's return passenger, and I wondered if I'd ever see either of them again.

Sitting primly alone in a petit taxi whose driver was in no hurry to leave this world, or get to the medina for that matter, I pondered my painful and ridiculous situation. What was I going to do with a house in the Marrakech medina? The place meant nothing but grief to me – as far as I was concerned, looked at coldly in retrospect, the whole venture had just been an expensive architectural opportunity for Dan to flex his design muscles, and now that he was no longer at my side it merely underlined my vulnerability and solitude. Restoring it, letting it, making a business out of it seemed like a hopelessly gargantuan venture, for which I had no appetite on my own.

Marrakech is not a good place for a solitary woman. You are not abused or badly treated, just invisible. Wife or mother might be acceptable, but I had finally and with relief resigned from both.

I set my jaw and walked back to my room with dignity. And sat in my room with dignity. And had dinner, breakfast and lunch with dignity, and wondered whether dignity was going to be my companion for the rest of my life.

I was certainly not going to beg Dan, or even suggest coolly and unemotionally to him that he rethink his decision to leave. Pride would never let me be with anyone who did not wish to be with me. That is why whenever the matter has raised its old-fashioned head I have felt ambiguous about marriage – after my only marital experience, when to my perplexed dismay I underwent a complete and unpredictable character change (being sub-missive, walking ten paces behind my husband, discovering myself to be a desperately inefficient but uncomplaining servant, that kind of thing), I am dubious about marriage. I have read a thousand articles itemizing its advantages to men and dis-advantages to women.

Slightly embarrassed by the discreet concern of Mohammed and Abdeltif, I decided that I had to get out of the hotel, and spent my free day visiting two museums in the medina, the Dar si Said and the Marrakech Museum. I loved them both. The Marrakech Museum, housed in the late-nineteenth-century Mnebhi Palace, was grandly portentous, showing an exhibition of cutting-edge con-temporary Moroccan photographs in cool pillared halls that are unfortunately roofed over, with a vast light fitting in the middle, like a baroque spaceship.

But the rooms, the fine tiled mosaic *zellig fessi*, the painted pineapple frieze in the hammam, and the frisky displays of dummies playing gnawa instruments or wearing wedding garb were engrossing, as were the cases – in magnificently painted rooms – of heavy Berber jewellery. I managed to spend quite a wad on books in the excellent bookshop, and eased my beating heart with tea and a cake in the small sunlit café.

Dar si Said palace, built at the end of the nineteenth century by Ba Ahmed, the vizier of Moulay Abd al-Aziz, and finished by his brother Si Said, had an air of being marooned in a 1920s time warp, with large hand-drawn maps, dotted with naive drawings and careful sans serif lettering. I expected to bump into Virginia Woolf or some other slightly whiskery Bloomsbury traveller with slender feet in sensible shoes.

The objects in the cases had amusingly amateurish labels, and the small stringed instrument labelled 'a kind of drum' stopped my gloomy maunderings for the space of a short titter. The walls of the high empty rooms were covered with carved wooden doors, Rabat rugs, Tensift carpets, embroidered kaftans, leatherwork, wedding chairs of perfumed wood, black and scarlet Berber shepherd cloaks. The whole place was magical, echoing with my solitary footsteps. There was a magnificent room, its walls and ceiling intricately rich with every kind of hand-wrought polychrome finish, with a fine pair of non-matching his 'n' hers thrones. There was a display of tiny painted cradles that made my heart lurch in a pang for my granddaughters Chilali and Maizie. And the garden, thick with tall palms and scented shrubs, with its gracious *zellig fessi* fountain and pool in a small hexagonal wooden pavilion, provided a peaceful moment of solace. Museums are always comforting, and for a couple of hours these two were a welcome diversion from the miserable black cloud called The Future.

On the way back I tried to cash some money, but all the cash-dispensers were in unusual agreement – no, they were not going to give me a single dirham. This was the end, to be stranded in this alien town with no man and no money. It was also a serious embarrassment, since I still had my bill to pay at Maggie's. I could not understand – I was convinced that I had loads in my account. Certainly enough to cover this withdrawal.

With his usual uncanny intuition for when a rescue was required, Abdeltif just happened to sashay into view as I was about to stumble glumly across the square, and asked what the trouble was.

'I can't get any money out of the machines. They are all telling me to refer to my lender,' I said, blushing that he should witness this moment of humiliation.

'Let us try once more,' he answered with

characteristic braggadocio. Standing beside me, he watched with increasing incredulity as I tapped in a number of dirhams. He looked uncomfortable. 'You want to take out £12.50?' he asked, puzzled.

'No,' I said, '£125.'

'Aah. Well, you need to put on another nought. You need to key in two *thousand* dirhams.'

If there's one thing I hate, it's being an incompetent poltroon. I had also not realized that banks had a lower withdrawal limit.

Back at Maggie's I sat in my room reading everything the hotel offered, desperately filling in the time until I was due to return to my new Spanish solitude the following day. With lightning speed I waded through several Royal Air Maroc flight magazines, something rollicking and rustic by Mavis Cheek, and as a grand finale *The Heart-Shaped Bullet* by Kathryn Flett, a flayed and painfully honest account of the demise of a marriage. It did not do anything positive for my mood.

I must admit that one of the things that was worrying me, aside from what I was going to do with this potential palace in Marrakech now that Dan and I were asunder, was that I was in a contorted way rather enjoying feeling sorry for myself. I never ask for help, *never* ring friends or turn up at midnight and sound off incoherently. I never drink and trash my ex loudly in restaurants. On the contrary, I get more and more silent and withdrawn. If things get *very* bad, I sometimes write it all down on pieces of paper – which turn up years later in my tax file or at the bottom of a drawer and are always fascinating, but the story is always exactly the same and I can never tell which of the five or so serious men in my life these documents concern. I'm not a cryer or a sobber, more of a numb zombie, and unnervingly, it was beginning to feel comfortable, as though this demeanour fitted me very well and I would have no problem at all vacantly staring my way through the next twenty years or so.

However, I had to face a slight interruption to this morosely satisfying prospect, since Abdeltif had insisted that I come and dine at his flat that night with Layla and his effervescent one-and-a-bit-year-old, Faruk. With a sinking heart, wondering whether I would be equal to being cheerfully bounced upon and overfed, I took a taxi to his place way outside the city walls.

Layla was effusively welcoming, and sat and talked briefly until we had exhausted our common vocabulary. This done with, she retired to the kitchen and I had a chance to make friends with Faruk, who had just discovered the joy of his new walker on wheels, which gave him an uncanny resemblance to the Red Queen in *Alice through the Looking Glass* – like a small tank he sped along the floor, aiming for painted tables and bookshelves and shrieking with laughter every time he crashed. He reminded me forcibly of his dad, though he was uncharacteristically shy when addressed directly. While Abdeltif channel-hopped on his enormous TV, and Faruk legged it for some priceless inlaid table, or hid, confounded by a smile from me, behind an armchair, the flat itself kept me busy. It was all dusty pink and eau de nil, a colour scheme dreamed up by Abdeltif and of which he was inordinately proud. 'It is *very* good. I think *everyone* will want their house like this. Oh, excuse me . . . *Salaam alaikum* . . .' His mobile needed him.

As he gabbled away, making some plan or other, I had a chance to take in the charms of the recently completed flat, which he had bought and then decorated as a surprise for Layla. One entered straight into an open space. To the right was Layla's kitchen, and to the left the bathroom. Ahead was a sitting room to the right, and to the left, separated from it by a low wall with a pink and green colonnade, Abdeltif's library, which housed the TV and a vast 1930s three-piece suite surrounding a low table. Once you took your seat, you sank immovably into the cut moquette and were further weighted down by enormous quantities of food.

In the sitting room was an elaborate bookshelf, housing a handful of gold-tooled books in Arabic, a very grand Koran on a special stand, and *The Country Decorator*, a book I had written several years previously, which was not hard to spot as the odd one out. Florid seaviews hung on the walls throughout, featuring lipstick-bright sunsets and patently unseaworthy boats floating on a neatly ploughed sea. Brocade banquettes lined the walls, and three large low painted tables made an impassable obstacle to crossing the room. No longer, however, since he has now sold them to me and they have become an impassable obstacle to movement in my house.

Pride of place was given over to a lamp confected from a piece of driftwood, covered in polychrome dribbles by his artist friend. Unusual lighting was Abdeltif's forte, and he also invited me to praise his tall terracotta minaret brilliantly illuminated from within by several light bulbs, which could be the Koutoubia or a less grandiose mosque, depending on whether it had its pinnacle in place. He demonstrated several times.

Layla had made a feast, the like of which I have never faced for quantity and deliciousness. I don't know how she did it – the shopping alone would tax the resources of weight lifter and octopus combined. Faruk was an enquiring and powerful wriggler, and most likely did not sit quietly in a pushchair while she carefully selected her vegetables. Her cold-water kitchen was lit by a single bare light bulb. Her sublime tagines were achieved using a few wobbly-bottomed aluminium pans on a single calor-gas ring.

Despite these handicaps she was a cordon bleu cook: she had made aubergines in tomato sauce (*zeilook*), peas in some thick spicy sauce, and quince in almond sauce that I recall as being particularly delicious. These were followed by tagine of lamb with lemon and olives (*tagine el lahm emshmel*). She hovered, smiling, pressing more and yet more upon me. I had been warned that the host's wife would lurk in the kitchen and never join in, and I had been told as a guest not to contribute anything, and absolutely not to do anything helpful. What I had not been told was that the correct response to '*Kul! Kul!*' (Eat! Eat!) was to belch loudly and say '*Shebaat*' (I'm full) while you can still move.

After I'd eaten enough for ten, Abdeltif accompanied me to the main road, hailed a petit taxi, and wedged me in beside a snoring man in the back, behind a snoring woman in the front. I had plenty of time to contemplate the grimness of the next few days, and wonder how I was going to manage on my own. The evening had been an unexpectedly pleasant diversion, but left to myself in the back of the cab I owned that I was feeling a little wobbly about the future. Even the immediate future – the walk from the square along dark alleys deserted but for howling cats and babbling glue-sniffers – did not appeal much.

Typically, thoughtfully, Abdeltif had arranged for his second-in-command, Mohammed, to meet me in

Djemaa El Fna, which was dark and empty by now. In companionable silence we walked back to Maggie's.

As we wrestled with the heavy door, I could hear the phone ringing. My heart leapt in the hope that this might be Dan – any kind of communication would be better than silence. It stopped immediately we achieved entry. Bitterly disappointed, I bid goodnight to Mohammed and shut myself in my room. He very kindly decided to stay the night, sleeping, I think, in the broom cupboard, to ensure that I would not be alone.

I was midway through brushing my teeth when the phone rang again and I could hear Mohammed pattering across the courtyard to answer it. Arabic. Then French. 'Non, elle est au lit, elle est très fatiguée.'

No, I wasn't, and with a light toothpaste moustache I charged out of my room, skittered down the suicidal stairs and sprinted to the phone. I was thrilled to hear Dan's voice, asking what time my flight was due to arrive. Neither of us mentioned the row, or the fact that he should have been ensconced with nice Miss Rich Philanthropist by now in some cosy flat in Islington. We both sounded cautiously pleased to be talking to each other. Our terminal row was over for another year.

My hopes soared. Maybe 95 Derb Al Qadi would not be the disaster I'd feared after all.

Extreme weather was another exciting annual event that marked our life together.

Whenever the electricity was on and the phone working, we would ring Abdeltif to hear how things were going. At first, of course, it was all good news – we had met ten workmen when we bought the house. By the following week there were twenty-six men working on the site, almost all the carefully handpicked specialists from his mosque who had brought Abdeltif's Neapolitan pistachio and strawberry flat to its heady level of perfection. I felt a massive surge of responsibility – single-handedly I was supporting hundreds of people, almost a village. It was a humbling and rather scary thought.

Maggie's architect friends reckoned that anything built in Marrakech would cost ten times as much to build in London, not that you'd be able to lay your hands on a *jibs* frieze master by riffling through Yellow Pages. Certainly the workmen did a hell of a lot of work for a pittance. I worried about the ethics of this, but I'm afraid that the logic of doing what Marakchis do when in Marrakech at length overrode all scruples. They were earning a good wage for a job they enjoyed, working in a team that was like family, and it looked like they would be in employment for at least six months. They seemed happy and worked together efficiently and effectively with much camaraderie. In this matter, as in so many others, I had to trust Abdeltif to recommend what was right.

But the enterprise was a complete leap of faith. We did not have an architect; big structural changes were being made without the benefit of a qualified engineer – although Abdeltif's good friend the trainee surveyor had done drawings sufficiently convincing to get planning permission, which had been awarded unusually speedily.

We also had no idea what kind of a house it was going to be, apart from Abdeltif's promise that it would be a palace. We had asked simply for traditional finishes and feared his penchant for over-the-top. But the most brilliant thing he had learned was to listen. When we talked to him he listened. In my probably warped experience, this is so rare among men as to need repeating. The other wondrous thing he did, having listened gravely and attentively, was to say, 'No problem.' He actually solved problems. What a guy.

The phone calls were usually cheering, but, as any fool could have predicted, they soon began to take a familiar turn. I began to ring Abdeltif rather less frequently when every call involved extras that seemed to cost thousands of dirhams, and I never knew whether they were what we had agreed to or something new. I could never compute how much he wanted during the course of our conversation – dividing by sixteen is not my forte. And I had no real idea of what he was doing at all, since we were in Spain and the house was in Marrakech. Being a sensible kind of person, you will say that this was asking for trouble, and that no one but a complete idiot would try to restore a house like this. With the benefit of hindsight, I am delighted to say that you would be wrong.

Maggie brightened our ignorant gloom by inviting us to stay at her hotel for Christmas, a prospect that solved a major yuletide problem: like a surprising number of men whose lonely benighted wives I have talked to, Dan is allergic to Christmas. Benighted wives and I have compared notes about how selfish it is of our respective partners to moan and groan and stage a mammoth whinge throughout December, how daft to make such a fuss throwing rattles out of prams, how lonely it is to be the solitary cheerleader, how ridiculous it feels to be the sole diner, toast-drinker and cracker-puller. They make more bother, we agreed, about Christmas than the most ardent pudding-maker and tree-decorator. At least if we were at Maggie's, I calculated, Dan would be unlikely to spend the dreaded day groaning in bed, and even if he did, I could have fun with the other guests.

We arrived on a cold and drizzly Christmas Eve, and were met by Abdeltif, who was curiously reticent about our house, apart from telling us how much more work was involved than he had estimated.

He took us straight to Maggie's, which was full over

Christmas, with her family and a couple of friends as well as two couples whom we had not met before. We dumped our stuff in our room and greeted everyone fondly, looking forward to whatever carouse she would have cooked up for us all.

However, we were also desperate to see how our house was progressing, so we grabbed an umbrella and sloshed off in our sensible boots through the muddy alleys to 95 Derb Al Qadi. Our excitement mounted as we passed the toothless cigarette man, the glue-sniffer and the crowd of juvenile foot-ballers, who all wished us 'bon soir'. It was almost dark when we reached the house, and we had to pick our way over the entanglement of builders' bicycles outside the entrance with extreme care.

Eagerly we pushed open the front door – and beheld a vision of complete devastation. It was like something out of the darkest eras of Victorian asbestos mining – dark-hooded figures squelched through wall-to-wall mud carrying buckets, by the light of three ten-watt light bulbs. Where there had been floor and wall tiles was just rubble. The hand-some doors had gone, as had the windows, there were no stairs at all, and the workmen reached the gallery by climbing up twig ladders. The painted ceiling had gone, replaced by grey cement. In place of the upstairs balcony there was nothing at all, just an unprotected four-metre drop. The one reminder of the pretty details that had seduced us were the curlicued wrought-iron window bars, and to these small plastic bags containing a yellow liquid were attached. I wondered aloud about them, until Dan murmured 'pee'. Ingenious, given that there was no loo and no plumbing.

Khaled bustled from the gloom at the back of the building, with a smile of welcome that faded from his lips when he saw our faces. We stood in the icy drizzle, damp, disheartened, and not a little afraid of what we had got ourselves into, while the hooded labourers continued to wander the site with their buckets, casting sinister shadows on the rough walls. Khaled attempted confidence, but his words did not thaw our frozen hearts. It was a disaster, from which I could see no way to extricate ourselves without losing everything. Dan wisely kept his opinion to himself – he just looked around aghast, and said nothing. In just over a month, they had completely destroyed our beautiful house.

We trudged back through the ankle-deep mud, tripping over manholes and slopping into puddles, in complete silence. But as we walked back to the hotel, the fine drizzle stopped. Once safely back among the civilized amenities of Maggie's we had several warming vodkas, decided that this had to be the nadir of our enterprise, that things could only get better, changed into something black and mud-free, and threw ourselves at the jollifications with all the desperate enthusiasm of drowning men clutching at a plastic bottle.

The nice businessman from Lake Como and his Swedish girlfriend enacted some Scandinavian ritual that I'm quite sure Carl Larsson has depicted – it took place at twilight, which is early in midwinter Marrakech, and involved both of them wearing white from head to toe. She had an ingeniously constructed cartwheel balanced precariously on her blonde hair, alight with candles. He was carrying a fistful of candles too, as well as his notes. We gazed up bemused and enchanted as they walked with un-flinching, ungiggling gravitas along the balcony running above us along the first floor, singing a Swedish Christmas song. Slowly they descended Maggie's tortuous staircase and stood, innocent and unabashed in the courtyard, still singing. Cynicism was peeled from our eyes, and the odd tear had to be quelled. Whatever happened to Christmas? I wondered. This is what it was once about, but it got lost somewhere between Mattel and Fisher-Price.

In the awed silence that followed – during which everyone hastily rearranged their lives and thoughts, with more love, more simplicity, more honest-to-goodness goodness – there was a scuffle at the front door. Abdeltif was the first to break free from his trance to open it. Into the hushed courtyard bounded Manu and three extravagantly peacock-clad confrères.

With their burnished dark faces and voluminous, all-concealing, scarlet, royal-blue and Barbara-Cartland-pink sleeveless gandoras, sporting red and black skullcaps encrusted with cowrie shells, they erupted among us, beaming perfect white teeth with a gleam of gold, eager and restless with repressed energy. Maggie arranged them, an electric life study, in a corner by the fountain, perilously close to an agave as spiky as a porcupine. Manu and his boys unpacked their instruments: tambours, *cracksh* (brass castanets), and the *gimbri* that I had seen before (fretless shoebox covered with skin from the neck of a dromedary, used for percussion with three strings for melody). They accepted Coca-Colas, settled themselves into comfortable positions on low seats and cushions while Abdeltif and Mohammed haloed them with candles, and began to sing.

It is probably customary to be stoned when listening to the mystical brotherhood of the Gnawa, but not essential, since the rhythm produces its own kind of dreamy euphoria. It is African Blues, full of the heartache of slavery and exile dating from a millennium ago, with lyrics that tell of loss and pain and injustice.

> The Sudan. Oh! Sudan
> The Sudan, land of my people
> I was enslaved, I was sold
> I was taken away from my loved ones . . .

The passion comes from long-remembered pain, but also from a belief that this music can heal all ills, cure madness, bring happiness. From time to time one of the quartet would rise to his feet and dance among the orange trees and bird cages, his eyes shut, weaving around obstacles, languorously waving his arms like seaweed underwater, music flooding his veins. I fretted lest they injure themselves on an eye-level birdcage or a crotch-level cactus spike, but they were way ahead of me, and wafted, floated their way out of danger, high on a dream of desert nights, pulsating stars, a thrilling emptiness of cold silence, with firelight flickering on sweating entranced faces.

They played and danced in their aggressive agave corner, never, as far as one could tell, impaling themselves on the bunch of upturned daggers that lurked malevolently in those giant plant-pots. How very English I felt, longing to be swallowed up, to drown myself in sound, to sway across the *mizmat* in diaphanous garments, arms drifting fluidly to the currents and icy syncopations, hips undulating like sand whirled in an eddy of wind. Instead I sat with my arms crossed, sipping my wine politely, nodding head, tapping toe, and very definitely *outside* the proceedings. My mind would keep returning to the scene of devastation along the derb.

Abdeltif felt no such reserve, and hurtled on to the courtyard, all kicking slippers and flinging arms,

123

feet colliding with candles, head glancing audibly against the bird cage, beckoning Dan to join him. They danced together with fine abandon until they had collected sufficient contusions, finally falling upon their drinks in a breathless, excited heap.

When the assembled hearts finally resumed their usual beat and Manu had whirled himself into exhaustion we applauded enthusiastically, Maggie paid them their fee, grumbling somewhat at Christmas inflation, and we fell to chatting with our fellow guests with a single-minded interest that might have made them wonder whether we were doing a surprise interview for *Hello!* We were unperturbed by the chill as we all settled down to dinner on the roof in Maggie's new pink tent, a comely interpretation of a Berber nomad's, with curtains all round, three big tables and many chairs. The Christmas Eve tagine was marked by the occasional excitement of a cat padding across the roof over our heads and tipping rainwater down the walls. We had all dressed up for the occasion, the wine flowed generously, and we became best friends surprisingly quickly. Maggie's husband succumbed to an unexpected burst of extroversion, and insisted that we all play silly games far into the night.

Oh, we were so grateful for the diversion, for those few brief hours of forgetting, of careless intoxication before the worries darkened like gathering vultures the following morning. Breakfast was quiet, there were remarkably few people to be seen, and those who appeared kept their own counsel. Dan and I were flabby and grey and had nothing to say either.

Despite the prohibition on presents, I wanted something frivolous to leaven our despair, and on Christmas morning insisted we go out into the town and buy the cheapest, most kitsch and ridiculous things we could find as stocking fillers for the other guests. The souk was functioning absolutely as usual – there was no sign of impending Yule apart from the inflatable Father Christmases that hung from every stall – and continued to do so on Father's Day, Easter Sunday, and every other day. We found a Pokémon shopping bag – in addition to being really naff, it fell apart within minutes; we found several variants on snowstorm globes – a couple of Dutch windmills, the Taj Mahal and a confusing underwater scene with fishes plying their way through a blizzard; we found some of the fanciest hair-slides that could ever have graced the tresses of a star-struck five-year-old, adorned with glittering shoes, twinkling bluebirds, diamanté hearts; and we found transparent plastic make-up bags decked with shoals of exotic fish and bouquets of improbable roses. Men were more of a problem. Finally we struck lucky with a job lot of fake crystals, confected as far as one could see from tinsel, anthracite and old potatoes, guaranteed to fascinate their recipients whether their interests lay in geology, glitter or forgery.

Clever Maggie had arranged Christmas lunch on the roof, and in honour of the occasion the sun made a welcome appearance, beaming down, drying and lightening the dark wet floors and walls of yestereve and making the tent steam. The tables looked properly festive, with red tablecloths, great tureens of oranges and tangerines wreathed by glossy leaves, bottles of wine in formation, glasses spattering fractured prisms on to plates. Again the magic of her bonhomie, good food – a turkey cooked to perfection in the communal souk oven, couscous, tagines – and plentiful drink dislodged our grey depression from its perch for a few grateful hours. It was a maverick day of fool's licence, when it was OK to ask intrusive questions; to make daft replies to simple queries; to tell the complete stranger on my left all about my younger son's penchant for football and fluffy girls, to laugh until everyone had a dentist's familiarity with each other's fillings; to grow maudlin and moon over the good times we had had in the past; to grow gloomy at the prospect of the future; to have a short bitter political alter-cation; and then to fall asleep.

As lunch finally drifted to its conclusion, Dan and I decided to look despair fiercely in the face and outscowl it – we walked through the slowly drying mud to our house in Derb Al Qadi. We braced ourselves outside the front door and opened it cautiously to a view of the courtyard, which was of course abuzz with workmen, since Christmas is nothing special in Marrakech.

By daylight the vision within was not entirely from hell – it was obvious that all the men knew what they were doing and were conscientiously following a tight timetable. They greeted us politely and continued with their work, carrying buckets, climbing rickety ladders, chipping plaster from crumbling walls. It was a scene of satisfying industry, even if the finer points of architecture were reminiscent of the Colosseum several millennia after the last gladiator had shut the door behind him. Khaled appeared, immaculate in his neat black leather jacket and trousers, from some hidden corner of the chaotic site, his briefcase pressed to his chest.

He smiled shyly, and offered to take us round. He had convincing answers for everything, explained the absence of doors and windows which were off getting their crusted old cocoa-coloured paint stripped, showed us the schedule of works, produced colour swatches and prototype tap fittings from his magic briefcase, described the intended finish in all the rooms, asked our opinion on light fittings, door furniture, door finishes, fanlight glass in bright colours from Turkey, and assiduously took notes in a special little black bound notebook. The place still looked like an asbestos mine, the walls were heaving porridge, the floors solidified mushroom soup, but we felt a waft of confidence in the calming presence of Khaled and came away almost positive. He seemed to be all attention, to be efficient, capable and to know what he was doing. The men appeared to work for him with goodwill and generosity, giving time and effort beyond the call of duty and certainly beyond the call of their pitiful weekly dirhams.

The startling thing to a European is that in the medina every building operation comes direct from the Middle Ages – there are no cement-mixers droning, no tile-cutters or electric drills screaming. Apart from the five ten-watt light bulbs and the heap of workers' bicycles, there is nothing to surprise a medieval time-traveller. The ladders are made of twigs; building materials come and rubbish leaves, swaying along narrow snickets, transported by donkeys; cement and *tadelakt* are mixed in great pools on the courtyard floor. And, as we discovered eventually, not a single centimetre of our riad was left as found. Everything was stripped, improved, decorated and replaced by deft, patient hands and primitive technology.

During our Christmas stay we visited our house once more, with tentatively rising hopes – even during these few days they had made visible progress, destroying the last vestiges of what had once been the hole-in-the-ground loo. The house was now nothing but an empty shell, things could only get better, and Khaled was, as ever, patiently reassuring. After all, they had only been at work for a couple of months, and they had accomplished so much destruction. However, the next stage was where things could go terribly wrong, and we would not be around to halt mistakes before they became disasters.

We left Marrakech feeling like people who had followed their instincts — straight into a midden. When friends and family asked eagerly how our riad in the medina was going, we could only mutter something inaudible and stare at our feet. Thanks to the distractions laid on by Maggie we had managed to laugh our way through Christmas. With the New Year, premonitions of doom rushed to fill the vacancy.

8

ONE MAN'S POISSON

April 2002 came.

In just two more months our house would be finished. Dan and I did an intensive magazine scour, leafing through ancient copies of *Interiors* and *Elle Decoration*, tearing out patches of colour for the *tadelakt*, jubilant with agreement, excitedly ripping ideas from their moorings – curtains, seating, lighting. Abdeltif rang daily with lists of extras, small things we had overlooked – painted *tazouakt* doors, glazed fanlights, *mizmat* tiles in the courtyard, two fountains, *jibs* frieze on the archways in the kitchen, carved *tadelakt* friezes in the bathrooms – and I sat fearfully by the phone, wondering what these things were, and what size of a hole these extravagances were going to make in our fast dwindling resources.

The answer was a mere pinhole compared to plan B. Within sniffing distance of Abdeltif's self-imposed deadline, the phone rang. 'There is something else . . . the neighbours want to sell their place. It was once the *doueria* of your riad, where the old women go. They separated it, blocked up the windows and gave it a different entrance. Once it is restored, it will make your riad into a palace. You will have another *big* bedroom, and we will make a gorgeous hammam, with a bath big enough for two, with *tadelakt*, soft lighting – so romantic. You must buy it – it will be *breelliant*.'

The *doueria*, the dower house, where redundant old ladies were put out of the way. Just right for me, I thought.

And yet, it would make sense of that great blank wall above the green bedroom. Windows on the other side would echo the gallery.

I put the phone down and sat very still. Dan ambled in from walking the dogs, and asked what was up.

'You'd be crazy to buy it,' he said immediately. 'We don't have the money to do it up. We've hardly got enough to finish the house as it is.'

It's an odd thing, but when he does this, dismisses an idea without really thinking about it, it almost always shoots me off in the other direction. 'Well, I think it might make it more lettable,' I told him. 'The riad would certainly look much better without that great empty expanse of wall. We could put in another bathroom and there's room for another big bedroom. It could even be a private place where we stay, when we're in Marrakech. Or it could be a romantic honeymoon suite.'

Dan gave me a crushing look. Red rag to a bull.

'We'd have enough if I sold the flat in Brighton,' I heard myself say.

Brighton was our last physical link with the UK, a dear little white-painted flat with a view – over the bedside false teeth in the old people's home opposite – of the sea, and – over the sprawling suburbs – of the Downs. It was my base when I was commuting between Malaga and London, working one week a month for *Country Living*. I loved the flat, which was the perfect solitary haven, loved Brighton, which seemed to me the warmest, brightest, most welcoming place in the British Isles, full of gossip and good coffee and artistic people trying to get by. Brighton was one of the few places where it felt fine to be a solitary woman, it had absolutely wonderful shopping, more Oxfam shops per square inch than anywhere else on earth, nothing particularly sinister ever impinged, and among the gentle decay there was nothing too ugly except the excrescences on the sea front, the towering cliff of blank windowless cinema and the streaky-grey-cement town hall, which I imagine must have been the result of *enormous* backhanders in the philistine Sixties and Seventies. From the flat I could walk to the station, to Waitrose, to the sea to watch the sun set over Hove, to have tea with friendly painters, to the cinema. But these had been wan palliatives for spending time alone in the UK, when my heart constantly yearned to be back in Spain with Dan.

'It should sell in minutes, it's so dinky and convenient. And we'd probably get quite a bit for it; every newspaper you read is banging on about rising house prices. Brighton is the smart commute to London for people who can't quite afford London prices. And they're about to build a new high-speed link for London commuters, aren't they?'

I certainly convinced myself, and on the crest of this confident wave, I rang three estate agents and asked them to go and do an evaluation.

Dan gave me an on-your-head-be-it look, and stomped off to finish a painting of the cactus grove down the hill.

Two estate agents went – foxy Eastender Mark, and tweedy vicar Alan – and to my surprise they both came up with the same surprisingly large figure.

Well, this was a result. I rang Abdeltif, predicting confidently that in three months at the outside, we would be able to afford the *doueria* plus all the work on both, and could he just carry on in the meantime and finish the riad? To my disappointment he answered no. He could not finish the riad until we had bought the *doueria* – if we were going to buy it – because the plumbing for both would have to be connected and there was no point in finishing one without the other.

There was a sort of logic to this, but what it meant practically was that major work on the riad just ground to a halt, though the odd artisan still chipped away at friezes or painted doors. There were times when the thought crossed my mind that Abdeltif might even have decided to come up with the *doueria* at this crucial moment to buy himself more time.

The whole thing was hypothetical anyway, since we hadn't even looked inside the *doueria* and didn't know if we wanted it. But with a sense of effectiveness, decisiveness and competence, I booked us flights to Marrakech. I felt like Bill Gates, masterminding some giant takeover bid.

I announced to Abdeltif that we were coming to check out the *doueria*, and would like to stay in our house. 'All we need is one room. Just a room and a bed, we're not looking for comfort. We don't mind what it's like.'

There was a shifty silence. I swear I could hear his great big Hobbit's feet shuffling around. Then in his husky *concerned* voice he said, 'I think this is not a good idea, Madame Miranda. It is not a good idea at all. You will be very uncomfortable.'

Pronouncing every syllable. 'It is not ready. There are still builders there, in every room. You will have no peace.'

I argued feebly for a bit, then, realizing he was adamant and beginning to worry just a bit about what we were about to find at 95 Derb Al Qadi, I suggested Maggie's.

The Riad Magi alas, was booked solid, so Dan and I decided to return to the Tazi where our passion for this place had begun and whose staff kindly pretended to remember us. We booked into the psychedelic suite with the painted furniture that Maggie had previously occupied, whose polychrome cheeriness I had envied then.

Abdeltif met us at the airport and drove us into the medina, stopping from time to time for an urgent phone call on his mobile. The route from the airport was being turned into a garden as richly detailed and intricately planted as any Persian rug. Against an improbably pure blue sky there were yellow puffs of mimosa, and sprays of amethyst jacaranda. It was a sunny day, hot enough already to make me wish that I was not wearing quite so many layers of black.

Abdeltif parked among the *carrossas* under the olive tree in the little square outside our local mosque. I felt a prickle of excitement as we approached Number 95 at the end of the alley. A

135

scrawny ginger cat had taken up residence outside the front door, contributing a sour top note to the thick odour concentrated in the narrow walkway. It glowered as we picked our way past it.

A buzz of activity was audible from within the house as we turned the key, and we were effusively greeted by familiar and affectionate faces. There was Khaled in his spotless blacks, briefcase at the ready, every single one of his perfect white teeth exposed in his pleasure to see us; there was Rachid, painting a ceiling in a jigsaw puzzle of little pieces, who smiled shyly as usual, and then proceeded to gaze at us in what we might have mistaken for rapture had we been big-heads; there was Bin Laden the plumber, with his massive beard and little blue skullcap – he smiled, but being a Muslim of the non-touching-women variety, kept his hands behind his back for our greeting; there was Abdel Akabir the electrician and Youssef Bekai, our perfectly turned-out *jibs* frieze specialist – there is about a kilometre of this hand-chiselled plaster frieze in our riad, crisply decorating walls inside and out, and out-lining windows and doors. And there was Buddr, Khaled's right-hand man, an innocent country boy who always smiled and said yes, no matter what your request. Half a dozen more men were perilously hanging from ledges or clambering up ladders.

Having concluded our greetings and asked after

missing faces and everyone's wives and children, we turned our attention to the house. What did we expect? At first sight we were torn between horror and horror. Much had been done – more demolition mainly. There was not the slightest possibility that it could be finished in two months, and we could only guess what the finished thing would look like.

Abdeltif registered our crestfallen expressions, and proceeded to itemize every operation. Repeatedly he told us how disastrously he had underestimated. As he talked, we realized that nothing at all was retained of the original building without having been subjected to thorough basic renovation and multiple skills thereafter. We could only register his shortfall and sympathize.

The walls were all new and reinforced, from top to bottom. The dodgy original stairs, roof and metre-thick ceilings had been demolished, and every single crumb of rubble had been removed by teams of *carrossas*, ambling through the narrow alleys and dumped God knows where, with the resulting mess of rubble and mud in the alley causing serious resentment among our house-proud neighbours. Electricity and plumbing had been installed but were not yet working properly. Installing drainage – or possibly disposing of rubble – had necessitated raising the entire courtyard twenty-five centimetres, plus all the doors and windows in order to give the waste pipes a workable gradient.

That didn't bother me so much as the fact that
nothing, not one room, was anywhere near finished.
Bare rubble walls greeted us on every side, most
walls, ceilings and floors shared the depressing look
of congealed mutton fat, there was no sign of our
magnificent doors, in fact even the elegant archways
that had housed them had gone, replaced with plain
rectangular spaces. The canopies that once shaded
the doors had gone also. Everything decorative in
terms of structure or finish had been destroyed or
removed. The floor of the courtyard was still
uneven slurry, stacked with buckets, bits of wood
and old bicycles, with a few corners where tiles had
been laid to gauge scale and colour.

It is true that we beheld a picture of industry –
lots of men bouncing up and down on twig
scaffolding, with buckets whizzing past their ears
on pulleys. But even so, there was a long way to go.
After the multiple telephone conversations with
Abdeltif, I had begun to imagine that – if we bought
the *doueria* and did it up – we would be able to start

letting in September, a good season for Marrakech, and timely to pluck us from destitution.

'I can see why you didn't think it would be such a good idea for us to stay here,' I said, with a winded attempt at a laugh.

'It does not look very good now, because we have had to do so much work on it, we have had to change everything. Everything. But from now it will go very quickly. You will see. We have finished all the preparatory work. A few days and we will have finished the bedrooms. They will be brilliant. Gorgeous.'

Unconvinced silence was the response.

Deftly Abdeltif changed the subject. 'Now we must look at the *doueria*. I have the key.' He dug into some secret pocket of his flowing djellaba and produced an old iron key.

We picked our way across the rubble and out of the front door. After a brief tussle, Abdeltif managed to open the neighbouring door, Number 96, and we stepped into total darkness which smelled strongly

of human piss. Knowing the Arab predilection for putting a hole-in-the-ground loo just inside the front door, I froze, waiting for sound, sight or smell to guide me. I could hear Abdeltif and Khaled feeling their way along the walls, and after a minute I could distinguish stairs and a faint stain of light from above. The source of the smell was in the blackness to my right, so picking my way along the left-hand wall, I stumbled up the stairs, with Dan following.

The stairs had high risers and tiny treads, took a surprising number of turns for such a small number, and were flanked by curious alcoves in which broken fridges and dented gas canisters reposed. At the top there was a minuscule landing, lit by a hole in the roof. A square of extra dust on the floor attested to the justice of the neighbour's complaint about our dust coming in, though it was a matter of degree, and it was plain that this building had lain empty for many years. Our dust was simply an extra layer on the suede-like finish of every horizontal surface.

There was a tiny room over the alley on one side, and a large long room over our green bedroom on the other, in which we could see by the half-light filtering through its door that three handsome arched windows with shutters had been brutally bricked up. Rarely have I been in a space more prison-like.

Abdeltif's rhapsodies had to do battle with rising waves of claustrophobia: 'This will be a wonderful bedroom – so big, with a view of the courtyard. This suite will have its own hammam, and out here on this landing we can have another fountain, with a carved border. And *mousharabi* – wooden fretwork – beneath the rooflight, very fashionable. Also having the *doueria* will make the roof terrace much bigger.'

Abdeltif indicated that we should scramble into one of the little cupboards, over the chipped brown-enamel cooking pot and the broken three-legged chair, and ascend the twig ladder through a hole the size of a washing-machine door to the roof.

'No way. I'll just guess what it looks like,' I said, feeling slightly panicky about this bit of ungainly rebirthing.

While the three men wriggled their way out into the sunshine, I wandered about in the strange interior, trying to envisage this room with windows, light, a view other than crude unfinished brickwork. Facing south, it would get all the sun there was. It was big, and the floor was tiled with old-fashioned chequered tiles in faded blues and greens. A little lurch of the heart suggested to me that it could be wonderful, but I was haunted by the thought of whoever might have lived in this bleak windowless corridor. There were clues – a notebook and some printed pages in Arabic. A broken cup. A battered raffia stool. It didn't look much of a life. But if we didn't buy this place, what would happen to it?

Well, I decided, it made perfect sense for us to bankrupt ourselves, hold up the completion for many more months, and buy something we had not intended to. I tried to convince myself that letting four bedrooms would be easier than letting three – after all, this was going to be our dependable income, this was how we were going to subsidize Dan's painting and my writing. We had to be sensible.

These thoughts occupied me for quite a while until I began to wonder what had happened to the others. Cautiously I felt my way down the vertiginous stairs, out into the alley and back through our front door, where I encountered Abdeltif, Khaled and Dan, who had found their way down along the roof terrace into our house.

'What do you think?' Dan asked.

'Do we know how much they want for it?'

Abdeltif claimed that he could mastermind the buying of the *doueria* without the sellers ever guessing that it was foreign money they would be laying hands on. 'I can get it for Marakchi price. Very cheap. You *must* buy it. You will always regret it if you do not. I will make it gorgeous. If you do not buy it, they will sell it to someone else, and there will always be trouble. I will talk to them today.'

Dan and I doubted that anyone else would be very keen, and we also doubted that Abdeltif's confidence about our secret identity was well founded, since everyone in the neighbourhood knew exactly who we were. However, counselling him to suggest that we were now quite poor, we told him to go ahead and find out what he could.

Half an hour later, as we were sitting in the sun waiting for our tagines at Chegrouni's, he sashayed up. What the vendors wanted was ridiculous – half as much again as we had paid for the entire house. But Abdeltif was convinced that he could bargain them down, and that the restoration would be relatively cheap.

'It is in good condition. The roof is sound – we will not have to take the roof off this building. And we can reuse the floor and wall tiles. The house will be worth *much* more with the extra rooms. And you will have a proper Moroccan hammam, in Marrakech-pink *tadelakt*, with a big bath, and columns.'

He went off to confirm to the vendors that we were interested, but not at *that* price, and returned almost immediately with a minuscule reduction. 'They say that the man on the other side wants to buy it, and he is willing to pay this much.' Suddenly the *doueria* became extremely desirable.

'OK,' we said through our lamb, figs and walnuts. 'We'll go for it.' We knew that the big sign saying 'suckers' was visible to all above our heads, but what the hell. The house would be a palace. One day.

*　*　*

Things moved fast. Abdeltif set up an appointment with the notary for two days later at twelve, telling us that by then we would have to have enough money for the deposit. As we already knew, the whole process took two weeks, and he suggested that I give him power of attorney for this transaction, so that he could complete on our behalf without us needing to return to Marrakech.

We returned to the *doueria* that afternoon, armed with tape measures, and tried to plan the interior. There was a problem with the original windows. When the building had been divided in two, the upstairs bedroom in the riad, which had previously been entered via the *doueria*, had become inaccessible, so a balcony had been built and a door made overlooking the courtyard. We calculated that the balcony ended smack in the middle of one of the blocked windows, so Dan found an envelope and started making drawings. There had originally been three equal-sized, symmetrical windows. Many envelopes later, he had designed three windows, the central one as it had been, flanked by an elegant pair of slightly smaller slender arched windows.

There was not a lot more we could do, even with the vague measurements we had managed to make, and Abdeltif called in one of many favours, and got his friend the engineer to make some accurate drawings overnight. Marrakech never sleeps.

Our next task was to pay the deposit, for which we had just enough money in the Marrakech bank, originally destined for the workmen. I have never yet discovered the opening hours of Moroccan banks. The bank overlooking the square was closed, despite large signs proclaiming it open. However, Abdeltif simply went round the back as before and banged loudly on the door. The bank manager himself answered, looking rather pink in the face, but he gave no other sign of displeasure at our unorthodox entrance. Surprisingly, the bank was full of people, and we were told that they simply shut the doors from time to time when they were crowded. Abdeltif stayed long enough to ensure that everything was going well, and then slipped off to make phone calls and organize our lives.

We completed our paperwork fast, and the bank manager, Hassam, asked if we would like to come and have a look at a couple of historic riads with him. We said we would be delighted, and feeling self-conscious and very honoured we followed him out of the back door into the sunshine.

'Please do not walk beside me. It is not fitting for you to be seen with your bank manager. If you walk just behind me, that will be fine,' he warned.

So, giggling slightly, we tracked ten paces behind him, feeling like an incompetent pair of private detectives. For a short man he walked surprisingly fast, and we trotted after him through the narrow alleys of the medina to an imposing riad, reputedly the oldest in the medina, which had been beautifully restored with exemplary good taste. The walls were very high and the place was very bare. Everything was white or carved polished cedar, there was nothing of the wild kaleidoscope of colour and texture that we were planning to have, this was all smooth planes and shadows. We felt childlike and rather humbled. Even the fountain consisted of the shallowest square depression in a polished slab of marble, with a minimal spout trickling a whisper of water. We wandered around like a pair of country bumpkins, clucking at this cathedral of genteel grandeur, while Hassam conversed with the curator.

Next we sprinted after him as he strode through the crowded alleys to a riad belonging to a willowy and beautiful French woman who was clad in drifting layers of white crêpe, and had a glossy chignon of thick black hair. Hassam brought us because she had done up her house to let and he thought we might be able to get some ideas. It was stylish, minimal and unmistakably French. Clean, fresh and simple. She had painted the whole place white, except for frills of carved wooden barge-board running along the top of the courtyard, which were bright blue. The bedrooms were very plain; each had its own little washbasin, and the beds were draped with great swagged curtains of brilliantly dyed muslin – orange, purple, saffron. This was more our level of operation, and we observed her bedroom arrangements, the bathrooms, the tiny plunge pool, the topiarized box plants and the cat shit with interest. There were many small mounds of the latter, due to some feline ailment that had stricken Felice, her Siamese. Our hostess's refined froideur indicated that we had not picked the best time for our visit and I was glad when Hassam's adieus signalled our departure.

We fell into line behind Hassam again, feeling rather hungry by now, and wondered how long he could keep up this breathless pace. Not for much longer, fortunately – he turned down a shadowed side alley and rattled on an inconspicuous door. It was thrown open, and a torrent of hugs and excited chatter greeted him. We were introduced to his sister-in-law, by whom, it transpired, we had been invited to lunch. She was a tornado of good will and interest, asking after our families, our work, where we would like to sit, what we would like to drink, were we hungry, and this was her son, and there, hiding behind a Buddha-like gentleman, was her daughter.

We nodded and smiled, and after loitering around trying to look relaxed, we were firmly seated on a chaise longue between a very glossy cultural attaché who spoke perfect English and a somnolent Buddha, the perfect double of the one at the other end of the sofa. I never know what to call these things – banquette sounds like railway speak but comes nearest to describing the low brocade-covered seats lining the walls of the entire room, stacked with cushions and populated with Hassam's extended family lounging like seals, within convenient grabbing distance of the large low tables at each end. There were occasional bubbles of talk, but not a relentless grilling – the twenty or so people present were perfectly happy to stare silently, laugh among themselves or fall asleep.

Two enormous salads were brought in and placed on the low tables. Everyone else dipped in and delicately picked off morsels of carrot or beetroot or potato in mayonnaise, conveying them to their mouths without splattering them on to their chests. Dan did not get the hang of this, and he began to look like the gutter beneath a vegetable stall. Vanity made me give the salad a miss.

After a respectable time the salads were taken away, the top tablecloth was whipped off revealing an immaculate one beneath, and two vast platters of the classic couscous with seven vegetables (*Seksu Beidaoui*) were laid before us. Everyone helped themselves, using of course only their right hands, pushing delicious morsels of lamb to each other. It's best not to wear black for this kind of event: little constellations of couscous show up in a Milky Way down one's front and it is not an attractive sight.

As so often in Marrakech, I was enchanted by this unquestioning hospitality from people whom we had never met before. No one else seemed to think it odd that two total strangers who do not speak your language turn up and eat your couscous.

Finally the top tablecloth was whisked away to reveal yet another, spotless and crisply calendered. Hassam joined us briefly in the lounging-around-eating-cakes-and-drinking-mint-tea ceremony, and then announced that, regretfully, he had a job to do and must return to the bank. Vaguely it crossed our minds that we too had something or other we were meant to do, and with great difficulty we prised ourselves off the brocade, thanked everyone, kissed several women, though I never correctly established who was who, or to whom we owed this bounty and generosity, and trotted along the stripy shadowed derbs in Hassam's wake.

By the next morning, Khaled had done several drawings of stairs and bathrooms with a queasy perspective, and Abdeltif had covered the small smudged Christmas card with numbers in three different currencies as his estimate for the work. It was runic but plausible, and we accepted his unorthodox guess, both of us signing and dating it wherever there was space. This grubby and increasingly dog-eared piece of card was the crux of the entire enterprise, and we referred to it a thousand times during the course of the next few months.

We convened chez Maître Yakub at eleven a.m. the following day, at his office outside the city walls. The vendor was there in person: a stout, heavily moustachioed seventy-year-old lady with an enormous mono-bosom and very short legs, which dangled some way off the carpet from one of the peeling leatherette sofas. At her side a gloomy man with a matching Saddam moustache, obviously her son, was idly scratching the last vestiges of a late tagine from his too-small too-short single-breasted once-black suit, whose jacket fronts and trouser seat were polished by age and frequent use. She was sprightly, flirtatious even, flapping her heavy arms about in a dangerous wave of dangling flesh, but he concentrated on his knees and the culinary archaeology to be done there.

The old lady and her son were being careful not to look as though they were about to laugh their way to the bank – but she was afflicted by natural effervescence like a rogue pit bull terrier with rolling eyes, and couldn't prevent herself from coming up with incomprehensible one-liners to which she slapped her thighs in solitary appreciation, while her boy concentrated very hard on his twill, trying to keep the dirham signs out of his eyes. I have no idea how much too much we paid for their little room.

Having been thus fleeced, we sat in the sun at a

café on one of the broad boulevards of the French quarter drinking coffee and orange juice by way of celebration. The sun, filtering through the jacarandas, warmed our shoulders as we read the papers – just two days old. Gazing up from the news, we admired the sharp art deco architecture in the French town-planner Henri Prost's radiating design for Guéliz. It was he who decreed that no building should be higher than a palm tree – and since it is illegal to cut them down, they occasionally erupt in the most inconvenient places. We observed the gaggles of coiffured and coutured women, by no means all French, who appeared to have been liberated from gloves, veils and djellabas by the sweeping modernity of their surroundings. When the French moved in to Marrakech in 1912 they left the medina well alone, building a crisply logical, tidily swept, fully mod-conned world outside the dusty pink ramparts of the mazy old city.

We decided to visit our house again and took a taxi into town. We stood aside to let a couple of rubble-laden *carrossas* past, picked our way over the bikes and mobylettes, ignored the hissing ginger cat and stepped over our threshold, where we were momentarily trapped by several cement bags and a welcoming committee of builders.

There were wonders in store: in the few days of our absence they had somehow got past the rubble stage and were into finishes. In one corner of the courtyard there was an astonishing lake of brilliant mint-green plaster, and before I could say, 'Yuk, what a vile colour!' Abdeltif materialized, smiling broadly, his hands clasped behind his back like a big-game hunter being modest about a brilliant shot. 'It is a gorgeous colour, I think. It will look wonderful. Khaled mixed it especially to my instructions. It is for the upstairs bedroom.'

Ah, yes, the room that we had decided to have subtle Wedgwood blue. Dan and I had spent hours leafing through old magazines to choose exactly the colours we wanted for every room, all along rather tasteful *blanc cassé*, chestnut-brown, Marakchi-pink and ochre lines, and had given Khaled carefully tabulated colour swatches.

Abdeltif beamed. 'You will love it, it will be a wonderful room. It will be gorgeous.' He shuffled a bit – insufficiently, in my opinion – and then relented. 'We will do the other rooms in your colours, but you must have *something* bright. Just wait, it will be breelliant. Come and look. You must trust me.' If there's one thing I have learned during a life of many bruises, it is to fear anyone who says 'trust me'. But in this matter, as so often in the months to follow, Abdeltif was right and I was wrong. The room is breelliant.

Somehow, the men had managed to begin the spiral staircase, and again, though this bore little relation to Dan's design, it had a wayward charm.

We picked our way up this bizarre corkscrew to the mouthwash room, and had to admit that once in situ the effect of the mint green was wonderfully exhilarating.

Looking down into the courtyard we could see a couple of men and a boy laying the first small square terracotta *mizmat* tiles around the perimeter, and fastidiously cutting the large glazed blue tiles that were to make the borders into triangles, with a reckless pile of wastage. Every tiny piece was cut by hand and fitted gently into its place in the thrilling geometry of the floor. Their work was so perfectionist, the finished courtyard so serenely beautiful, that we felt prickles of excitement.

Abdeltif described the projected glories of what he called the Pink Salon. We followed meekly, expecting further misunderstandings. What we beheld silenced us absolutely: the magnificent double doors had returned, their original dull cocoa stripped and repainted with intricate strapwork, dark glowing arabesques and touches of gold, all painted with infinite patience, slow, careful, by young Rachid. Handsome studded bands of brass held python-sized bolts. Within the big doors in their broad plaster arch, the little ones opened in a pair of narrow arches, opulent, richly glimmering, with different designs outside and in. They were like a jewel casket.

Abdeltif hustled us through the doors, enjoying

our rapture, but in a hurry to see what we would make of what lay within. In just two days painters and plasterers had been busy creating a real room, with a ceiling finely painted like an intricate Berber rug, and walls of glowing satiny *tadelakt* the dusty pink of old ladies' rouge. They had made a seat in the alcove – a throne, actually – and deep windowsills of fine indigo and white *zellig fessi* – tiles cut in tiny pieces and laid in a scintillating patchwork. All the colours sparked little riffs with each other. A line of crisp carved *jibs* frieze topped the *tadelakt* like icing on a wedding cake, snaking round the window recesses and the richly decorated arched cupboards.

I spent some time opening and closing doors and shutters, gloating. It was quite simply a delicious room that looked good dimly lit, brightly lit, and with all doors and windows opening out to the gallery and the wall where our *doueria* windows would one day be. There was nothing we could say. It was entirely breelliant.

'Abdeltif, it's wonderful. It's a bleeding work of art. We never thought we'd own anything so beautiful.'

'The whole house will be like this. The workmen love it, they are very happy to work here for you. Look, they have done this frieze and this *zellig fessi* for nothing, for a present, because they like to be here.' He indicated the base of the gallery pillars, which were sheathed in minute gleaming hexagons of different blues, each one cut and positioned individually, and waved his arm to show the extent of the carved frieze. There was miles of it, all stencilled on the plaster and then fastidiously incised by hand. Incredible. How could we have doubted him for a single minute?

Khaled bustled up with our swatches, and re-assured us that the other rooms would indeed follow our colour guidelines. We walked from room to room, holding up the postage-stamp-sized bits of paper, trying unsuccessfully to visualize a whole wall of ox-blood or ochre. From his briefcase he also extracted a curious collection of plumbing fitments – handmade taps and spouts of beaten brass to go with the little brass hand basins we had already seen.

Abdeltif, who is more of a chrome and onyx man, obviously felt uncomfortable with this foray into ethnic plumbing. 'I am not sure, Madame Miranda. The thing is, will they work?'

Khaled seemed confident that they would, so we decided to have cute ethnic rather than boring old functioning plumbing.

We drew designs for the Berber doors for the mouthwash bedroom – we had seen a cupboard made in the dark, carved multicoloured Berber style and were very taken with it, and had asked Khaled to copy it for our doors. We discussed glass for the fanlight and painted wardrobes.

'You must use sandalwood or cedar, Madame Miranda. Not cheap rubbish which will break. Pine, pah.' He grabbed a spare ceiling offcut and broke it in half with his bare hands: 'Look, it just splinters. In this climate you need hardwood.'

I felt a money haemorrhage coming on, and had to sit down alone in the pink room for a while. Khaled's assistant Buddr tapped lightly on the door a few minutes later, bearing a cup of sweet and restorative mint tea.

That night we invited Abdeltif and Khaled out for dinner. Moroccans would far rather be entertained at home, but since we had no home, this was the only way we could return some of their hospitality and thank them for their amazing efforts. Abdeltif picked somewhere smart and French, and the two of them sat surrounded by glass and silver and napery, looking like a pair of naughty schoolboys, quite nonplussed by the menu. The waiter described every dish, and a lengthy discussion ensued. Finally, having made their much-debated choice, they sat back, swigged their Coke – 'Mmm, *delicious*' – and smiled.

Dan made a touching speech about the glories of the riad, and Abdeltif beamed. 'Yes, Mr Dan, we have a brilliant team, I picked them myself, you have seen their excellent work in my flat, it is perfect, and they work well together because Khaled is a brilliant foreman.' He slapped his brother-in-law powerfully on the shoulder, which occasioned a certain amount of discreet choking on Khaled's part, through which he smiled gamely.

At this moment the waiter put the much discussed grilled mullet in front of Abdeltif, who drew back, his face registering dismay. 'What is that? I did not order that. It is fish, I think?' He prodded it suspiciously with his fork. 'I don't eat fish.'

Patiently the waiter brought a menu and pointed out Abdeltif's choice, under the heading 'Poissons'.

'But I didn't know it was fish. Please, take it away. I cannot eat it.' He said this so sorrowfully that I offered to swap my chicken for his fish, to which he agreed with alacrity.

Dan and I allowed ourselves a moment of triumph – Abdeltif and Khaled were masters of their trade, the riad looked wonderful, and the *doueria* with the elegant windows we envisaged looking on to the lemon trees and fountains of the courtyard would finish it off perfectly.

I could see Dan picturing himself as a sultan from Suffolk, wafting in a lordly way through the shadowed verandah in flowing robes, and cheerfully, optimistically, we all drank – not Coke in our case – to our future palace.

9

STAFF PROBLEMS

2002 was the year when we waited – for my Spanish book to come out, for the sale of the Brighton flat, for money from any source. I discovered a brilliant wheeze and cashed in my minuscule pension up to the 25 per cent limit. But there came a point when I had to say that until the Brighton flat sold, we couldn't give Abdeltif another penny. With characteristic generosity, he said, 'No problem – I have money at this moment; I will lend you the money for the extras. That would be better than to stop work now, and lose this wonderful team of good men who work so well together.'

Mark, the estate agent in Brighton, came up with cast-iron convincing reasons why a) the flat would definitely sell quickly and efficiently in his capable hands, and b) why no one actually wanted to see it, and those who did preferred any other flat but mine. He continued to do this for six months as Dan and I became increasingly desperate, and then I switched to Alan the vicar to represent the flat. House prices everywhere in the UK were rocketing that summer – but it was not until we slashed the asking price of ours by 20 per cent that anyone showed a glimmer of interest. I didn't mind, the asking price had always seemed absurdly greedy to me, but since both agents had independently come up with the same figure I had reasoned that they knew better than I. But I minded that we had wasted six months while Dan and I lived on beans and were afraid to use the phone.

In July, when we were at our most impecunious, we received a summons from Abdeltif, saying that we had to go over immediately and buy furniture in order to be able to let the house, which he was confident would still be possible in September. We had to go also to check out the work on the *doueria*, and, with an audible purr of pride, Abdeltif said we must meet our new manager.

In twenty years of full-time work and single-handed boy-rearing, I had never employed anyone – not cleaner or nanny, psychiatrist, personal trainer or life coach – to help, on some obscure PC grounds that escape me. I certainly wasn't about to start now.

'No, Abdeltif. We don't need a manager.'

There was a silence. I could hear him scratch his chin.

'Madame Miranda, you *must* have a manager. Everyone has a manager.'

'I'm sorry, but I refuse to have a manager. There's no reason on earth why we need one.'

He sighed. 'You cannot leave a place like this empty. It will be broken into and destroyed. People will take things.'

'But everything will be insured.'

A ladylike cough from Abdeltif.

'That is not all. People will break in and use it as a brothel. It happens quite often. Then you will lose your licence and will be forbidden to let it. The riad may be taken away from you.'

Put like that it made sense to have a manager.

'OK. I suppose you are right.'

'You will need a full-time manager and a daily cleaner.' I was sweating at the other end of the phone. How much were these people going to cost? We couldn't afford to buy a bottle of wine in Spain where it is cheaper than water, and Abdeltif wanted us to employ two full-time staff. Three, as it turned out – we had to have a guardian too.

Imperturbably he continued. 'He is very good, you will like him, he will be very good with your clients – he speaks *excellent* English. His name is Ramadi. He is a scholar. You will love him. Here, say hello to him.'

160

There was a brief scuffle at the other end, and then someone said, 'Hello, Madame Miranda. This is your manager Ramadi. It is, for me, great pleasure to be working for you. I am sure that it will be very good and that I am the right man for the job.'

'Ah, yes. Hello, Ramadi. I'm sure. Fine. Could I speak to Abdeltif, please?'

'If you wish, but I will replace Abdeltif for you here, you will not need to talk to Abdeltif any more because I am here.'

'Right. OK. But just now I'd like to have a word with him.'

'I will see if I can locate him. Please hold on, Madame Miranda.' There was a long wait, while I could hear shuffling and shouting. Finally Ramadi returned.

'Abdeltif has gone to the mosque to pray. I will ask him to ring you when he returns.'

Yes, it seemed that somehow we would have to get the money together to pay another visit to 95 Derb Al Qadi, and soon. This was when we reached the bottom of the barrel, and resorted to borrowing money from Dan's mother. Not only did she very generously lend us several thousand pounds, but Dan's ex-wife Elly contributed to our profligate wastrel fund and lent us several thousand more. This made me very uneasy – it was all too reminiscent of the Awful Debt I had incurred on buying my house in Spain, when two weeks before exchange of contracts on the sale of my London house and consequent wealth, I had borrowed a large sum from my sister, confident that I would be able to repay her within a month. Thanks to the Arsenal football club putting an untimely blight on my house, it had taken over two years.

Things seemed to be on the verge of going seriously pear-shaped. Nothing was moving on the flat sale front, either.

'Your second bedroom really does not compare favourably with most of the others. And most clients don't want to have to climb up five flights of stairs,' said Alan the vicar. If this were not condemnation enough, he continued, 'It's a bad time of year; nothing sells in high summer. There are problems with the rail service, so we're not getting any London clients at the moment. And we've got a glut of two-bedroom flats on our books right now.' Great. 'We could drop the price again.' The newspapers were still effervescent with the excitement of the property boom, and he was asking me to drop the price again?

'OK. How much should we drop?'

'Oh, not much. Say another ten thousand pounds?'

Ouch.

Dan was deeply embroiled in a book he was illustrating, its deadline imminent, and he was unable to take any time off. I really did not want to go alone to Marrakech in the sizzling dog days of July to deal with bossy and opinionated men, so I invited my younger son Spigs to come with me, reasoning that it might be a good idea to fight fire with fire.

He agreed with alacrity, so I booked flights for both of us and, with a hard knot of panic in my stomach, proceeded to make lists of what we needed to do, take and buy. The money Dan had borrowed would barely cover the necessities in terms of furniture, but without the essential beds, tables, chairs, etc., we would never be able to let the house in time to rescue us from imminent penury. It was a classic catch-22. I had a passion to get the thing moving – this was, after all, our cast-iron business investment, our pension, our means to subsidize writing and painting. If we could just survive until September – only two months away – we could let the house and we'd be fine. Such innocents!

When Abdeltif met Spigs and me at the airport in the early afternoon of a roastingly hot day, he was accompanied by Ramadi, who was wearing a jacket that seemed to have been borrowed from a shop, since it was still emblazoned with labels and the price ticket kept springing out of the collar, and a cloud of aftershave so dense and choking that I wondered what olfactory disaster it was intended to mask. I attributed his hand-wringing Uriah Heepishness to nerves, and concentrated on trying to discover from Abdeltif how far the house had progressed. He was disconcertingly vague.

It was a bad start, which became worse when I said firmly that Spigs and I intended to stay in the house for the week, no matter what condition it was in.

'Abdeltif, I really need to stay there now. I've got to get the feel of it, to know what it is like at different times of day. We don't need anything fancy. We'll just buy a couple of mattresses and we'll be fine.'

Abdeltif was just saying how much Layla was looking forward to having us stay with them when Ramadi interrupted.

'You cannot stay in the house now. I am staying there as guardian and it would not be right for you to stay. No, you must stay with Abdeltif.'

I gawped at him. 'Ramadi, it is my house. I will be staying there with my son. I have not hired you as guardian; in fact I have not hired you at all yet. We have to make sure we can work together first.'

Abdeltif spoke to him with some urgency in Arabic, and then said to me, 'He is very dedicated. But he may be right. The house is not ready for you. There are problems with the plumbing.'

A distant alarm bell rang.

As always, Abdeltif was hospitality itself, and

insisted that we spend the first night at least with him. It was wonderful to see Faruk again, who was newly cheeky and extra boisterous on meeting Spigs. Layla in her headscarf and long djellaba was sweet and loving as usual, and had constructed a feast for us of multiple delicacies, including my favourite, tagine with preserved lemons and olives.

The following morning we climbed into Abdeltif's monstrous wonderfully air-conditioned car and breezed into town, rightly apprehensive about the heat that would smite us when we stepped out of it. We worked up quite a sweat during the quarter-mile walk to the riad.

For Spigs, whose first visit to Morocco this was, everything was thrilling. 'People travel on donkeys, I can't believe it. It's like being in a different century. Look – that bloke's selling water from an animal skin. Shit, look, he's got a snake, it's a big one! A python. What's that? It looks like an ostrich egg. Can't be. Hey look, that old bloke is selling false teeth. Look at those spices! Wow. They've got every-thing. What's that grey rubbery stuff?'

'Tripe, the lining of a cow's stomach. It's a great delicacy here.'

'Cool.'

He was very taken by the serpentine route to the house, and showed no disappointment when we gathered outside the scruffy front door.

'Is this it? Needs a bit of work, but it looks solid.'

The Entrance Hall at 95

His words died on his lips as we were let in by one of the workmen. He just stood and gaped. So did I. The transformation was astounding.

There was a long silence. 'It's a fucking palace, Mum. You said it was good, but I never thought . . . I just couldn't get my head round . . . I didn't think it would be *this* good. Just look at the work!' Spigs used to manage a branch of Paint Magic, my sister Jocasta's business, and prided himself on his familiarity with all known decorative finishes and paint effects, and his general sense of style.

'I've never seen anything like this, Mum. It's amazing. Look, someone has carved all that plaster. There's miles of it. And look, that pillar is covered with hand-cut tiles. It's fantastic.'

The main part of the riad was nearly finished – as it should have been, since it was supposed to have been completely finished the previous month, when we had scuppered our contract with Abdeltif by buying the *doueria*. The floors were tiled – the exterior floors with *mizmat* – small terracotta squares with a decorative edge of glazed, coloured hand-cut tiles. Every room had sumptuous walls of *tadelakt* in the rich colours we had requested – except for Abdeltif's mouthwash room, which vindicated him entirely, looking deliciously cool and fresh. The waterproof, marble-smooth, coloured finish *tadelakt* is applied to the walls of hammams – Moroccan bathrooms – and, since its discovery by

167

interior decorators, to every other kind of wall as well. It consists of plaster mixed with powdered pigment and marble dust, applied in a thin layer. When dry, it is polished by hand with olive-oil soap and a smooth stone until it achieves the sensuous, slightly undulating smoothness of leather sofas in gentlemen's clubs patinated by generations of pin-striped bottoms. It seduces the hand, you just have to stroke it, and the colour glows deep and lustrous. Doors, ceilings, stairs, they too were all beautifully finished.

'Abdeltif, it's absolutely gorgeous, you've done brilliantly.' I gave him an effusive hug.

The house was a dream but for two things. There was a small problem with the window frames, the painter having decided that we could not possibly really want the subtle grey-blue we had requested, convinced that a startling turquoise would be preferable. Also the elegant narrow trio of windows that Dan had designed for the *doueria* had been replaced by three asymmetrical dumpy windows with all the grace and charm of a buffalo's bum.

'What happened there?' I asked Abdeltif, who shuffled his feet, sought and found a Marlboro in his voluminous garments, and taking a calming drag said, 'I think they are very nice windows. Typical. Just right for the house.' Short pause. 'We lost the drawing. Don't you like them?' I did not, and they were even worse from inside the room, meanly cutting out the view of the courtyard below with chest-high sills.

'Where's Khaled? He's got the drawings in his briefcase. He is so conscientious. I'm amazed that he would let this happen.' More shuffling and another Marlboro later, Abdeltif muttered that he and Khaled had had a falling-out, and that another of his brothers-in-law, Mbarek, had taken over.

'But Khaled has made the house the place it is. All the best ideas have come from him.' Khaled, I realized in that instant, had been quality control, had kept the whole thing together, and had maintained the great relationship with the workmen who respected him and loved him.

I was devastated. Khaled was our right-hand man, source of all good sense and information. Mbarek, our new foreman – a tall, dreamy and saintly non-touching Muslim – had drifted down from planet Vague. The only visible workman was Rachid, the boy-genius painter, although making mint tea seemed to be what he was now principally engaged in. Mbarek's other handicap was that he spoke only Arabic and pretend French. So when I made some suggestion about the colour of the cushions, for example, in French, he would nod ferociously and then do something quite unexpected. Instead of the cinnamon pink that we had agreed, they ended up white. He was, I think, completely out of his depth as far as actual building went, possibly consulting

Allah from time to time on the finer points of plumbing.

I measured the house for beds, furniture and curtains while I mulled over the dumpy windows, the disastrous absence of Khaled and the odd placement of the cooker hob, which was standing proud of the magnificent expanse of marble in the kitchen, precariously balanced on four bricks.

There was a lot of measuring to be done. As I toiled from one room to the next, Ramadi kept telling Spigs that I was doing it wrong, or that he'd already done it and my measurement was wrong, or that it was not necessary.

Spigs turned to him after quite a bit of this and said, 'Look, mate, there's no point talking to me. It's my mum who pays your wages, not me.'

Abdeltif pranced off with Spigs to get something to eat, while I continued with my labours. It was very hot, and after an hour of sprinting up and down stairs with my tape measure, I sagged on to a fountain, mopping my brow and longing for a cold drink. But Ramadi bustled up from some secret hiding place and started filling me in on the references and bibliography of his dissertation. He repeated the praise of his tutor for his work, and reminded me that he had a BA in English, with literature as his option. I'm not sure what kind of literature – nothing sounded familiar to me, but at least he spoke English.

My bottom set rigid on that fountain while Ramadi expanded on the theme of his wonderfulness. I might have needed emergency measures had not Spigs and Abdeltif burst through the door, like a pair of tumbling puppies, bearing chicken and salad, chips and long cold drinks. Tall, shy Mbarek joined us and we sat in the shade of the gallery and marvelled at the handiwork of our little palace. Spigs was as happy as a chap with a season ticket to Tottenham. He kept gazing around and sighing deeply. This place, the Kingdom of Boys, was paradise for him.

After lunch I announced that now we needed to buy mattresses. Ramadi, who may have been given a short talking-to by Abdeltif, sprang to his feet and announced that he would help, and that he knew the very place.

'Well,' I thought, 'perhaps I've been too hasty in condemning him. He's young, and it takes time to learn how to get on with people. Maybe he'll settle down.'

We speed-walked the mile or so to the mattress place in blazing and shadowless forty-degree heat. When we arrived at the shop it was closed for lunch, as were all the shops in the entire city. They would remain so for a further two hours. It surprised me, to put it mildly, that Ramadi and Mbarek had not previously spotted this daily feature of life in Marrakech.

I elected to take Spigs to Le Prince to eat divine cakes confected of honey and almonds, sesame and chocolate, and drink coffee in air-conditioned splendour, arranging to meet Ramadi at the mattress shop when it reopened at five. One more incomprehensible lecture about his dazzling dissertation and I would shatter into a million stinging pieces.

For two hours Spigs and I debated the shortcomings of our manager.

'He couldn't manage his way out of a wet paper bag, Mum. He's hopeless. And it really annoys me how he always talks to me, as if you weren't there. I mean, I'm not his boss.'

I could not but agree. 'But what alternative do we have? We're only here for a week. I don't think that even Abdeltif could find us a replacement in a week. And Ramadi may just be showing off because he thinks it's impressive.'

'Well, if that's how he behaves to impress you, it doesn't look good for when he doesn't feel he has to impress you. I mean, how is he going to behave when you're in Spain and strangers are staying at the house? It won't go down well if he refuses to treat the women as equals. English women aren't used to that kind of behaviour, and won't take it well.' Spigs knew because he had tried it himself. But he was older and wiser now.

We munched thoughtfully, surveying covertly the peacock clientèle – gorgeous young Marakchi women with impossibly full lips and glossy hair, toying with small, balding, sweating men in small shiny shoes. George Grosz would have felt at home. Now we knew where the ladies of the night spent their days. I just could not get to grips with the rules that governed female behaviour in Morocco. It probably comes down to the universal truth that even in Muslim countries beautiful women can and occasionally do exploit their looks regardless of the local mores, to gain freedom, wealth and independence. Bleeding obvious, really.

We returned to our quest. Ramadi was not at the mattress shop when we reached it, though Mbarek was, so we went through the routine brandishing a measuring tape, and reeling back at the prices: mattresses are an expensive commodity in Marrakech. We were getting more and more hot and bothered in a claustrophobically windowless and stuffy attic storeroom. However, I was determined to have big comfortable beds – there is nothing worse on a hot night than to have to be glued to your partner whether you want it or not. For affection to flourish in hot climates, you need space and distance. We were standing amid a choppy sea of mattresses when our manager reappeared, looking ruffled and defensive, with no explanation, no apology.

We continued with our researches, and bought two mattresses in the end – both too big and too pricey for our budget – with a couple of rock-hard polyester pillows thrown in. A crumbling geriatric was summoned from nowhere to transport our acquisitions back to the house on his tiny cart – he headed off, his tiny bent back pushing what looked like Stonehenge, forging into a deadly swirl of traffic.

Layla had very kindly lent us bedlinen and towels, and on our return we awaited the mattresses with apprehension. To my surprise, the crumbly one was at the house with his grotesque load before we'd managed to find a receptacle for a drink of water. By now it was dark, so we made up our beds on the floor by the depressing light of a couple of ten-watt light bulbs, Spigs grumbling about Ramadi's bloody-minded choice of the best room.

'You'd think he might offer it to us. After all, it is your house.'

'I think he thinks it's his.'

'Yeah, that's his problem.'

Then we pranced out into the night, leaving Ramadi and his maddening antics behind, and thoroughly enjoyed our indifferent chicken tagines high up on the roof restaurant of the French café, with the entire kaleidoscopic drama of Djemaa El Fna below us – smoke spiralling up from the busy crowd at the outdoor dining tables, the huge circle of rapt fascination surrounding the storytellers, the ostrich-egg man and the false-teeth man still plying their wares, the stalls bursting with a multicoloured jumble of leather, metal, glass and ceramics.

A delicate breeze wafted as we pondered ice cream, and regardless of petty problems, we felt just about on top of the world.

10

FIFTEEN TIMES TABLE

I had not wanted a manager, had not seen the necessity for one, but Abdeltif had brought the entire force of his hefty personality to support his argument that life without a manager in Marrakech is inconceivable. He intimated that a manager was an essential protection against danger to person and property. Patiently he explained that a manager was vital to prevent inconvenience and incomprehension; indispensable to explain and mediate; to run the house and eliminate problems; to fix leaking pipes and sparking electrical fittings, find firewood, gas bottles, cooks and cleaners; could in fact save money by ensuring Marakchi prices in the souk rather than the fabled dollar rate. Without a manager speaking the native tongue, how could an ignorant foreigner expect to arrange trips, find taxis, shop, negotiate the thousand and one bureaucratic and political pitfalls that beset a newcomer in this mysterious land? How could one possibly think of letting without a manager smoothing the path and bribing judiciously? What kind of shameful scrapes – from non-collection of rubbish to non-observance of essential feasts – would the naive outsider endure? What would people think? Above all, we would be giving much-needed work to people, we would be philanthropists, we would make friends. Allah would smile upon us.

Foremost among a manager's many tasks was breakfast.

The following morning Spigs and I awoke early and wandered around looking for Ramadi. On not finding him we assumed that he'd gone to the mosque, and we made a short shopping list for breakfast – coffee, milk, bread, butter, eggs, vanilla yoghurt. We were just about to set off on this shopping adventure when the man himself emerged from his bedroom, yawning.

'Ah, Ramadi. Would you mind getting us some breakfast?'

'I have just got up, Madame Miranda,' he said to Spigs severely. 'I must shower.'

'Oh, OK. We'll wait.' And we did, for forty minutes, until Ramadi was sufficiently groomed to buy some yoghurt.

Almost immediately there was a flurry at the door and Abdeltif swept in wearing a stylish black brocade salwar kameez, Hobbit sandals and Nike socks.

'We are going to buy tables today. We go in my car, out to the country where they are made. How many do you need? You have measured?'

Don't know and no were a feeble response, so Spigs and I did a lightning tour, coming to the alarming conclusion that we needed fifteen tables. I have never set out to furnish an entire house from scratch before, and it made my knees tremble contemplating such vast numbers – we'd need at least twice as many chairs. Oh God.

My special notebook that I had brought for all this information soon became an angry tangle of crossings-out, underlinings, red top priorities, blue less importants, irritated scribblings, unhinged doodles, miles of muddled maths as I tried to convert dirhams to pounds (divide by sixteen), and small meaningless drawings showing details, but of what I could not later fathom. I felt as though I was trying to hold a swarm of bees together with my bare pen. As soon as I felt secure about having worked this part out, another would erupt. No sooner were tables OK than lamps blew up; the minute I'd sussed cupboards, bed bases started throwing a tantrum. Round and round in circles like a demented sheepdog I went, tackling the problem from every angle, making lists, floor plans, elevations and endless measurements.

Anyway, today was just tables. No worries. We piled into the Pajero, Ramadi firmly waiting until we'd scrambled into the back before placing himself at the front next to Abdeltif. At least it gave me and Spigs an opportunity to make faces and roll our eyes whenever he said something pompous, which he did with gratifying frequency.

We drove for about an hour, along the ruler-straight road that led to the Ourika Valley, until Abdeltif found the place he was looking for: an upmarket interior-decoration outlet housed in a garage, with very handsome wrought-iron candelabra, hideous tables made out of polished fossils, and one or two very expensive mosaic tables of the kind we wanted. Abdeltif was torn between flirting with the elegant proprietress and denouncing her for gross extortion. Giving her a last winning smile, he muttered his way back to the car and we all piled in as before. Just one slight difference. Spigs was suffering the first intimations of an inconvenient stomach condition, which took his mind off the matter in hand somewhat.

We visited another establishment – more mosaic tables, but just as pricey, and then Abdeltif turned back to the city.

'We go straight to the manufacturers. You will get Marakchi prices. I will do this for you – you cannot pay those foreign prices.' He was genuinely disgruntled, and toying with the idea that he should go alone because our very presence added many noughts to the total.

'They take one look at you and they see dollars. Two things – you must not say anything, and you must not show interest in what you want.'

'How am I going to choose then? Will we have to communicate in code?' I asked, astonished.

'No, that is ridiculous. You can use your note-book, and you can write "Yes" or "No". That way perhaps the table man will think you are mute.' Or daft, I thought. I could just see it, with me scribbling away 'Yes – but rectangular, not round, 200cm by 75cm and in blue and white, not pink, but with the edging pattern of that ochre table over there . . .' and so on, with every one of the fifteen tables. Good plan, Abdeltif. Added to which I knew that he – like many sensible people, including myself – could not read my writing.

As we sped back to the city I thought of a solution. 'Abdeltif, if we are going to see the man who actually *makes* the tables, they'll be much cheaper than those shops we've just seen anyway. I really don't mind paying a *bit* over the odds for them. Better to do that and be able to choose the right ones than try to communicate like spies and come away with disasters.' He grunted reluctant assent, parked the car in a dusty and very shuttered-looking lane, and we did another thousand-yard dash in the blistering dust. It was Sunday, and the table place, along with all the other workshops, was closed.

A hallucination of a long glass of cold iced water beaded with condensation swam into my mind, and from Spigs' face I guessed that his guts were having some kind of revolution, but Abdeltif was not finished, not by a long chalk. Striding ahead with Ramadi and Mbarek, who had materialized from nowhere, Abdeltif marched us to the Jewish quarter, where it was business as usual, to buy material for bed linen. Mbarek – our self-appointed tailor – was polite, and asked me through Abdeltif if I had strong feelings about sheeting.

'Yes,' I replied. 'I want 100 per cent fine woven cotton. Linen would be even better, but absolutely no polyester. White.'

And so I ended up buying about a thousand yards of cream polyester cotton, with a texture like hessian. It was and is a mystery to me – we had actually agreed on the material, fingered it, the shopkeeper had extolled its virtues, and then we came away with something quite different. These things happen with surprising frequency in Marrakech.

No matter, it was a result. We had the beginnings of our bed linen.

Wandering through the Mellah, where every carpet-seller claimed to be an intimate of Mick

Jagger, who must at one time have had a place there, we were persuaded by a spindly but insistent gentleman to patronize an alarmingly tasteful place for lunch – Riad Bab Firdaus – in whose palatial splendour we were the sole customers. We gorged unwisely on a handful of salads, startlingly sweet cheese briouats and kebabs.

This done, Spigs and I decided to broaden our horizons and ambled through the heat to the Bahia Palace. Of course, being Sunday, it was shut, but on our way back we stumbled across one of Marrakech's best secrets – Maison Tiskiwin, which was not only open but manned by its founder, the venerable Dutch collector and inadvertent anthropologist Bert Flint. He had lived in the finely decorated *dar* on rue de Bahia for fifty years, during which he trawled the Sahara from top to bottom, finding fantastically beautiful embroidered Kasar Hausa robes in indigo; cream gandoras from Mali; camel saddles and Berber tents from the Sahara; old carved doors and painted lockers from all over. He was a diffident and endearing man, and Spigs warmed to him and his inspiring collection as he stood in the midsummer sun, in his old waistcoat and hat like a sock, explaining his mission to show that Morocco is an African country as well as an Arab one. He had contributed generously to the painter Tom Phillips's exhibition 'Africa: The Art of a Continent' at the Royal Academy in 1995, and was busy preparing a catalogue of his own collection, due to come out by 2006. The passion and personality of Maison Tiskiwin contrast well with the grand, empty, uninhabited palaces open to the public that surround it.

We had set aside the following day for our final putsch on the furniture-shopping front. The heat smacked us with quite unnecessary violence – it rose rapidly to forty-two degrees, and poor Spigs was in a state of acute gut-wrenching and dared not stir more than three metres from the loo. His supportive company was out of the question.

Ramadi and Mbarek strode out into the shimmering whiteness with never a backward glance and I sprinted to keep up for about a mile in shadowless dusty streets hazed with heat, until we arrived in the purlieus of hell. Despite this being the wrought-iron-chair emporium there were none to sit on, no shade, and the blazing furnace of the forge inches to our left. In fact there were none of the actual articles to be seen, just a dog-eared catalogue with amusingly approximate drawings and fuzzy photos of wrought-iron furniture. I was sweating so much that I could not see: my eyelids were dripping with stinging salt. Blindly I ordered twenty-eight chairs of five different varieties along with a sofa and two armchairs for the mooted Berber tent on the roof.

During the forced march to the table man, no

matter how much water I slurped, more seemed to pour from my body. Mbarek and Ramadi strode ahead while I pattered unhappily in their wake. To my great joy, Abdeltif met us at the table-maker's and, observing my state, fetched a chair, provided mint tea, and generally raised my spirits as he always did.

You might think that choosing tables would be a simple thing, requiring just the selection of size, height and shape. But in this case I had a pattern book of *zellig fessi* designs of confetti-sized pieces of cut glazed tiles in colours that made my head spin. It was like choosing from the Book of Kells. I was so hot and bothered that the exquisite patterns took on a hallucinatory vengeance, tiny tiles dancing before my eyes, twined borders writhing snakily, chequer-boards flashing positive and negative like an Escher print. I chose fifteen surprisingly satisfactory tables, the task being made immeasurably easier because Ramadi, who was occupied in indignant discussion with Abdeltif, did not assist me. There remained only table and bedside lamps to get, and my job was done.

We adjourned, thanks to the presence of Abdeltif at a more congenial pace, to a wonderfully cool basement for chicken and salad – you can have anything as long as it's chicken in Marrakech. Afterwards Abdeltif had things to do, and Mbarek had prayers to recite, so it was with the undiluted chaperonage of Ramadi that I went to the ceramics and lamp stall on the outskirts of town. Here he excelled himself with remarks of the 'this is blue', 'this is big', 'this is a lamp' variety, until I asked him to wait for me outside while I tried to match colours and sizes with locations in the house. Again, the problem was the wealth of choice – there were a million different colours and patterns for the simplest bowl, and I was torn between wanting one of everything and going for cool monotones. As for the lamps, there was the additional thrill of trying to find ones that actually worked – the bases were the most beautiful glowing *tadelakt* orbs in pinks, oranges, purples, acid green, but they were haphazard in the matter of electrics, and of the final choice, only three could be lit without mortal danger.

Mbarek shimmered into view to help with the transport arrangements, and we bundled into a taxi with a boot load of newspaper-wrapped ceramics. They found a *carrossa* with a bent geriatric at the other end when the taxi had gone as far as it could, loaded him up, and strode off again on their long manly legs, while I shuffled behind on my short, chunky ones. Getting, it has to be said, increasingly furious with the pair of them, until I could bear it no longer and peeled off to ring Dan from a téléboutique. My need to talk to him was so acute that I very nearly wept when there was no reply.

Spigs was a little grey, but rallied at our return, and later recovered sufficiently for us to escape to the Café France and gratefully eat something that was not chicken. We sat, in an obliging breeze, discussing our managerial problem. It was not going to work with Ramadi. I kept getting the impression that it was he who unwillingly employed me. But he was Abdeltif's choice, and I certainly did not want to hurt *his* feelings.

On the way back from dinner we rang Abdeltif, and explained our dissatisfaction. He was no pushover, and pointed out that we'd only known Ramadi for four days, that he was young, that he had sterling qualities and that *no* self-respecting Arab man can be seen to listen to a woman. Slightly taken aback, I agreed to stick it out for the rest of our stay, to see if things did not improve. Abdeltif promised to keep a beady eye on his protégé, and to find a replacement if on mature reflection I really could not work with him. It was beyond me to imagine what deus ex machina could transform this truculent misogynist boy into a smiling, competent, helpful and thoughtful adult.

The next day, our penultimate, was labelled 'Marjane'. This is an aircraft-hangar supermarket some miles out of town, crammed with things that fall apart. Our mission was to get all the para-phernalia for civilized life – bottle-openers, towels, dish-scrubbers, glasses, etc. Ramadi found us a petit taxi for the journey, which passed uneventfully.

On arrival, I suggested to Ramadi that he wait for us outside, or have a coffee, and we would assemble in an hour outside the front entrance. I was terrified that he would insist on accompanying us and pointing out every spoon, cup and towel en route. I would have to debate with him via Spigs about why I had chosen this cutlery rather than that, and acknowledge the bottomless stupidity that caused me to select a large heavy frying pan in place of a small tinny one. I might have had to attack him with the special bendy knives that are a Marjane speciality. He glared at me, but spotting that Spigs and I presented a united front, he assented and marched off, rigid and trembling with suppressed fury.

Spigs and I had a really good time in the air-conditioned wonderland. He is always good company on an adventure, but he surpassed himself on this comprehensive spree – we piled two trolleys with teetering mountains of necessities, and had a brief panic at the check-out when it appeared that my credit card was about to get funny with me, suffering from shock at the stupendous and unprecedented amount of money I was suddenly demanding, but it recovered, we paid and heaved our loot out to the front of the store to find Ramadi. He was nowhere to be seen. Spigs left me with the trolleys and did a thorough recce. Not a whisker. We were in the right place at the right time waiting for the wrong man.

'Come on, let's go and have some coffee – they've got a good coffee bar, it's the best thing about this place,' I said to Spigs – joyfully, actually, because my feet were double their normal size and lightly baked.

So we had a coffee, checked for Ramadi, had another, checked for Ramadi, looked for a loo, found one, checked for Ramadi and went ballistic. There were several reasons for this. One was that I couldn't remember our address – pathetic, I know, but there you are. Another was that when I approached a petit taxi, he answered with a brusque negative, pointing out that we had too much stuff to fit in his cab. The grand taxi likewise. So there we were for two hours, on a boiling humid day, stranded sweating in the car park of Marjane some ten kilometres outside the city, with two trolleys laden with household goods and no means of getting home.

'I'll ring Abdeltif. He'll come and collect us.'

Hampered by our overloaded trolleys we asked in the supermarket. No, they did not have a public phone, but perhaps there might be one at the petrol station? No, I certainly could not use the shop phone, no matter how much I paid.

Leaving Spigs with the baggage, I tackled the petrol station. No, they did not have a phone.

The nearest was four miles away on the main road to Casablanca.

A light unseasonal rain began to fall and the air suddenly became very cold. I trudged back to Spigs and we stood, stumped, with our mountains of household goods topped by the most expensive kettle I have ever clapped eyes upon (whose spout dropped off on its maiden boil). I could not think of any way out of this mess.

'Well, we could set up a tent with the towels and just live here. We've got food and drink, and plenty of knives and forks,' Spigs said. I was not amused.

Far in the distance, beyond the six-lane highway, we spotted a swaggering, strangely familiar figure – after three hours, Ramadi had decided to amble back.

Spigs's face set into a rictus of fury, for which I was very glad not to be the recipient, and he streaked across to Ramadi barely touching the ground. I saw him having several uncomplimentary words with the errant manager, and they returned in a toxic haze of rage, resentment and mutual loathing. It felt dangerous to be anywhere near their volatile and highly flammable aura.

With an impressive show of surliness, Ramadi commandeered a small taxi-van with an open back and we stacked our stuff within. He was about to swing into the front seat beside the driver, as was his wont, when Spigs said firmly, 'No, you come in the back with me.' Whenever we stopped at a traffic light, I could hear harsh words being spoken, and hoped I had put the kitchen knives out of sight.

Ramadi and Spigs were both alive when we reached our square, Spigs still incandescent and Ramadi by no means chastened. As he swaggered off to get a *carrossa*, Spigs hissed, 'He said you treated him with disrespect when you asked him not to come into the shop with us. He said that the people at Marjane had not allowed him to wait in the store, and he was humiliated at having to hang around outside.'

'Not enough,' was my unkind reply.

We managed to get all the stuff back and paid the *carrossa* men – it took a small team of them. What we needed desperately, right then, before any more excitement, was a cup of tea. Triumphantly I filled the Armani kettle, put it on the wobbling hob and turned on the gas. What gas? There was no gas, no connection. I had a shameful girly moment when tears seemed the only answer, but Spigs put a protective arm round me.

'Come on,' he said. 'Let's just go out and have tea at the Prince. You'll feel better when you've had a cup of tea. And then we can ring Abdeltif. And Dan. It'll all be all right. The house is magic, and these are only little problems. Abdeltif will sort them, you'll see.'

Shirley Conran once remarked that if you want to

find a good man, you have to grow one, and at this moment she was completely vindicated.

We sat in the Prince and ate cakes, tried out their almond milk (very good) and had a vigorous discussion about our plight. There was no ambiguity about our conclusion, but it was very necessary to let off steam, so we both said the same things over and over again, feeling a little better each time, until we were sufficiently restored to go back to the house.

We picked up the usual chicken and chips on the way, I rang Dan, who was manly and reassuring, then returned to find all the lights on but no one at home. We took our picnic up on to the roof, seeking cool in an evening that had turned decidedly sultry. Then we collapsed gratefully into our beds and slept.

The next morning, after breakfasting and waiting an unusually long time for even Ramadi to awake, I did a little investigation and discovered that the bird had flown. He had left me a copy of his very angry dissertation on the subject of foreign colonizers (French, but the principal still applied) and a curt note. A wave of relief flooded us with optimism and energy.

Poor Spigs had so far spent most of his first visit to Morocco either slogging or suffering, so we plunged into the souk to enjoy ourselves in the acquisition of a few trinkets: a scarf for Spigs's beautiful Spanish girlfriend, Maria, and a couple of eccentric outfits for my granddaughters, Chilali and Maizie, emblazoned with the appropriate legend Girly Team.

As a reward for Spigs's heroic support I dragged him out for our last dinner to a rather smart, very Moroccan restaurant, the Douiryia in the Mellah, whose ethnically clad waiters made a joke that very nearly backfired, given his internal state, when they denied having a gents' loo. There was a distinctly uncomfortable moment before they relented and slapped his shoulder in mirth.

This tricky incident was more than made up for by the appearance of a gorgeous belly dancer uncannily like Nigella Lawson, in regulation sequins and orange chiffon, with a large gap between her front teeth. Spigs opined hopefully that a gap between the teeth denoted rampant sexuality, but to his disappointment she did not drag him amorously into a broom cupboard. He was manfully indignant about her treatment by the rest of the staff, who appeared to think her no better than she ought to be and were noticeably lacking in respect, though this may just be the itinerant belly dancer's lot in life.

In good spirits at last, thanks to the weighty load that had been lifted with the departure of Ramadi, we sipped our wine and lolled on the red brocade cushions, trying to ignore their strange texture

(Spigs thought that they might be stuffed with giblets), working our way through a gargantuan set menu which ended with strange papery puddings and far too many petits fours. We ambled back home, making a brief detour to leave a note under the door of Maggie's hotel, asking Abdeltif to get in touch as soon as possible.

Once at the house, we took another bottle of wine up on to the roof terrace, and in the extraordinary hush as velvety darkness enshrouded the city, we talked about many painful things long buried – about what had gone wrong between me and the boys' father, about how badly Spigs felt he and Leo had coped and what an angry pair they had been during the long years when I was their acting parent. Spigs praised the courage and affection I had shown.

'You were rock solid, Mum.'

There was a long pause.

'We kicked the cat.'

And in case I had not understood the message: 'You *were* the cat, Mum.'

It's odd, how this laconic statement wiped years of grief and soul-searching away. For the first time in possibly twenty years, I felt I could lift my head up high. I was so grateful that the Ramadi nightmare we had endured was as nothing. On the contrary, it had been the catalyst for something I so needed to hear. We sniffed, wiped our eyes, and then giggled. Thank you, Ramadi.

* * *

Abdeltif came round early the next morning to do battle on behalf of his injured friend. I was impressed by his loyalty, but it did not take long for him to see that there might be another side to the story, and he acknowledged that Ramadi had been very angry.

'I think he went with a fluffy girl, while you were at Marjane. It is what boys do. He is no longer a friend of mine. He told me that you behaved with disrespect, but I think maybe the shoes are on the wrong feet.'

'But how will we do without a manager? You said it was essential to have someone here all the time.'

'No problem. Mbarek will stay in the house until I find a manager. I have someone in mind, a good man who works at present in a shop. He is very smart, a snappy dresser, he speaks very good English, and he will be perfect. Now, I will take you to the airport.'

That trial was over, but as I discovered a few months later, a new and far more alarming one was just taking its first breaths.

11

TRAVELS WITH A TRANSIT

August came. The Brighton flat did not sell. We were penniless.

Dan's son, Ted, came to stay with a friend, Rachel, but though we made vats of Pimm's, watched the annual meteorite showers and attended the *verdiales* in Villanueva, we were not good company. Even the summer *feria* in Almogia, tarnished by an unpopular sponsor, was a half-hearted affair compared with previous years – to Dan's disappointment there were no Brazilian dancing girls clad only in fishnets and feathers, just Señorita Guapa being crowned with a Barbie tiara. Dan's art classes and two lots of paying guests kept us alive, and the worst of it was the tightwad meanness that this incurred. There was no question of making grand gestures – the grandest we dared was to take Ted and Rachel out to Paco's for chicken and chips.

Of course there were good things – I adored Dan's art classes and did one painting that makes me prickle with pride every time I look at it: a pink and steely grey fish on a plate. May mean nothing to you, but for a Pisces it was profound. Another good thing was an elfin Mexican painter and his Irish wife who came to stay, via the pages of *The Author*. We briefly came to life during their week of residence. Immediately they left a deadly torpor set in, until an ex-colleague of mine from *Country Living*, Carl, and his actor friend Stevan came for an all-too-short holiday. Their stay was a brief oasis of peaceful pleasures – cooking, painting, drinking and laughs. This happens rarely enough in a lifetime – I should forget all the other tribulations of that year, and acknowledge that we ended up quids in – I do, I do. But for a fidgety person, there is nothing more corrosive than scanning an endless flat horizon and seeing no cloud of dust approaching. Stevan had unsnagged a tangled life by becoming a Buddhist – in a relaxed kind of way – and he taught us to chant, a technique for alleviating fretty waiting to which we took recourse many times over the following months.

Alan, the estate agent selling the Brighton flat, was upbeat, claiming that nothing ever sells in August but as soon as people returned from their holidays the flat would flash off his books. Abdeltif asked with increasing seriousness about how the sale was going, and continued to subsidize the restoration of the riad, but with noticeably less brio.

We bought a van – as a sensible economy, we thought – with our last euros, especially to go to Morocco at the end of September with a cargo of furniture preparatory to letting. It was a sleek indigo Citroën Jumpy, new-looking on the outside, and as we discovered later, very second-hand and mongrel under the bonnet. Naturally we took no advice, nor did we peer knowledgeably into its oily interior – just requested that the aerial be tightened up and the CD player replaced with one that worked. We envisaged using it for intrepid forays into the Moroccan interior, trailing to Marrakech via Fez and the Atlas mountains, we foresaw trips thriftily laden with furniture for the riad, coming back laden with rugs for the finca. We imagined taking the van around Spain, visiting Toledo, the mountains of the north, perhaps driving back to the UK, taking our time, enjoying the ride, camping in it with the dogs.

In the event, what we had to do immediately on taking ownership – apart from ignore the stunned snickers of Arturo Daley – was *hire* a van to take the furniture to Marrakech: the Spanish had just invented a new piece of bureaucracy, resulting in a delay of three months between buying the van and being able to use it outside Spain, a period that neatly coincided with the expiry of its guarantee. A pity, in view of subsequent events.

Grumbling a lot, we hired a wonderfully dependable Ford Transit and loaded it with books, bedding, cushions, my mother's Chinese bentwood chairs, pictures and the sort of things we hoped would make the riad into a home. I recall a little frisson of excitement when it looked as though I might not have enough cash to pay for it, but we somehow managed to squeak by with a couple of euros to spare.

Insured to the hilt and unusually confident in our immaculate hired van, we took the familiar route to the pink city, wondering what we would find at the riad in view of our seat-of-the-pants money situation. The great news was that Khaled was back, but we were worried about the dome over the stairs which Abdeltif had told us about by phone. 'It is gorgeous,' he rhapsodized. 'There is nothing like it in the medina – it is carved plaster on the inside, with coloured glass and a big brass lantern I bought specially in Fez. Very special. With coloured glass. And on the outside the light comes through the coloured glass – it is like a jewel. You will love it. Everyone who sees it loves it.' We remembered stipulating quite clearly that we absolutely did not want coloured glass.

Apparently the fireplace was also causing problems by belching black smoke both into the sitting room, thereby blinding the occupants, and on to the washing lines next door, thereby enraging a whole new set of neighbours.

In the event, we arrived to find a committee of house-proud ladies in the derb outside our house, all complaining about the mess we were continuing to make, and entirely mollified by the boxes of chocolates I had brought them. The whole squaring-up scene dissolved into giggles and kissing all round. I have yet to meet a Moroccan woman who is not generous, honest and disarmingly friendly, despite the lack of a common language. Many Moroccan men speak French, Spanish and English, but very few women have any other language but Arabic – a reflection of their confined circumstances and second-class status. Despite not having a single word in common, you always know where you are with a Moroccan woman; never a safe assumption with a Moroccan man.

How times have changed. Back in 859 when women were people, one of them, Fatima bint Mohamed ben Feheri, founded Al-Qarawiyin university in Fez, the first in the world. *A woman. The first university in the world.*

The Prophet respected women – he was asked, 'Who should you honour and befriend most?' He replied, 'Your mother, then your mother, then your mother, then your father.'

Having been introduced to all the mothers and daughters of the derb, we approached our own door and executed the special entry salsa, braced against whatever nightmare we might find within.

As we came through the front door we bumped into Abdeltif, who was euphoric, babbling with excitement about the things they were doing and how wonderful it all looked.

'*Everyone* comes to the house. Everyone *loves* it. We have put *tadelakt* in all the rooms, not just the ones we agreed, for nothing. It is a present from the builders. And on the roof, I have not put the little hut that Mister Dan drew' (an elegant, restrained cupola, absolutely simple). 'I designed a room, it is like a jewel, with a carved dome, and coloured glass, it is my present to you, you will love it, everybody loves it. It is *breelliant*.

'The stairs are unlike anything else in the medina, they are beautiful. And the kitchen . . .' (which Dan and I had designed to be cool and functional, with sensible downlighters over the worktops and lots of light and efficient, scrubbable surfaces). 'The kitchen . . . has brass lanterns, and *zellig fessi* on the walls. Marble. It is wonderful. You will love it.' A short pause. 'There are some extras. Not big. The brass lamps, I bought them in Fez, very good value, the best coloured glass. Red and blue and yellow and green.

'And the lamps on the roof – there are twenty of

them . . . it comes to . . .' He did a calculation. 'I will write it down for you,' he said finally.

My heart sank.

The place had been transformed in the two months since I had visited with Spigs – the court-yard had a fountain, a shallow carved stone goblet with fluted edges in the middle, and a blue and white *zellig fessi* alcove on the remaining blank wall with a lion's head spouting water. Four large but spindly orange trees were struggling gamely with life on a building site. They proceeded to die by millimetres, bearing out what seasoned gardeners are apt to say and hotheads to ignore, that it is always best to plant small trees that catch up, rather than big ones that die slowly. Our huge doors were back in place, and painted as finely as a Persian carpet with strapwork in spice colours: browns, ochres, deep reds, interwoven with bands of gold. The dumpy *doueria* windows had been replaced with Dan's elegant trio – involving who knows what demolition and rebuilding. All had Wedgwood blue shutters in place of the virulent turquoise, and their wrought-iron lace work was pristine white. Sizzling-pink bougainvillea cascaded from huge pots, and pleasantly undulating little terracotta tiles were laid on the diagonal underfoot. The major work had been done, and there were just one or two specialists putting the final cosmetic touches to the completed building, like Youssef Bekai the *jibs* frieze expert, clad as always in spotless black and unperturbed by the surrounding chaos, still carving out the endless frieze that ran around the walls at dado height and round every door and window, like a broad band of Valenciennes lace.

Everywhere we looked there were marvels – individually hand-cut tiny octagonal *zellig fessi* tiles clad the base of the pillars lining the gallery. The walls of all the completed rooms were as smooth as marble to dado height, resonant with the vivid pigments of *tadelakt*; each was finished with a differently patterned carved *jibs* frieze, and plain paint above. The bathrooms were entirely *tadelakt* in classic hammam style, with barrel-vaulted ceilings, shiny brass basins and taps, and decoration everywhere – bathrooms are very important in Morocco. They looked inviting, freed of Ramadi's shaving detritus. The kitchen could hardly be called brightly lit, but its brass lanterns shed a romantic glow over the gloom beneath the knife, and the acreage of marble made up for less than cordon bleu cuisine. Both the downstairs bedrooms had had their walls finished with *tadelakt*, one soft turquoise, the other dark library-leather green. Abdeltif's mouthwash room glowed as cool and fresh as a mint granita. The grand pink salon was finished, and the dining room was dark brown, like being bathed in chocolate – which sounds disgusting but was in fact sexily opulent.

The stairs had had to be built from scratch, and they were distant cousins of Dan's design: the wide light well we had envisaged with a table and chairs and a couple of plants had mysteriously failed to materialize, making the spiral quite tight and extremely dark. It was, however, a triumph up to the first floor, after which the banisters went somewhat awry. We picked our way gingerly up the intricately tiled steps to the gallery, marvelling at the ironwork, the cut tilework on the pillars, the carved and painted Berber doors on the upstairs bedroom.

Abdeltif, who had joined us, laid a hand on our arms and said in hushed religious tones, 'They have done these doors as a present for you. For nothing. So you will be happy. So this will be a palace.'

The newly painted gallery ceiling was dark, rich and intricate. It was one of the two original painted ceilings in the house, but whereas the one in the pink salon (Abdeltif's name for it, not mine) had been in good condition and had just needed a bit of restoration around the edges, this ceiling had at one time been taken to pieces and put together all wrong. Rachid had painted over it, the colour as richly sumptuous as the confused puzzle it replaced.

They had done so much. There were plants everywhere – on every balcony, by every door, up the stairs. Mbarek had made seating for the two sitting-rooms, and fat white cushions for all of the banquettes, the twenty-six chairs, sofa and two arm-chairs. Rachid had painted wardrobes and bed-bases for every room, there were rugs on the floor and each bedroom had its own table and chairs at which to sit and breakfast in peace, sulk, apply eye make-up or write a brace of haikus. Everything, top to bottom, had been scrubbed and polished. Abdeltif's low glass-topped painted sandalwood tables – loathed by Dan – formed an impressive obstacle in the gallery and caused a flurry of expletives every single time he grazed his shins on them. There were shelves and drawers in the kitchen, which unfortunately showered your knees with cutlery whenever they were opened. There were shelves in the bathroom with a fluffy cargo of towels from Marjane.

The *doueria* had a gorgeous hammam in Marrakech-pink *tadelakt* – a bath like a tiny proscenium, with pillars to each side and discreet downlighting. Abdeltif pointed out that it was just the right size for two, and that the sides of the bath were the ideal place for candles and an aphrodisiac brew – flutes of chilled Coca-Cola, perhaps. There was a wall fountain being installed on the landing outside the bedroom, edged with bands of carved sandstone. Khaled had ordered fine *mousharabi* latticework screens for the bedroom windows and the rooflight. The *doueria* had a wonderful, calm air of detachment – with just a few modifications to the stairs it would be finished.

There were small problems. Although the cooker was now flush with the grandiose marble worktop the gas jets hissed, removed your eyebrows and then expired. The metal chairs all wobbled and screeched hideous protest on the tiled floor, the small dining-room was so overpowered by the oval table and dining chairs that you had to breathe in on sitting down, and once in place no one could move. Where we had asked for halogen downlighters in the kitchen Abdeltif had installed brass lanterns with coloured glass. In fact, there were brass lanterns with coloured glass – of the type that Dan and I specifically did not request – everywhere. They were the stunningly inefficient sole form of lighting, apart from the *tadelakt* lamps I had bought with Ramadi, which, should you try to turn them on, ran a frisky voltage through your body and remained unlit. But these were peccadilloes, and we had to admit that the place was breathtaking.

'Ah, Mr Dan, you have not yet seen the dome. You will love it. Everyone loves it. People say, "We have never seen anything like it" when we show them. It is unique.'

We had been avoiding the dome. Apprehensive again, we slogged up the strangely skewed stairs and, looking up, saw an extraordinary carved white plaster hemisphere at the top of the stairs. The sun was slicing through green and blue glass inserts, casting glowing strips on the opposite wall. An enormous brass lantern was suspended from the apex.

'What do you think?' Abdeltif was as excited as a child at Christmas. 'It is breelliant, don't you think? Look at the sun coming through the glass. Like a jewel,' and before Dan could formulate a remark that would do justice to the exquisite workmanship and to his own feelings of astonished revulsion, Abdeltif hustled us outside.

'You must see the outside, you will love it, there is nothing like it in the whole of Marrakech.' We could see why. It sprouted, an incongruous crenellated Tardis, at the corner of the roof, bristling with spotlights and bizarre turrets. Fortunately, while we were standing, lost for words, Abdeltif heard Khaled somewhere in the building and bustled off to arrange for some tea.

Dan and I had a chance to get used to this strange alien presence. 'We can only call it magnificent. Abdeltif is so proud of it. It's his chef d'oeuvre. And it *is* magnificent, in a weird sort of way. He's done wonderful work, that's all there is to be said. Our own little *tadelakt* Tardis.'

Fortunately Abdeltif is not one of the non-touching Muslims, so I gave him a huge hug and a major gush when he emerged from the Tardis. 'It's wonderful, Abdeltif. The riad is the palace you promised. We are so happy and so *relieved*. You've been as good as your word; better, thanks to all the things that your team has thrown in for nothing. I can't believe the workmen have been so generous, and so speedy.'

He beamed, and put his arm round Khaled's shoulders. 'This is why,' he said. 'They do it for you and for Khaled. They just want it to be breelliant.'

Khaled, who had been out on some research mission, joined us and the four of us sat on tiny wicker stools – us in the sun, the two Moroccans in the shade – gazing well beyond the Tardis to the view of the rooftops and snow-covered Atlas mountains. Khaled's right-hand man Buddr brought us mint tea, while we discussed the progress of the building. It was an unsullied pleasure, now that we had seen the direction it was taking and the quality of the craftsmanship. Porridgy walls had been transformed into mirror-smooth *tadelakt*; floors of rubble had succumbed to little squares of terracotta and blue glazed *mizmat*. Coarse and ugly had metamorphosed into the sort of thing you see in glossy books with titles like *Marrakech, the Poetry of Pink Clay*, written by learned Germans with Von in their names.

Dan and I spent a happy afternoon playing house, finding the right places for chairs and pictures. We were on the roof, taking a break from our industrious decision-making, when there was a disaster. Abdel Akabir, the electrician, had been hard at work with his juvenile apprentice, Cheb, fixing exterior lighting. They scaled impossible heights and teetered on narrow ledges casually chucking yards of cable to each other like steeple-jacks. Skinny Cheb had clambered out on to the canopy over the door to the green room, a good twelve feet above the courtyard tiles.

'I know he'll be all right,' I said to Dan. 'They've done it all a million times before. I just can't watch,' and covered my eyes.

There was a silence, a crash, and then Dan said 'Shit!' and I heard the sound of running feet.

I looked down, heart thumping, mouth dry. The canopy was on the ground, torn in a hail of rubble from its moorings, and Cheb was lying in one of the citrus beds. Everything stopped, freeze-framed. There was an extraordinary stillness and silence.

I ran down to the gallery and was relieved to see that he had got up and was standing on one leg, doubled up in agony, clutching the other. Khaled had cold compresses already. Lovingly, a trio of builders shepherded Cheb into the nearest bedroom, and there was a great deal of coming and going. Khaled said firmly that there was nothing we could do and a doctor was not required. We had painkillers and chocolates – Cheb was very grateful for the latter, but refused the former, preferring Khaled's more familiar herbal concoctions.

An hour after the accident he was back at work with an impressive bruise and a theatrical limp.

There was something about his mute stoicism that refused to be cleared from the mind, despite the fact that the next day he appeared as good as new. I continued to keep a beady eye on him during the rest of our stay, and Khaled promised to pay special attention to his well-being, for which purpose I left an extra box of chocolates in the fridge.

For once, in my tetchy prejudiced life, I regretted the lack of health and safety regulations. The workmen in the riad routinely took the most appalling risks, and we were incredibly lucky that this was the only accident to have occurred. Well, the only one we knew about.

This trip to the riad – apart from Cheb's fall – was all pleasure. I forced Dan to come and do some restaurant research, and we dined on excellent French food in the romantic Rôtisserie de la Paix in Rue Yougoslavie one night, followed the next by a meal at Mosaique, where we were the solitary recipients of very attentive service from the owner, two waiters, a cocktail-bar waitress, the chef, his assistant and three musicians. We applauded and tipped with wild abandon. Dan threw caution to the winds and ordered the surprise menu, which did not turn out to be a platter of sheep's eyes as I had hoped, but a tagine remarkably like my lamb with prunes and walnuts, except with almonds.

* * *

We sped back to Spain in the trusty hired Transit, convinced of imminent success in our enterprise. Any minute now, droves of eager Moroccophiles would be begging to stay at the riad, we could repay our loans and I could stop worrying about money. The one vital thing we lacked was a manager, and Abdeltif had assured us that he had the very man in mind, a sophisticated polyglot, fluent speaker of any language one cared to use, born and brought up in the city and wise to its ways. We could not actually meet him just then because he was working in a men's clothing shop and had no free time. 'But he is perfect for you, you will love him.' He was ready to start at the beginning of December.

'Hey!' we said to each other on getting home. 'We've done the difficult bit. The rest is plain sailing.' And we celebrated – prematurely – with a menú del día down at Paco's.

12

CHRISTMAS POX

In October a tiny star glimmered feebly in the darkened sky. Someone was interested in the Brighton flat. Not interested in the asking price, but kindly prepared to take it off our hands for twenty thousand pounds less. We had not been there, had not seen it for over a year, and I wondered what state it was in, and how hard Alan had worked to get this insulting offer. We accepted it immediately.

Gradually, we allowed ourselves to believe that the pieces were beginning to shift. There might be a future if our buyer did not have second thoughts. With cautious jubilation we started to make plans: finish the *doueria*; persuade the editor of a newspaper to do a feature on buying in Marrakech – to which she agreed with gratifying enthusiasm; get my elder son Leo to put the riad on the Web; pay a flash visit to the UK to visit much-missed friends and relatives.

The buyer had second thoughts. Some other property was more seductive. We slumped. Penniless and paralysed, we thought things could at least get no worse. 'What doesn't kill you makes you strong,' we muttered to each other on the grey days that followed.

I had radically improved my Freecell score and taken up smoking again by the time our potential flat-buyer's more des res fell through, and *faute de mieux* he returned to us. He made a game attempt at an even more derisory offer, and I made a game attempt to resist. Alan the vicar – tried beyond patience by my vacillation – got firm with our buyer, who paid his 10 per cent to the solicitor, and there followed eight weeks of acute anxiety while his surveyor poked every hole and prodded every bit of woodwork, making dark prognostications that threw the whole operation into delay, panic, and attempts at further negotiation.

Alan stood firm, bless him, and finally, towards the end of November, the flat sale was completed and we were in a position at last to repay all our loans and move on. We asked Abdeltif to finish the *doueria* as quickly as possible. There followed a flurry of extremely expensive and complicated payments to him and Hecham, our newly installed manager – the perfect man in every way, according to Abdeltif – via Western Union.

Immediately on receipt of the money for the flat I cooked up a new scheme to ensure that we would be broke. In a moment of madness I offered to pay for Spigs, Leo and family, and Dan's children Doris and Ted to come out and join us for Christmas in Marrakech. I still thought, a few minor details aside, that we were outrageously lucky with our beautiful riad, and wanted to share it with my favourite people. They all agreed, imagining balmy evenings under the stars, dreamy five-star luxury with every whim catered to. Dan made quite a few escape bids, his first and almost successful ploy being to point out repeatedly that we could not afford it, which was of course very true. The second possible let-out was that there was no certainty that we would be able to use our malevolent Jumpy van.

In fact the plan threw Dan into a depression that lasted until the end of January, and very nearly finished our relationship. He hated Christmas with fervour, and the prospect of being surrounded by family in a place whose plaster was barely dry and bankrupting ourselves in the process struck him as dangerously crazy. As it turned out, he was absolutely correct.

What follows describes a Christmas from Hell. Read on, if you have been suffering from one fabulous Christmas too many.

* * *

We planned to depart for three weeks on the Monday before Christmas, to arrive a few hours before Leo and his family, having crammed the Jumpy with all the essentials for life. After a three-month mystery delay our van papers were cleared – thanks to some quiet but insistent pressure, including a refusal at six thirty on the previous Friday evening to leave the nefarious garage from which we had bought the beast – in the nick of time for our trip. We pranced home full of self-congratulation.

Over the weekend we jammed the Jumpy with an alarming amount of stuff – high chairs, toys, wendy house, duvets, bedding, lamps, radios, computers, guitar, books, crockery, glasses and knick-knacks, games, Christmas decorations, fabrics, cushions, a bed and mattress for Chilali, a cot for Maizie, and electric blankets against the fearsome cold that our newly installed manager Hecham had described. Finally we resorted to poking tiny things into the interstices – *turrón*, CDs, and bedside lights that refused to work on arrival.

Stevan, our actor friend, arrived the night before our departure, to spend Christmas at the finca, and consolidate his fond relationship with the dogs by looking after them for the three weeks of our absence. Carl, my erstwhile *Country Living* colleague, was due the day after we left, but we were going to overlap for a couple of days from 3 January.

Brilliant planning, I thought, just time enough to have one or two of Carl's curries and a few laffs. Stevan gave the dogs a thrill by prancing about in a pair of Rudolf antlers – they always appreciate a bit of novelty headgear. He had brought with him the Elizabeth Taylor book of jewellery, a present from Carl, over which I drooled briefly before stuffing it into the last gap in the van to show Dan's daughter Doris, a fellow jewellery fancier. She likes real. Diamonds are fine by her. When she was a waitress, she always favoured folding tips.

Stevan looked rather small and a bit wobbly as we abandoned him to dog-duties, so it was with many hugs and kisses that we left him and slithered weightily down the track. As we descended towards the coast, the weather became grey. It was, as usual, drizzling in Gibraltar, where we collected the insurance documents.

It continued to drizzle all the way to Marrakech. Dan did the journey calmly, patiently, in perfect time, and we found Hecham waiting for us at Chegrouni's as arranged. About my height, thin and wiry, clad in a sharp black suit, he had a fine set of glittering white teeth which he showcased at every opportunity. He summoned multiple *carrossas* for our baggage, and got us into the house with the minimum of hassle.

'Beliv me, Mr Dan,' he said, 'you will love the house. Everything has been done for your convenience.'

What awaited us was not exactly a shambles, but a sad, dirty, neglected-looking place, with mud and grit everywhere, filthy lavs and kitchen, and insufficient usable beds for us and Leo's lot due to arrive that evening.

I asked Hecham what it was that he had done for our convenience. He led me to one of the *zellig fessi* tables.

'Look,' he said proudly. I looked. It looked like a tabletop. 'I have painted the grout. It is now dark, not white. Much better.'

'Ah.' I thought privately that a little cleaning and bed-making might have been even more convenient.

I moved furniture, found bedding, made beds, cleaned the loo and bidet as best I could with no cleaning materials, made a few discoveries such as the gloomy one that the bidet discharged straight on to the floor, found homes for the stuff from the van, failed to get half the lights to work, panicked about Leo having no idea where he was coming to and no contact number should anything go wrong, and worried about what we could eat.

During this anxious whirlwind Hecham followed me around with a catalogue of extra problems that I might have missed, lecturing me about how much I had spent, and warning me not to tell Abdeltif that it was he who had alerted me to the crumbling *tadelakt* in the dining-room and the sorry state of the plumbing. Glumly I remembered Abdeltif's strictures about the absolute obligation to have a manager, and tried to recall his reasoning. 'Damned if you do, and damned if you don't,' I muttered under my breath, as I heaved bedding around under Hecham's watchful eye.

It was raining quietly but insistently, bringing joy to the locals but dropping a pall of utter gloom and misery on this house. I scurried about, tramping mud into every room, feeling more tense and miserable by the second. I had wanted to make a wonderful cosy welcome for Leo and the girls in the green room on the ground floor, but Hecham had set up the upstairs room, so I made up beds and a cot there. Everywhere I looked things needed attention – non-functioning lights, muddy floor, doors that would not shut, an unconnected electric oven, electric sockets hanging out of the wall at perfect child height.

Perilously close to tears, I did not know where to start. Somehow, in the few months between the desertion of Ramadi and the arrival of Hecham, the riad had begun to look unloved and sad. This wonderful treat that I was inflicting upon my beloved family seemed to have lost its sparkle.

Dan, who had holed up in one of the few habitable rooms, complaining gently because he did not have a desk, a light, paper etc., relented and put the cot together.

At least Hecham offered to get a quick and easy

takeaway for everyone when we got back from the airport, so I crossed dinner off my worry list and toiled on, trying to make cold, messy and unlived-in look cosy and inviting.

Well after dark I realized with a jolt that my watch had stopped and I had no idea what time it was. Hecham established that we were still in good time to meet Leo and the family. He insisted on driving me to the airport in the van, clipping wing mirrors as we passed and bearing down aggressively on cyclists, other cars and pedestrians, occasionally enlivening the journey with a short tirade of gratuitous abuse.

'Ah well,' I thought, 'boys *have* to show off as soon as they get behind a wheel. He'll calm down.'

We arrived on time and there was quite a wait, during which I convinced myself that the plane had crashed, chatting inanely to Hecham to take my mind off disaster scenarios. He was concerned to demonstrate what a thoroughly good guy he was, and told me solemnly that what he really abhorred above all else was lateness. He just could not abide people who were not punctual.

Eventually people started trickling through, and my anxiety abated. But the arrivals petered out and there was still no sign of Leo and his partner Saki. I was convinced that they had missed the plane, or that one of them was ill.

As it happened, Maizie, their one-year-old

daughter, was. Hecham and I waited until the queue dispersed and there seemed to be no one else coming through. Finally registering my panic, he had a word with one of the officials lounging by the exit, who nodded, and accompanied me through the barrier. And there, in a tense little huddle, was Leo's brood, looking terrible.

Maizie barely had patches of clear skin between spots caused by some mystery allergy, and though momentarily stunned and quiet, she was in a bad state.

Leo had taken her to the doctor that morning, who had said, 'There's no way you can travel with her, not until that has cleared up.'

Courage or foolhardiness? They had been terrified that she would be forbidden to fly, and the strain of deciding to go ahead with the trip must have been immense. Maizie had slept all the way from Gatwick. Chilali, her two-year-old sister, was bouncing about with gossamer confidence, poised for tears at the slightest provocation.

We piled into the van, and Hecham drove back slowly and carefully. I was appalled by the risk Leo had taken and at the same time touched to the extent of having a brief lip-wobble.

We got back to the damp desolation that was our house; Dan had lit a fire that had obscured everything in a blanket of eye-stinging smoke without contributing any warmth. Hecham disappeared to get our supper. For an hour or so, everyone was busy settling in and comforting the girls, who were alarmed by this peculiar dimly lit place. As time passed, fractious became frantic. Finally, after two hours, Hecham returned jubilantly with an unexplained friend and a complicated Moroccan feast. Now, at midnight, we just wanted him to leave us alone, but he was determined to make a big production out of the humble takeaway we had requested, with flourishes and pretentious table settings. We sat like Easter Island heads, staring vacantly and numbly munching.

After twenty minutes of this we shuffled off to bed. Maizie screamed all night, and I was as rigid as an umbrella spoke, fretting about her mystery pox, aware of every snuffle, cough and wail, appalled by the responsibility and convinced that she was going to die in the night. Where would we find a doctor? Ignorant foreigners that we were, we would not even be able to find Hecham's house in an emergency.

The next day dawned grey and cold. Maizie was worse. Both girls were desperately clingy. The house looked like a sad, wrecked folly as rain dripped on our heads from the door canopies and we had to plan the driest route from one room to another. More and more small disasters in the design area became apparent, such as the difficulty of making the dining-room work – room too small, table too big – or the propensity of all the plumbing to drip on to the floor in depressing small local floods. I was convinced that the girls would injure themselves on steps or stairs, sharp metal table corners or unprotected rooftop.

Hecham arrived with breakfast surprisingly late. When I asked mildly why, when we had arranged nine, he had turned up at ten, he glared at me and said, 'Beliv me, Madame Miranda, I have been to the hospital with my niece.' Naturally I felt like a creep. Especially when he produced from his pocket a gift – the first of several – a blue plastic clock bearing the legend 'Nurofen'.

'Oh, Hecham, how thoughtful. Because my watch broke. Brilliant.' I set it for ten thirty, and so the time remained. Mid-afternoon I asked Hecham if maybe the clock needed a battery? Indignantly he snatched it up, checked the time on his watch, and reset the hands for half past four. 'There. Now it tells the right time.' And swept off.

That afternoon we intercepted a wood cart and bought a small pile of wood, with which Dan made a successful small fire in what Abdeltif dubbed 'the Winter Salon', smoke-free thanks to his construction of a cardboard hood. Saki and I sat with our bottoms in the fireplace and emerged cheered but lightly kippered. We set the blue clock at eight thirty, fed it a new battery and placed it prominently on the mantelpiece.

I turned on the grill to cook dinner and all the lights fused. We stumbled about in the dark hunting the fuse box, and were rescued by our guardian angel, Khaled, who claimed to be just passing by, though as we are the penultimate house in the Derb, I can't imagine where he was on his way to. We established that if we attempted to use the oven, dishwasher, or a hair-dryer – let alone two electrical appliances at the same time – everything went dark. During dinner preparations, the timer knob fell off the virgin cooker. Afterwards the brand-new dishwasher refused to work. The fridge, teetering on a curious lordly plinth, seemed to be fine. Nurofen time remained serenely at half past eight.

I managed to cook something or other, and the second long night began, Maizie's parents surprisingly calm despite her recurring sobs. Every door that banged, every experiment with the CD player, every footstep clunking the crooked manhole cover in the bathroom provoked fresh screams. In brief bouts of sleep I dreamed of chequered dogs, while a vaguely familiar woman commented disapprovingly on the size of my hips. It was the second night without proper sleep, and there was another barrage of organization and decisions to be made the following day. I was beginning to feel numb in the extremities. Dan dreamed of a multitude of women queuing to kiss him and praise his good looks.

I had a new thing to worry about – Spigs and

whether he was due on Friday as Dan suddenly asserted, or Saturday as I had written in my diary. I pictured him arriving in the scary strangeness of Marrakech airport with no one to meet him, no contact address or telephone number, no recollection of where he was going, and probably no money. Fortunately I was right and Dan was wrong.

One good thing was the arrival of Fatima, Hecham's sister, a pretty, sweet-natured, giggly woman, built like a hippo. She spent the next morning and the following days scrubbing floors, walls, windows, clothes, pots, fridges, baths etc., in between doing some very fine Moroccan cooking – a lamb tagine for Spigs's arrival, a couscous the following day, then chicken with lemons and olives, all delicious though somewhat parsimonious with meat, and always involving an appetite-enhancing wait of about six hours.

At the beginning of our stay Hecham provided breakfasts, consistently late, but amazing: flat bread spread with butter and honey; dark, solid, moist Berber bread with a granular surface; plain doughnuts strung together fetchingly on a grass stem. Brilliant orange lentil soup was a surprising element, there were saucers of the fabled argan oil in which to dip things, *smen* – a powerfully rancid buttery substance revered by the locals that tasted better than it smelled, as well as *amlou*, a delicious concoction of spices, honey, almonds and argan oil.

Tiny almond and sesame cakes occasionally made an appearance, followed by glasses of extremely sweet mint tea.

To my concern Fatima worked until well after dark, washing floors by bending from the waist and shimmying a grey cloth around, presenting her stunningly large bottom to the world. She tackled washing in the same mode, doubled over and scrubbing the benighted garments on a washboard, using a thick paste of Omo. Clothes came back from this drubbing radically transformed, many a fine garment reduced to a stiff but absorbent rag. Chilali's vests reappeared about twenty-four inches wide and six inches long, and dousings with un-diluted bleach may have contributed to the subsequent disintegration of the Marjane towels. Fatima's hands, after three days, were red and raw; she grudgingly consented to wear the rubber gloves we bought. The whole medieval process was horrific to watch, and I planned to get a washing machine as soon as possible, no matter the assault on the fuse box.

On the third morning, after the first night's sleep when Maizie did not awake once, she and I were rejuvenated. On rising, the first thing I saw was a relatively spot-free Maizie helping Chilali to dig the earth out of the citrus beds with a spoon and put it in a saucepan. It looked as though they had been engaged in this task for some time, judging by the sprinkle of earth around the courtyard. Some time later I heard Dan yawn, throw open the doors and stride into the courtyard from our bedroom downstairs.

'Hello, girls,' he said cheerfully. 'What are you doing?'

There was a moment of silence, then Chilali said, 'I'm putting the earth in this pot with a spoon.'

'Aah,' said Dan in his special Horribly Patronizing Voice. 'Putting the earth in a pot with a spoon. Good idea.'

There was another silence, and then a somewhat waspish reply: 'Well, I am only two.'

Later that morning, Hecham's contact from the local police, Moulay Idrees, arrived, and politely ate cakes while we discussed our residency and Hecham's residency and the phone. In order to legitimize our new manager, we invented a portentous document, averring that Hecham was indeed our employee, and lived in 95 Derb Al Qadi. We signed it, and I put it in a folder.

Hecham seized the opportunity to try and persuade us to draw up a six-month contract of employment, but I had an intimation that it might be wise to wait a bit and see how we got on.

As it happened, this proved to be the wisest decision I made during the course of that benighted Christmas.

13

YULE DO

With the arrival of Spigs and Dan's grown-up children Ted and Doris, the place started, for the first time, to feel festive. Maizie and Chilali finally slept soundly and we no longer had to tiptoe – it was possible to have audible music; Dan lit the fire, which blasted out heat instead of a painful low dark cumulus; Doris made risotto and we played racing demons to the disgust of everyone except Leo and me. I found it very touching, Leo's insistence that we do the things that came from a more fun and less troubled era, before overworked adult and bullish adolescents had transformed our life in Islington into abrasive hell. I had brought some children's books rescued from the boys' rooms, and Leo wandered out of the sitting-room jubilant, carrying a dog-eared favourite: *The Worst Person*, asking me to do the voice for the Ugly Creature. I felt quite tearful that this should matter so, and that he had faith in me to remember how it sounded, which I did.

It dawned on me that the tension I was feeling came from suddenly having unaccustomed servants. Well, from having *these* unaccustomed servants. From having Hecham ostensibly at our beck and call, hanging around and demanding money for shopping expeditions; and Fatima, slaving obtrusively: sweeping, washing, making beds, collecting socks, cooking, scrubbing, drying, probably mangling, ploughing, threshing, grinding and winnowing as well. Having servants has never been an ambition of mine, though Abdeltif's arguments were persuasive and I was happy to be providing employment, and, as he said, making their families happy and pleasing Allah. I have never been a successful capitalist; now

I was being forced into the role of an exploitative Western one to boot.

On Christmas Day I spent a peaceful morning observing Fatima's widescreen bottom and baby-sitting Maizie, while everyone else plunged into the souk. Maizie woke up at three, having slept for three hours, and slowly, solemnly, deliberately, ate half a mango, quite untroubled by finding herself alone with me. She waded out of her nappy, explored the courtyard and peed on an ivy, all with a look of deep concentration. I admired her doughty little legs and solid square bum – now perfectly spot-free – and carried her up to the roof to potter about in the Wendy house in the warmth of the healing sun.

The others bounced back soon afterwards, and rushed up thrilled by their purchases – embroidered slippers, crocheted skullcaps and Berber make-up for Doris. Chilali came up to the roof, and joined Maizie and me in the Wendy house, where we

229

discussed its appurtenances. Sitting very tall with her legs straight out in front of her, Chilali turned to me gravely with a revelation.

'You know,' she said, 'Daddy's pooter's boken.'

Doris and Spigs were the only serious present-givers. We sat on the roof in the sun and felt very spoiled. Doris gave us comics and bath goodies, beautifully wrapped. Spigs had sat up all night before he left Malaga painting wooden boxes for us with bold Inca motifs. He had wrapped them in clingfilm for the journey, and tragically most of the Incas came off with the wrapping. Having warned everyone that this was to be the year of Scrooge – since, having paid for everyone's tickets, we were broke – we tried not to allow it to embarrass us. No one seemed particularly bothered – relieved, if anything. To my surprised gratification, Dan gave me a small prettily framed distorting mirror – for which I had to pay as he had run out of money.

The next few days were passed in shopping for trinkets, reading and writing. We cooked surprisingly successfully in the stygian kitchen, and in a heady burst of Christmas extravagance ate out at Dan's favourite lunch spot: the Snack and Café Berbère, restaurant panoramique, overlooking Derb Dabachi, where Maizie and Chilali had a happy time feeding the cats with their kebabs and dropping cutlery into the fountain.

Slowly we began to notice a pattern to Hecham's behaviour. For most of the day he functioned reasonably, but he was always late and bad-tempered in the morning, and any task we set after dark would take a mysteriously long time. When we demanded to know the reasons for these delays, he would weep on Dan's shoulder. 'Beliv me, Mr Dan, I could not get the food for you because all the shops were shut. I tried, beliv me, I went all the way to Marjane.'

Dan pointed out that when he left – three hours earlier – all the shops would have been open.

'The traffic was very bad, beliv me,' Hecham would protest, wiping his nose on Dan's jersey.

Spigs and I became quite familiar with all the local takeaways.

One evening Hecham burst in, animated by a BIG IDEA, clutching a plastic bag filled with strangely repellent small objects wrapped in clingfilm which exuded a powerful smell of lavatory cleaner. They were sweating unattractively in their plastic jackets and were coloured pink, blue, yellow and cream, with the greasy glaze reminiscent of the skin of someone about to vomit. They looked a bit like floating candles without wicks.

Hecham handed them to me with a flourish. 'These are for you, a present, for the bathroom.'

I assumed them to be bath salts, and hurried off

to put them in a discreet pile prior to binning them.

A few minutes later, Hecham and Dan were locked in serious confabulation – these were not bath salts, they were prototypes for his friend's gap in the market business – they were little plaster moulds, coloured and scented, to strew about the place causing small pools of chemical stench to disguise more organic smells.

'Yes,' said Hecham, expanding to the brilliance of the idea. 'We can make perfumed Barbie dolls, and flowers. You can stick them on the walls, and they smell for one year. How much do you think they cost?'

Unable to think of any sum of money small enough, I admitted defeat. 'How much?'

'Just one dirham, just one dirham.'

'For all of them?'

He looked at me pityingly. 'No. One dirham each. Very good price, no?'

Wisely, I think, Dan did not decide to invest his remaining eleven pounds in Hecham's business venture.

To revive our drooping spirits after the departure of Ted and Doris, we went on a trip to the vaunted Berber market in the Ourika Valley, a few hours' drive from Marrakech. I pictured handcrafted jewellery, embroideries, leather bags, and a rainbow of rugs. Perhaps spices and delicious things to nibble. What we actually found was flour, odd things made out of old car tyres, many small dented aluminium cooking pans and teapots, old clothes, second-hand knickers and shoes, naff machine-made acrylic rugs, vegetables, old bicycle parts, miniature shovels in quantity, plastic sandals which Hecham said were the Berber's favourite footwear, and spherical terracotta pots. Try as we might, we just couldn't find a single thing to buy. However, the setting was stunning in the clear sunlight, with a wide river-bed and a narrow sparkle of clear water down the middle, surrounded by hills neatly flecked with fruit trees, and with an enclosure – a sort of car park – full of donkeys.

We stopped at a surprisingly smart hotel further along into the Ourika Valley, and sat out in the sun among luxuriant gardens, enchanted by the snow-topped peaks above, the simple painted farms surrounded by fruit trees set in emerald grass, the sparkling little river and the excellent coffee. The place was awash with tourists in buses, coaches and hundreds of big taxis.

Leo, Chilali and I had quite explosive colds by this time and were fast running out of loo paper. My eyes were streaming. Dan and Hecham were still busy bonding, and after coffee and a smoke, Hecham's driving – always edgy – became decidedly unpredictable.

We had lunch in a streamside open-air café whose

proprietor was a friend of Hecham – lamb and chicken tagines with potatoes yellow as sunflowers, thanks to turmeric. Cats threaded their way around the table-legs, the valley was grassy and green and studded with neat little trees, above which the sun glittered on snow.

This diversion over, we drove to the next stream-side village. Rugs were what we were after. We shot past many a rug-dealer with rugs we fancied until we came to Hecham's chosen vendor, a small intense man with a passing likeness to Dustin Hoffman. We had been marched past rugs that we really wanted, particularly a black one with a brilliant orange square in the middle, but there was no diverting Hecham, who led us up steep, rough and winding alleys into the hillside, until we found ourselves in the last house in town, on a small, unbalustraded roof with a twenty-foot drop in every direction, and an admirable view of satellite dishes, flapping knickers on washing lines and taxis waiting below. My eyes and nose were streaming as Maizie and Chilali made energetic suicide bids on that roof, and the sun got lower behind the snow-covered hills. Even in the sun it was surprisingly cold. Dustin and Hecham wanted to go through the whole routine – mint tea, to be followed by a tour of the house and the hammam and a glimpse of Berber women at work. From where we sat we could see a couple, swaddled with floral garments, winnowing grain on a narrow rock ledge above our heads.

As darkness fell and the air grew colder, we persuaded the sales duo that just the rugs would do fine – they trundled up from below with about fifty, and after much pantomime we agreed to buy four. Two finely woven from some lustrous fibre – vegetable silk – excellent for asthmatics, apparently, in saffron and faded-denim blue embellished with runic embroidery; a wonderful deep pile mutably scarlet; and a rustic version of a Persian flower garden in faded blues and pinks. Hecham floored me by asking, 'Do you want me to bargain, or do you want a friendly price?' Naturally, not wishing to appear like tightwad cheapskates, we opted for friendly. Friendly worked out at probably twice what we would have paid at Liberty.

When we finally and gratefully reached home after a hazardous drive, Hecham dropped us and took the van off to the car park, returning several hours later as we were clearing away the remains of dinner. To our dismay he staged a five-star melodrama, flinging his arms round Dan, calling him his English father and leaving a snail trail all over his last remaining good jersey. Dan fell for it absolutely, embarrassed but flattered to be Hecham's hero du jour, calling Hecham his Moroccan son. Saki and I gagged.

Wiping his eyes, and with many a 'beliv me, Mr

Dan', Hecham followed his tears with a histrionic confession: he had been given a hefty commission on the rugs we bought. With this princely sum he proposed to take us to Essaouira. He had arranged to take a friend's grand taxi. When we asked why not just go in the Jumpy van, Hecham mentioned casually, too casually, that it had a problem with the radiator that his friend was fixing. We thought this odd, since he had not mentioned it when he took it to the car park. Brushing our nitpicking concerns aside, he warned us that we would have to start at first light in order to have a fun-filled day by the sea, so we all went to bed sensibly early.

The morning of the great Essaouira trip, we were all up and ready just after eight. By ten we were still waiting for Hecham, and Dan and Leo decided that this was the perfect opportunity to have a fight, shouting and pushing each other about. They had cleverly spotted that what we all really needed was a full-scale yuletide battle, after which no one would ever be able to speak to anyone else again.

When the pushing subsided and things seemed to have calmed down, Spigs and I decided that hunger had got to these two normally peaceable chaps, and bought us all breakfast. We had just finished when Hecham turned up, looking furious, with breakfast. No mention was made of Essaouira. The day was set fair for general disgruntlement.

Hecham created a diversion by shouting at Khaled about various things, including fixing stops on the appalling kitchen drawers, which still fell out of their sockets, showering feet with knives and forks. Luckily Marakchi knives are not made for cutting purposes. Khaled obediently summoned a couple of carpenters, who took over the kitchen, filling it with cutlery, sawdust and the cheery mayhem of drilling and sawing.

Having created complete chaos, Hecham then disappeared for an hour, and returned sizzling with excitement.

He handed Dan an unwieldy newspaper package. 'Open it, it is for you. A present.' Inside the grubby newspaper were three metal spaceships on little legs.

'Thank you, Hecham,' Dan said, bemused. 'Very nice . . . what are they?'

'They are for tea. Every house must have them. So this will be like a proper Marakchi house.'

'Ah. Tea. What do you do with them?'

Hecham was getting a little impatient with his English father. 'You put tea leaves in this one, mint in that one, and sugar in the other. Simple.' Hecham lined them up proudly on the worktop.

Dan is the saintly patron of lame ducks and three-legged dogs – he never has any money in Marrakech because he spreads his bounty recklessly among the poor and needy. But he was undoubtedly the man of

237

the household, and still, despite the evidence, root-ing for Hecham. There was something about Hecham's transparent ineptitude that brought out the protector in Dan, and, this championing of hopeless causes being a role Dan valued, I really did not want to intervene. I was torn between sincere admiration for Dan's goodheartedness and suspicious cynicism about Hecham.

As our manager disappeared to check the progress of the Jumpy, Dan said, 'He's a good boy – he just needs a bit of guidance. I think he's learning. He's working really hard to sort the van.'

I kept quiet about my growing suspicion that Hecham had caused its problems and contented myself with a groan when he rang late that night to say that it was not fixed – that it would, in fact, require another three days.

Why, the sensible reader will ask, did I not simply tell Hecham to go?

Dan's inexplicable fondness for him aside, there was Hecham's frequent tear-soaked declaration that he alone kept his elderly and ailing parents in food and medicine. That he paid for his niece's operations and the roof over his drunken brother's head. If he was telling the truth and we sacked him, we might be consigning his entire family, including good innocent Fatima, to who knew what fate.

I was feeling my way in a country where women are expected to be invisible, inaudible and definitely powerless, and like it or not, we needed a manager. I had realized the truth of Abdeltif's sage strictures – so many operations I take for granted at home were out of the question without an Arabic-speaking intermediary: checking plane flights, finding a taxi, buying car parts, getting the engine fixed, organizing the delivery of a washing machine, taking issue with a guarantee, finding and collecting gas bottles. Above all, without a manager we could not communicate with the essential cooks and cleaners who, being women, spoke only Arabic. In addition it was common knowledge that without a manager, empty houses (particularly those of foreigners) in the medina became vulnerable to thieves, vandals and, worst of all, amateur bordello keepers.

Also Hecham was my second manager. Even supposing that Abdeltif could snap his fingers and instantly find another to look after the riad in my absence, what guarantee did I have that he would not be even worse? In this promise-anything world, how would we know the good solid heart-of-gold candidate from the meretricious toe-in-the-door contender with plans to run a whorehouse, with a weakness for alcohol, or afflicted by rampant kleptomania to support multiple wives or buy top-of-the-range automobiles. We did not have the time or the arcane insight required to trawl those mysterious alleys for the one trustworthy man who

14

THE PRINTS OF DARKNESS

The plan had been for Dan, Spigs and me to return to Spain on 3rd January, leaving Leo and Saki with the riad to themselves for a few days. I was looking forward to seeing our dogs, and Carl and Stevan. But the Jumpy – and Hecham – had other ideas. When Hecham told us that it would take three more days to repair the van, I was quite unreasonably upset. I rang Stevan and Carl, and asked them to take the dogs to the kennels on their departure.

In a panic I tried to find some alternative means of getting home quickly. Being Christmas and the busiest time of year, the regular plane flights were all booked. Such was my desperation to leave that I even tried to track down a private plane to charter. Abdeltif's suggestion was to get Hecham to hire a car and drive us to Tangier – a fine idea but for the mystery absence of Hecham, who rang eventually to swear that he was labouring to fix the van.

First he claimed to have had the radiator mended. The existing one he described as 'crumbly as cake' – he had a Polaroid of what looked like a clairvoyant's ectoplasm to prove it – but his men had cleaned it out, filled it with some magic potion, and it would get us back to Spain.

Then he said he'd had the gasket fixed – bursting in at midnight to show Dan the old burnt-out one – which had involved taking the entire engine to pieces.

Finally, he told us the dynamo needed attention.

He turned up unexpectedly at around one in the afternoon of 4th January, swearing that all problems were solved. Speedily we stacked the back of the van with our stuff. The engine seemed to work, but there was a hefty new dent in the Jumpy's already weathered bodywork, about which Hecham was extremely vague.

I felt terrible creeping away while Maizie was having her siesta and not saying goodbye, but leaving was definitely top priority. As I was handing a somewhat begrudged four hundred dirhams to Hecham in gratitude for I'm not sure what, Khaled puttered up on his Mobylette. I was touched that he had come to wish us bon voyage, but what he wanted was a thousand dirhams to pay the builders.

We piled into the van and set off, with Hecham on a motorbike as outrider for a kilometre or so. We stopped at the first service station and filled up with diesel, and I inadvertently spent a fortune on nuts and biscuits. We continued our journey, Spigs solemnly munching his way through the priceless ginger nuts.

'Oh shit!' As we overtook a lorry the temperature gauge suddenly rocketed. We stopped, waited till it cooled down, and then refilled the radiator with mineral water. We got as far as the military compound and then it started boiling.

Dan put his head in his hands. 'We're fucked.'

We had managed sixty-four kilometres.

We bought six large bottles of mineral water, turned the van round and filled the radiator. Again two miles back down the road. And a couple of miles further. And so on, at ever-increasing intervals all the way back into Marrakech, stopping once for a while at a picnic site decorated by wild lavender and ixia.

A motorcade approached, with two big bikes at the head of it, whose riders firmly signalled oncoming traffic to pull over. A tiny caravan followed them and about fifteen smart new smoked-glass-windowed cars, one of them probably containing the new king.

We moved on when the insane overtaking began to terrorize us.

Next stop was by a sewage plant in the Palmeraie.

Finally just by the Koutoubia in the thick of rush-hour traffic, where Spigs and I left Dan to take the van back to the garage. We walked home in silence.

Coming back wasn't as grim as it might have been: I was thrilled to see the girls again. Dan appeared in surprisingly good spirits, having left the van locked outside the closed garage: it obviously needed a new radiator; potions didn't do.

After some discussion, Hecham acquired a train ticket for eight the following morning so that Spigs could get back to work and his bereft girlfriend Maria. But having delivered the ticket, he immediately came up with a better idea: he would take his friend's taxi to Casablanca to buy a radiator and drop Spigs off there.

These are two different operations, I said; best get Spigs on his train and *then* sort the radiator. I queried whether it might not be an idea to look for a radiator at the Peugeot/Citroën place by Marjane that we had passed on our return.

No, said Hecham, there was certainly not going to be a radiator at the Citroën parts outlet in Marrakech. Casablanca was the only possibility. It also turned out that we had melted the gasket, which involved taking out the entire engine again, because no one had thought to tell Dan that he must not under any circumstances use the accelerator.

Neither Dan nor I were surprised when it turned out that the Jumpy was six days outside its guarantee.

The best thing, apart from seeing Maizie and Chilali again, was Khaled's invitation to come and visit one of the houses along the derb, which belonged to a French family and was run by an extremely nice woman called Hassania with a beautiful ready smile and bright, observant black eyes. The house was restored in the best of discreet modern good taste, all white and neutral, with a dinky plunge pool in the courtyard beneath a fountain, all done in white *zellig*, a couple of bench seats along the sides making a sort of cool jacuzzi. White, plain, neutral, beige – that was the prevailing smart ethos, but it did not worry me a jot that we were the vulgar, joyous end of the colour spectrum. Aspire as I might, I'll never be a convincingly beige person.

'Madame Miranda is a very nice neighbour, you can see – look at her face,' Khaled said to Hassania, explaining that the way I talked and dealt with things was a sign of my general gorgeousness. I was too astonished to set him right.

Hecham ambled in at nine thirty the next morning, bearing no breakfast, well after the train that Spigs was due to catch had gone. He gave no explanation for his delay, but proposed to drop Spigs off at Sidi Kacem on his way to Casablanca, where he could catch the train to Tangier. I did not realize that Sidi Kacem was practically as far as Tangier, imagining it to be just outside Casablanca. It was not until Leo showed me on a map that I saw how crazy the idea was.

However, Spigs and Hecham set off in his friend's cab. I said goodbye with trepidation, since it was rainy, the roads slippery and Moroccan drivers suicidal. I watched them go with a heavy heart. I need not have worried – on the way out of town, Hecham came up with a better idea, which was to drop Spigs off for a later train at Marrakech station, and go to the Peugeot/Citroën outlet near Marjane for the requisite parts.

Leaving Dan in bed, I decided to spend the day with Saki, Leo and the girls, starting with lunch at the new 'French' restaurant, the Alhambra, on the square, which was warm and comfortable and ambitiously overpriced. I ordered goat's cheese salad, which turned out to be tiny wedges of curiously sweet bread, spread with some sort of vaguely onion goo, and topped with tepid Dairylea.

Watching umbrella-topped figures outside scurrying through puddles, I was so grateful to be somewhere heated that I couldn't have cared less. The girls were exemplary, spurred to good behaviour by two execrably screamy French children at the next table. For the first time during this yuletide nightmare I felt relaxed and happy.

The sun appeared when we went for cakes at the Prince. Things were going so well, we decided to attempt the Saadian tombs. They were shut, so instead we visited a Berber herbalist. We were introduced to the shop by a wily puppy of a woman, all rolling eyes and swaggering behind, who took us in and handed us over to her friend, whose demeanour and face were an unattractive cross between Barbie and bulldog, lips outlined in regulation brown. Instantly and impassively she went into her spiel, recommending anti-freckle creams for Saki and weight-reduction pills for me. Neither of us was enchanted. She indicated that I should try a pink salve on my lips, which I did, taking a smear from a much-used pot – good for herpes, she said belatedly. Good for getting herpes, I guess. She handed us a list of cosmetic essentials from which we chose amber: 'an Cubic parfume for The Body', white clay: 'Mix with rose water for removing black spot, fever button, dry face, and Wrinkless', and essential oil of orange: 'For stress (nerves) . . . 3 droops in a glass of water to drink.' With the prospect of an entire bottle of tranquillizing droops, we felt we could face anything.

We happily wandered the souks, where Leo the Taciturn revealed a startling talent for bargaining. In Morocco an article does not have intrinsic value – the object is not priced, the prospective buyer is. Leo and Saki bought *two* magnificent scarlet woollen rugs for 3,000 dirhams by dint of saying truthfully that they could not afford the 3,500 they were being asked for one. On a previous trip, Dan and I had managed the same feat for 10,000 dirhams – but I had been wearing my pearls and had a gold Visa card. The secret was Leo's perfect willingness to walk away. Moroccan stallholders have a precise intuition for the gleam in the eye, and know exactly when 'no' means 'mmm'.

We bought presents for all Leo's friends and Saki's family, and then happened across Dan, looking rather perky, princing it with his guitar at his friend Moulay Omar's spice stall in the magic souk. Marrakech medina is such a tiny village.

At that very moment a fight broke out between two women stallholders, involving attempted GBH with baskets and hats and a chase through all the stalls, causing much dispersal of turmeric and shoals of flying lizard skins.

'They smoke too much marijuana,' murmured Moulay Omar disapprovingly. 'It makes them aggressive. There are always fights among the women.'

That excitement over, we all sipped mint tea perched on wooden boxes at the back of his shop, gazing out peacefully across the sun-slanted square at the backdrop of cinnabar and indigo rugs draped across shop fronts and jars of mysterious spices and unguents within. Moulay Omar did a brief tour of

Spices

his wares: myrrh and sloe calmed restless spirits, he confided, and demons could be summoned with certain herbs and skins. He was longing to tell us about spells he had known, things one could do with headless chickens and red wax, easy hexes for beginners. I tried to prevent him from telling us the full horror story of Aisha Qandisha – a particularly scary, man-hunting, cemetery-scavenging ogre with camel's legs, a woman's body and bloody wounds beneath her eyes – but the girls' interest was fortunately waylaid by an examination of the caged chameleons. Moulay Omar was disappointingly reticent about love potions.

I asked about the pile of dried hedgehogs.

'You must burn them,' he replied, astonished at my ignorance.

'What for?'

'For the evil eye. To frighten the evil eye away from your house.' Obvious really.

Since there was no sign of a sale in the hedgehog department, Moulay Omar was not going to let me go until I had bought a bottle of the fabled argan oil and some henna. The henna came from one of the pugnacious ladies and looked convincing enough, but the oil had to be brought in from a neighbour's shop decanted into a plastic Coke bottle. It struck me as being a curious colour and having an odd smell and by the time everyone in the shop had pressed their more or less whiskery noses against it or dipped their more or less filthy fingers in it, pronouncing it best quality, I wasn't sure I wanted it at all. But Dan plonked down the money for it, and more or less said, 'Now git.'

We did, ambling past perfect pyramids of scarlet, dun and ochre spices, past tiny shops whose grid of sagging shelves held a brilliant rainbow of old-fashioned sweet jars containing pigments. Maizie and Chilali were fascinated by the tortoises, the festoons of sweets and the underwear stalls, where sequinned belly-dancing outfits winked naughtily among drooping thermal drawers.

To his embarrassment, we came across Dan again, now playing his guitar for the delectation of his new best friend Jamal, who ran a musical instrument shop. Dan, as Maggie once said, 'is happy in his skin', meaning that he fits in anywhere quite un-selfconsciously. I envied him his ease in this Kingdom of Boys.

Hecham rang from the garage as we shuffled back into the riad, and the news was not good. Apparently there were no Jumpy radiators in Morocco, so the garage was going to make one, and not a feeble plastic one, but brass, which would be much better but would take an extra two days. Oh, and something else had broken in the van, costing, curiously enough, the exact amount that Hecham had left over in his pocket from the non-trip to Casablanca. The taxi trip itself to Casablanca, Radiator City, was history and not worth mentioning, though Hecham swore that Spigs had caught a train in plenty of time for the boat to Spain.

Hecham staged one last brief eruption that night while we were peacefully eating Dan's never-fail chicken casserole. He was bearing a gift to make everything all right – two goldfish.

I was curious as to why he had wanted to put Spigs on the early train in the first place, if a later and more convenient one would do, and in reply Hecham frowned indignantly. 'Beliv me, Madame Miranda, Spigs will already be in Malaga.' I was glad to hear it, though still puzzled.

Dan had a serious fatherly conversation with him,

suggesting mildly that he had problems with his time-keeping and pointing out that Leo and his family needed to catch a plane the next morning. We would need breakfast at eight thirty.

'Yes, yes, Mr Dan, you will see, I am a changed man, all problems are over. I will be here with breakfast at eight thirty.'

With this comforting promise, Hecham left.

An hour later our tranquil evening was shattered by a desperate phone call from Spigs, who had finally arrived in Tangier, alone, practically penniless, unable to speak Arabic or French, well after the last boat had left. He was taken by a dodgy taxi-driver to a hotel with no phone in the seediest part of town. He had wandered the sinister back-streets and found a phone, but did not have enough money to phone Maria, which I did. She was distraught. So was I.

At nine fifteen the following morning, when we had finished breakfast, Hecham strolled in. I asked what had happened to the changed man and eight thirty, then told him about Spigs.

'Beliv me, Madame Miranda,' he said, 'the train takes seven hours from Marrakech and arrived at seven.' I could not bear to address another word to him.

Leo and family made it with minutes to spare.

As the imprisoned days ticked by, with the Jumpy laid low by one mystery ailment after another and still no prospect of getting to Spain, I began to see Marrakech as the home of secrets and lies. It seemed that no one could manage transparency; everything was whispered deals. I have always valued my independency, fought my own battles, and I hated being entirely in the hands of others. Garage mechanics have always been agents of evil alchemy for me, even when the satanic, sump-oil-covered creature and I speak the same language. How much worse here, when the latest drama revolved around a defective *kelas*, and I did not even know what language we were speaking. To this day I do not know what a *kelas* is. What could we do but laugh about the whole horror ride? What a kaleidoscope of little nightmares, shifting, changing, becoming more intense and darker as I looked.

We didn't yet know the half of it.

But while our tribulations preoccupied us, Khaled had been busy getting his men to create a palace. There were some imperfections, but actually very few, and while we had stayed, making their work difficult, they had been busy on the *doueria*. Rachid had painted the ceiling patiently, slowly, meticulously; the *tadelakt* boys had completed an extraordinary Marrakech-rose bathroom with a huge *tadelakt* bath like a little stage with arches and columns, a perforated dome with glass inserts to let in shafts of sunlight, *zellig fessi* around the basin, a finely tiled floor, and a window with a curly grille. The fountain on the *doueria* landing was a miracle – two tall handsome young men made it out of sand, presumably with some kind of binder – stencilling a design and carving flowers and patterns upon its pillars. The carved sand motif was carried on around the walls at low dado level, a technique called *tahajart*. The rooflight on the befountained landing was glass blocks above and intricate turned wooden *mousharabi* below, so the sun entered in narrow slices. The bedroom had Rachid's beautiful painted ceiling, off-white walls, the original chequered Harris tweed tiles on the floor, and *tadelakt* up to dado level. The windows were veiled with *mousharabi* for privacy and to prevent small children from hurling themselves to the ground below. It would be a very superior suite.

As well as all this, the men continued with the roof, adding another pair of terraces with carved *tadelakt* and brass lamps. Most days over Christmas we had gravitated up to the roof, where we could lounge on our grand sofa and eat at the big round table, warmed by the sun. I liked all the rooms in this house; there was not a single duff one. All the bedrooms were lovely, the upstairs salon was divine, the gallery cool and gracious.

Dan rang Doris for her birthday on 7th January. He joined me later, cheeks tear-streaked, doubled up with chest pains. I ran through the heart-attack scenario, but concluded that we were dealing with extreme tension compounded by a talk with his daughter. I made him lie on the bed, wrapped him in a blanket, and massaged his head with argan and arnica. He responded very well, relaxing almost immediately, the chest pains went and he recovered his spirits. I worried about his health: a couple of months previously he had fainted, forcing me to admit how very much I loved and depended upon him, whatever I tried to convince myself. He had been astonished, on regaining consciousness, to find me attempting to give him the kiss of life.

As soon as he rose I insisted that we go to the elusive Saadian tombs: after so much ghastliness we needed to see something beautiful. The guidebook said they shut at one, so I hurried us along to get there. In fact they shut at eleven forty-five, and did not reopen until two so we sat out in the biting cold eating kebabs.

In 1581 the French essayist Montaigne, in Italy for treatment of his gallstones, saw the Carrara marble being shipped to Marrakech for the columns of the El-Badi palace and the nearby tombs, paid for, weight for weight, in sugar. No European clapped eyes on the marble columns again until 1917, when the French did an aerial survey of the city and accidentally came across El Mansour's Saadian tombs close to the palace, immured but intact. Today the simple columns still support the carved and painted cedar ceilings of the two richly worked and sumptuously decorated pavilions built to house the dead. Ismail the Bloodthirsty's fingers itched to plunder these as well as the rest of the El-Badi palace, but he did not quite have the bottle to desecrate the tombs of the dead, so with a snort of displeasure and a couple of petulant beheadings, he walled them up instead. If he could not benefit from their beauty, no one else would either.

In the cold and after all the hyperbole, looking at the tombs took ten minutes, and that was stringing them out. Though undeniably beautiful there was not much to see, and any atmosphere of solemn gravitas was shattered by a caterwauling tomcat looking for a female, shuffles of aimless tourists, and the freezing chill that suddenly descended.

By mid afternoon, on our return to the riad, Hecham claimed to have found the perfect replacement engine part, which fitted like a dream and cost only three hundred dirhams more than the previous one.

'Beliv me, Mr Dan, it is the bog's dollocks.' So much for Dan's language coaching.

I extended the car insurance for a further week.

That afternoon Hecham and Khaled trawled the latter's personal scrapyard and found a *kelas* that worked. Brilliant. I had enormous faith in Khaled's calm and methodical approach, his overview, his intelligence.

Hecham promised us a wonderful gift, his best yet. My heart sank. What could possibly surpass the Nurofen clock, spaceships, sweaty smelly things or goldfish?

We did not bother to pack, and Dan trudged around singing snatches from 'Hotel California' – something along the lines of being able to check out any time you want, but never being able to leave – until he was asked to shut up.

Unbelievably, Hecham arrived at nine forty-five the next morning, having rung from Ben Saleh Square to ask how many *carrossas* we'd need. It really seemed as though something was about to happen. We threw all our possessions into bags and set off in the bright sunlight, following our *carrossa* man, who had a slight altercation with a donkey cart coming in the opposite direction laden with building materials.

Suddenly the air was sparkly, the children sweet, the house palatial and gorgeous and I nearly didn't want to leave. But I fought with myself, and as we burst into the open dazzle of the square with its view of distant snow-covered mountains floating like knife blades on the horizon, the boulevards lined with orange trees spangled with fruit, I knew quite definitely that I wanted to get home to our dogs.

Hecham, who had accompanied us to the garage, presented us with the wonderful surprise he had threatened, his last and least-desired present – a disposable camera with which he had recorded all the labours of his motor-mechanic friends. As we discovered later, there were many pictures indicating that the garage only worked during vampires' hours. There were sinister, shadowy black crusty things, and sepulchral grey greasy things. There were hands, shiny and dark with oil, holding small rusty things, and a flash-lit variety of motor parts looking like the scene of a nasty nocturnal accident, laid out on a rag. The Prints of Darkness.

To our incredulous amazement, the Jumpy, with an almost entirely new engine, worked. Dan drove brilliantly as always, there appeared to be no sneaky secrets, like only drive at twenty mph or do not use the accelerator, and we arrived at our usual hotel in Asilah to find as usual no hot water and no soap, but abundant good will. Fantastic. They brought up a tiny radiator to stave off hypothermia, and Dan managed to have a restorative hot bath once the water was on.

We had an alarm call at six thirty a.m., which seemed like a very bad idea at six thirty a.m. However, we tottered downstairs – my eyes always water when I have to wake up too early, and they did, rivulets. The elfin-faced young night manager was sleeping swaddled in a blanket on a sofa in reception, his face grey with cold. He had never known such cold. 'It is coming from Russia,' he said darkly. We stumbled out into the rimy dark street, dumped everything into the van and left, breakfasting on cashew nuts and dates.

We said goodbye to the African coast as the sun rose, setting off a glittering crystal display, scintillas of frost on grass and dunes, reflecting rosy on great flooded pools dotted with the silhouettes of trees.

Carl and Stevan had left us a wonderful welcome before returning to England – coppery carnations and grey olive foliage in a jug on the table; paper chains criss-crossing the ceiling; chocolate coins next to the bed; and a collection of presents on the table with a great big message in multicoloured squiggly felt-tip – 'Welcome Home Dearest Mr Dan & Ms Miranda with love and kisses XX Carl and Stevan.' There was, clockwise from left to right, curry powder from Goa – 'Only need one teaspoon!; Popadums take 1 min in microwave; Lavender lotion in gorgeous box'; Dr Hauschka facial stuff in a nice tin – 'Pretty lady likes pretty products'; candle for workroom 'to aid creative thoughts' – the candle was a cedar Dyptique that I've always coveted; limited edition 'pen for creative writing' – a stunning blue Parker 51 with a silver top and a gold-plated bit. A silver-grey tassie, even – whatever that is.

While I grilled some salmon I found in the freezer, along with spinach and carrots in butter and garlic, Dan lit the little stove in the kitchen, which immediately filled with dense clouds of choking black and stinky smoke. He persevered, and eventually we sat down to eat at a little table by the stove, our bottoms comfortingly warmed by its radiant heat. The boys had even left a bottle of fine sherry in the fridge, which, though cold, had a definite warming effect. *It was so good to be back.*

Christmas in Marrakech: a shifty sense of nothing being quite what it seemed; money straying into surprising pockets; in-your-face, too-close, too-quick bonhomie. Disturbing dimly lit meetings at night; drizzly days hanging around waiting for news in a state of anxious impotence; Christmas fisticuffs.

Also sunny mornings, with the girls quietly and with dogged determination digging the earth out of the pots on the terrace in the sun or chattering happily as they removed the leaves from the hibiscus or dropped CDs into the fountain. Maizie fascinated by the answering machine, her gentle but persistent curiosity with anything that had buttons – phone, cooker, computer, tape player. Chilali snuggling up to Saki with the remark – which pleased neither of us – 'You've got Grandma's elbows.' Sitting with the girls, buried in cushions, reading *Leo the Late Bloomer*; the three of us wedged into the Wendy house, discussing Barbie's (maddening) ballgown; Spigs's Aztec boxes painted with such care, and Doris's twinkling beribboned presents. Playing cards with assorted boys, Pictionary with Ted, the etiolated orange trees getting a battering as we played badminton in the courtyard; the builders borrowing the pressure cooker to cook something that smelled delicious over a tiny charcoal brazier. Making Fatima giggle with our attempts at Arabic. All of us squeezed into the candlelit dining-room, eating her sumptuous chicken with honey, pomegranate juice and toasted almonds (*djaj bil assal wa roman wa luz*, in case you want to try your luck). Fatima's good round bottom in the air as she washed the floor or beat the hell out of our clothes.

It was aversion therapy for Christmas junkies, but we had survived; and even though Dan still considered most of it was my fault, he was willing to concede that the Jumpy's delinquency was not.

15

GULLIBLE'S TRAVELS

Bruised after Christmas, we settled back thankfully into our happy tedium in Spain, relishing our privacy, the simplicity, the absence of drama.

But it was too good to last. We were, as usual, careering into another financial crisis, and like it or not, we needed to return to Marrakech to take some photographs for a newspaper which had shown interest in featuring the house for its property page; also to take pictures for our website, now that the building was – Hecham swore – finished and habitable. It was a small assignment, four or five days should do it, and to save time we decided to fly.

We rang Hecham, who insisted on meeting us at the airport, despite our protestations that Abdeltif had offered to collect us in his car. A friend of Dan's and three of her mates were staying – our first lot of paying guests – and while they spent a few days in Essaouira, we could stay in the riad to take pictures. In order not to overlap, we were staying the first night at Maggie's – an unaffordable piece of carefree irresponsibility that I was looking forward to. This was to be our first visit for fun, rather than anxiety.

'We'll have to try out some restaurants too,' I said, hoping that masquerading my favourite thing – a *dîner intime* with Dan – as research would make it acceptable to him.

Our journey started and ended inauspiciously. The morning of 1st February was freezing cold, with a searing north wind. Dan had inadvertently broken the feet off one of the enormous suitcases I had bought for this trip the previous day, so that it simply keeled over. I had chosen the cases for their astounding size and cheapness – they were the size of small bungalows – and it never occurred to me that he would ignore their wheels and try to drag them up the steps on their little plastic feet. In this, their maiden voyage, the suitcases were stuffed with blankets, towels, bedspreads, knives, snooker cues, a tripod, coat-hangers, and an incredible wealth of lavatory paper. All the small but surprisingly heavy paraphernalia that was essential to give the riad a loved, homey look. No clothes.

We crammed the mutilated suitcases into the Jumpy along with the dogs, ready to drop them off en route to the airport, and Dan turned the key. Nothing happened at all. Not a flicker. The Jumpy had done it again.

Change of plan. Dan took the dogs out of the van and pushed them into the jeep. There was room for dogs plus one suitcase, or me, but not all three. Grimly he sped off for the kennels along the hair-raising top track, leaving me awaiting his return. Having deposited the dogs, he was back in minutes. We wrestled the suitcases into the back of the jeep, worrying lest we run out of petrol before we reached the airport. We did not, but staggered out with the bungalows with time enough to reconnoitre the duty-free for moisturiser, noting that the J&B whisky we had bought for the Marrakech van mechanic was roughly twice as expensive in duty-free as in the local *venta*. Malaga airport was being transformed into a giant shopping mall, where you could splurge your remaining euros on Lacoste, Dior, 'local gourmet specialities', and hideous tourist trinkets for twice as much as they might cost in Harrods.

With panic on my part, and schoolboy excitement on Dan's, we boarded the Beechcraft toy plane and bounced from cloud to cloud, travelling via Tangier, in whose tiny airport we stopped for about ten minutes. I was delighted to get in and out of this nefarious city without being fleeced. Landing at Marrakech, however, was to prove considerably more expensive.

The transfer from toy to normal-people-sized plane at Casablanca was very quick – too quick for the bungalows. Once at Marrakech airport we watched the carousel go round again and again, until the final eviscerated golf bag disgorging beige two-tone shoes was removed and we stood blankly watching plenty of nothing. At this point two things happened – bear hugs out of the blue from Abdeltif, and an official announcing that there was no more luggage to come, and we had better file a complaint. There was no sign of Hecham either.

We gave the large, jovial airport official our details: two mammoth suitcases, navy blue with red ribbons on one, purple on the other, broken feet, etc., and he promised to ring us.

'Madame, if the luggage is in Timbuctoo or Alaska we will find it. It will be on the next plane.'

Amazing. I crossed finding suitcases off my worry list and meekly followed Abdeltif to the duty-free shop, where he relieved us of eighty-one euros to buy cigarettes and Dune for men. I wasn't sure why these purchases were necessary, and something told me that we had bid a final goodbye to those rather necessary eighty-one euros.

Abdeltif's face, though plainly pleased with his contraband, betrayed a wrinkle or two of disquiet. We agreed that it was strange that Hecham hadn't appeared, since he had promised all of us that he would be at the airport.

'I have left many messages, but he has not rung me back. I think it is impolite.' Abdeltif's face betrayed a greater worry than the finer points of decorum. However, he had his monstrous four-wheel-drive thing, and reeking of Dune we piled in and took off for Maggie's.

It was sunny but cold, and Maggie's courtyard was in shade, so we huddled in our room with an ineffective electric radiator whimpering in the corner, and smoked and worried some more. Abdeltif ordered lunch for us, and sat with us while we ate. His face was as greyly furrowed as a basset hound's. Having ignored it for as long as possible, I asked what was the matter. It was, of course, Hecham, Hecham the mysterious, who had not returned calls for three days, had not advised Abdeltif of his absence from the airport, and had generally been as unpredictable as usual.

Despite our nightmare Christmas, Dan and I were unwilling to land our manager in the shit. Terrible twilit pictures of Hecham – the self-proclaimed solitary family breadwinner – wiping theatrical tears on Dan's jersey and swearing utter loyalty, would get in the way of any rational decision. So we murmured vague noises of doubt, to which Abdeltif listened attentively. We did not confirm or deny his tentative suggestions, but the following inter-rogation made me feel very uneasy, and it was not difficult to read between the lines.

'So, are you happy with Hecham? Does he do what you ask, solve problems, help you?'

Well, not exactly. But because Dan was Hecham's champion, I decided to let him deal with it. Dan looked uncomfortable.

'How is he on time-keeping?' Abdeltif continued. 'Does he arrive when he says he will, or when you ask him to? Can you rely on him?'

Dan coloured slightly, and recounted the tale of Spigs's disaster. I added one or two other instances of mystifying morning tardiness. Abdeltif's diagnosis clicked another factor into place.

'And when he arrives, does he bring breakfast? Is he in a good mood?'

No, we both had to acknowledge that Hecham was pretty unpredictable in the breakfast-and-good-mood department. 'He is often quite surly, actually. In fact, most mornings, if he does turn up, he does not speak to us at all,' I added.

'Ah.' Abdeltif looked at me as inscrutably as a Chinese doctor making a tricky diagnosis, acupuncture needles hovering.

The only incontrovertibly good thing Hecham had done was to get the van fixed. But the thought did lurk at the back of my mind that his belligerent driving could have led to inattention to the temperature gauge, and might have contributed to the problem in the first place.

'He did get the van fixed,' I offered weakly.

'At *my* garage. *We* got the engine fixed. I was there every day. I drove him to find the *kelas*,' Abdeltif pointed out. 'He had to get the van fixed there when he drove it into a taxi outside a nightclub – he took your van every night and drove it around with his friends. One of my policemen friends told me about that. He only told me because he thought Hecham was a relative of mine. One night he drove into a taxi and ran away. You could have got into trouble – it was your van, and there was no one to accuse because he ran away and hid. They might have fined you or taken your licence.'

Hecham's explanation for the dent in the van had indeed been extremely vague. All those mysterious absences and evasions were falling into place.

Money, women and alcohol – these were the downfall of many a good Arab, concluded Abdeltif, after more questions and a series of shame-faced responses from me and Dan. And Hecham himself is fond of a drink, he added.

'It is also not good that Fatima his sister is employed as your cleaner,' he continued.

What shocked me most of all during this exchange was the revelation that the purgatory to which Hecham had subjected Spigs might simply have been due to a hangover. According to Abdeltif, there had been much drinking and many hangovers. And fudging, lies, incompetence and demands for money to feed what is in Marrakech an expensive habit. Not to mention crashing the van and contributing no doubt to its internal problems.

Not for the first time since we had come to this city of smoke and mirrors, where illusion rules and transparency is a quaint foreign concept, we felt that we had an enormous brightly lit sign over our heads: 'Suckers'.

Abdeltif had not finished with us. After a brief absence he burst back into our room with all his Riad Magi books to show us how things *should* be done. He had kept a record of expenses, employees and contacts, complete with photostats of their IDs and a weekly set of marks out of ten.

Dan perked up considerably in the presence of Abdeltif. My heart, on the other hand, sank. I muttered to myself, 'Dan and I are probably constitutionally incapable of running a riad. How on earth can we learn to be steady, methodical, and punctilious about records and accounts at this late stage in our messy and untabulated lives?'

Fishing, hopeful, I said, 'Now, if someone like Khaled could be the manager of the riad, I'd have no worries.'

Abdeltif leaned back expansively and uttered an Abdeltif rune: 'Ah, yes. Khaled. He comes from a different market. One is from the spice market and the other from the leather market.'

I wasn't quite sure how this reflected on our plight, but assumed with some disappointment that

Abdeltif was saying that Khaled was out of our league. We pecked away at the problems for a while longer, until I got up the courage to ask Abdeltif directly, would Khaled consider working for us? To my surprise, Abdeltif was on his feet in a flash, scurried out with his mobile, and came back beaming.

'Yes, Khaled is happy to do this.'

I was overjoyed. Khaled was a sober and sensible adult who took relationships seriously, who could inspire others to work for him, who had never, as far as I could judge, put a foot wrong. Always respectful, happy to listen, eager to help, he was the perfect man for the job, except for the small problem that he spoke no English.

Thank God we did not fall for Hecham's hustle to get us to sign a permanent contract, I thought. Thank God he was consistently rude and unhelpful towards me, ensuring that I did not fall for the slippery charm that had befuddled Dan.

He had spotted Dan for a soft-hearted sucker and me for a hard-faced bitch, and backed the wrong horse. Dan has enormous influence on me, and can blind me to the evidence of my eyes, but fortunately in this case he had been too vague to put any pressure on me to legitimize Hecham's position. The more I thought about it, the more appalled I was by our close shave.

As it had been Abdeltif's idea to appoint Hecham

and thence Fatima, we gratefully accepted his offer to sack them on our behalf, which he did discreetly, humanely, merely confirming a conclusion that Hecham had seen coming and Fatima accepted with good grace.

Our home was finally our home. The faultless Khaled would be our manager – he had already collected our suitcases from the airport, where they had fetched up as predicted. We had to celebrate the departure of Hecham, and I managed to persuade Dan to dine out. We had nothing edible in the riad anyway.

As we searched for something thermal to wear, the phone rang. It was Abdeltif calling on his ailing mobile from what sounded like a giant laundromat. He said he was out of town, and would we like him to buy a sheep for the forthcoming housewarming feast? What housewarming feast? According to Abdeltif, any new house (or car, donkey or wife) should be bloodied by a slain sheep if its owners were to have any kind of good fortune. He was shocked by our ignorance. The day he had chosen coincided auspiciously with the major Muslim festival of Eid El Kabir, the 'Big Festival'.

'How much?' I shouted.

'Very cheap' he yelled. 'Only 2,300 dirhams.'

'Where will you put it?' I shrieked.

'On the roof,' he bellowed. And then we were cut off.

I was not sure what we had arranged, but we thought we'd better stay until we heard from Abdeltif, not wanting him to be shut outside the riad with a dead sheep. I feared that the cats would get it on the roof, but it was an absolute cert they'd do so in the derb. So we waited and rang and waited and wished that there was something edible in the house.

The door-knocker finally clattered at about ten, and Dan sped out to welcome the travellers. I did not want to be involved with a dead sheep, and lurked behind closed doors. From the courtyard there came the sound of scuffling and a strange clacking noise. Hoping that it was not Hecham taking the safety catch off a colt .45, I peered cautiously out. By the orange tree a large, petulant-looking ram was refusing to cooperate, backing pettishly into Mohammed's knees like an enormous radio-controlled bolster. I did not think it would have much trouble with predatory cats. Mohammed, a sweet, innocent young man, always impeccably dressed in spotless black, had had to cradle the beast's head all the way from the farm to prevent it from damaging Abdeltif's Pajero.

Abdeltif, Khaled and Mohammed decided that the *doueria* entrance was the very place to keep the sheep, and I suddenly realized that our little house-warming was not going to be a discreet affair with Marmite pinwheels providing the major excitement.

As our four-legged guest showered the *mizmat* with coffee beans, Abdeltif did a convincing mime of breaking its neck. The very next day they intended to sacrifice the docile beast with its impressive curlicued horns, barbecue its innards for lunch and roast the carcass in the communal souk oven – we were going to share it with our team of thirty or so builders, labourers and decorators. I had a short attack of claustrophobia, and wanted, not for the first time, to go back to Spain.

Abdeltif and Mohammed admitted to being very tired and refused our invitation for dinner. We shut the sheep into the *doueria* hall, struggling hard not to bond with it – it gazed at us fixedly with strange orange eyes and stood aside politely to let us pass – and made off hungrily for Djemaa El Fna and food.

That night we fell into bed exhausted. We had disposed of a malevolent manager, but acquired a well-mannered ram. What dramas would the next day bring?

16

CARELESS SLAUGHTER

Eid El Kabir is the high spot of the Moroccan year. It occurs two lunar months after the end of Ramadan and celebrates Allah's humanity when, having presented Ibrahim (Abraham of the Bible) with the ultimate test of loyalty by demanding that he kill his son Ismail (Isaac), He relents and they slaughter a ram instead. It is always a ram, Moroccans eschew female meat, which is why the testicles are always proudly displayed at butcher's shops along with the carcass. The city is always abuzz with anticipation for the feast of Eid El Kabir, which takes place on the tenth day of the month of Du al-hijja, the month of the Muslim pilgrimage to Mecca. The entire Arab world takes a week off to celebrate: banks close, hospitals evict patients, trains leave their tracks and everyone goes home to their mum. In Morocco it is not unusual for people to spend 20 per cent of their annual income on this celebration.

In the medina, the streets were the usual circus, with a special ovine addition for Eid El Kabir: wherever you looked there were old men carrying serene-looking sheep on their shoulders, pushing them uncomplaining in prams and *carrossas*, or cautiously navigating the derbs on mopeds with sheep draped languorously across the front watching the world whiz by without great interest. There were sheep on leads, small children dragging them by their horns, women pushing them along the alleys with sticks. And everywhere you looked there were little piles of greenery – clover and straw – being sold as sheep feed. In honour of the carnage to come, the knife-sharpeners, with their huge cake-shaped carborundums spinning with a rasp to set the teeth on edge, were doing great business at every street corner. As Dan and I walked past one of the ancient doors in our derb, we both leapt sideways as a loud and indignant bleat greeted our passing.

This year it happened to coincide with our house-warming. There are three things for which Allah's blessing is mandatory: transport (car or camel), getting married or moving into a house. The way to get Him on your side is to slaughter a sheep. Ideally the sheep-slayer should be the most religious or oldest person you can lay hands on.

In this case it was Abdeltif, who arrived on the morning of the auspicious day, sombre in flowing black with a black turban. Mohammed, his lieutenant, accompanied him, in black too and maybe a little apprehensive. Gradually the builders assembled, coming from nowhere in ones and twos, all of them apparently with a well-rehearsed role.

Khaled bustled up wanting the sharpest and biggest of our knives.

'Is this the biggest you have?' he asked, fingering it with some disdain, and took it away to be properly sharpened.

Abdeltif had killed his first ram at his wedding four years before. 'I enjoy it, I get benefit from God when I sacrifice for Him. It was absolutely good at my wedding. When you take the knife and you put the sheep facing East, you don't show him the knife, or sharpen the knife in front of the sheep, which would kill him twice; you don't show him his brother being killed, you know, for his feelings. It is always a ram. It is much better to sacrifice a beautiful male sheep, with good horns and no flaws. You say, My Lord, it's from you and to you, and then you cut his throat. Then we skin him, gut him, and take him to Djemaa El Fna to cook.'

After a fair amount of acting tough, Abdeltif was hyped for the kill. The animal was unceremoniously laid out on the *mizmat*, facing East, with its throat just over the opened drain entrance – a nice touch.

They held its head, and Abdeltif cut its throat swiftly and cleanly, blood spurting neatly into the drain just where he wanted it. The ram continued to make a horrible rasping noise and danced and jerked for several minutes, even though its windpipe was hanging out of its throat.

Dan was at the bank, but I was there wielding his Nikon as his proxy to document this important occasion, feeling distinctly queasy. Abdeltif, typically, wanted a picture of himself beside the corpse brandishing the knife, and disappointed by the paucity of blood – he looked as though he'd just had a little accident with his editing pen – he dived in up to his elbows and glowered ferociously for the paparazzi. Me.

Next Bin Laden the plumber made a small incision in the animal's rear leg, and blew into it while everyone else beat the carcass with a wooden spoon to loosen the skin. When it was as inflated as a walrus in prime condition, Bin Laden, by now divested of his designer plumbing gear, ripped the skin from the beast.

On the coast they take the skin to the sea, crowds of people, beating it with sticks to clean it, then lay it, covered with salt, in the sun on a roof for a week or so to cure, and finally give it a hairdo with a special comb.

The chief builder who had masterminded the spiral staircase sluiced down the courtyard while the carcass hung politely from the balcony above, not dripping – sleek and neat and headless. The other men in black lounged like Salli brigands at one of the tables, an occasional cacophony of mobiles jerking the scene into the twenty-first century.

Abdeltif sidled up to me looking distinctly shifty, wanting to know what was going to happen to the head. 'Because it is very nice steamed.'

I said with no hesitation that he was welcome to it, but that I'd like the skull as a cute Georgia O'Keeffe ornament when he had picked it clean. He also offered me the skin, which could be made into a lovable fluffy rug for just eighty dirhams. I agreed with alacrity – at least something good might come out of this grizzly bloodfest. Neither rug nor skull ever materialized.

Images of the event remain, whether I want them or not: Mohammed rolling back his sleeves and plunging his arms deep in the animal's guts; tenderly handing the balls to one of the other men to cook; the carcass swinging gently neck-down in the entrance, wrapped in a rather twee patterned plastic overcoat.

Contrary to my fears, it proved to be the happy occasion they had promised: the men were jubilant, swigging Fanta with wild abandon and laughing, slapping each other's shoulders, or standing hand in hand as Moroccan men do, commenting on the progress of the sizzling gizzards on the barbecue. Mohammed busied himself over the tiny charcoal brazier, making delicately browned patties and beautifully presented kebabs of the working parts of the sheep, which were enjoyed by the assembled workmen with many a swagger and lewd cackle, presumably topping up their testosterone levels to ram-like proportions. At one point Dan was urged by Bin Laden to eat a sinister white kebab. It was a solemn silent moment – plainly a great honour was being awarded to the generous patron of this festivity. Asking what it was composed of as he chewed valiantly, a general discussion ensued, from which Abdeltif concluded that it was ram's penis. Now Dan will try just about anything, but there was something about this particular bonne bouche that diminished his appetite.

When it was clear that Dan's penis had got the better of him, Abdeltif kindly replaced it with a kebab of good old straightforward liver.

Hitherto this had been an all-male event, but once the sheep was safely dead, two very charming smiling women conscripted for the occasion by Khaled – Hassania from five doors down the derb with her friend Nassima – bustled in to wash, chop and boil a roost of chickens in a huge pot balanced precariously on a terracotta charcoal burner dangerously positioned just inside the kitchen door, where there was maximum traffic. Private ovens are an unheard-of novelty to most Moroccans. Everything is cooked either on top of a charcoal burner, or dragged off to the communal ovens half a mile away. The two women quietly chatted to each other, sounding like wood pigeons; very soothing.

Dan had returned from the bank earlier with lots of money – that day we drained the lifeblood from all our accounts to pay our builders. We were nearly at the end of our money haemorrhage; just one more dizzy dip into the coffers, we thought, should do it.

On his way back to the riad, he had also invited Jamal the music-shop owner to the forthcoming fest, and skipped off later to invite his friend Moulay Omar (purveyor of argan oil in the magic souk). We also invited Hassam from the bank. Madame Zakina, the housekeeper of the smart riad across the derb, introduced me to Rebecca, her boss, who promised to drop in for a few minutes that evening. Small, French, vivacious, Rebecca had an enormous smile and fizzed with energy in her designer linen.

I admit that I was apprehensive: we appeared to be throwing an enormous teetotal party at very short notice, and this party was going to be a little different from any I had encountered, although Rebecca told me later that she had gone through the same ritual to bring good fortune to her house.

I laboured under a huge weight of unaccountable anxiety that day, feeling that the responsibility for everything lay athwart my tiny shoulders. Dan was prancing about being David Bailey, taking photographs for the newspaper article and ordering this quilt to be put here or that table there, while I ran up and down, doing his bidding and getting seriously overheated, while trying to stay on top of the party situation and fretting about all the stuff I had to go through with Khaled. (The sumptuous double-page spread with Dan's photos was finally published in the property section of a London newspaper on my birthday, 19 March. Auspicious, I thought. The following day, George Bush invaded Iraq, and thereafter sensible people stayed at home.)

Acknowledging after several hours of this that I was not my usual sweet self, Dan invited me out before I laid about me with the sheep knife, and we went to Dar Imlil opposite the silk-weaver's shop for a necessary cup of tea in a peaceful citrus-sweet courtyard. The owner was taking his ease in the garden and was in an expansive and philosophical mood. As we sipped mint tea and ate petits fours, he regaled us with stories of his life as a merchant.

'The best thing in life is business,' he told us. 'Be happy with what you have, and you will have much to be happy about.' The sky was overcast, there was a trixy little wind, and I mentioned that I was feeling rather cold. 'The best blanket,' he said, looking wistfully at the heavens, 'is if you are not alone.' He continued to pepper his discourse with unnervingly

281

apposite aphorisms, such as 'Life without problems is not a life at all,' which he rather ruined by following it with 'Ça c'est la charme de la vie.' I could not agree, but there is something wonderfully calming about saying *hamdoolillah* (phonetic rendition of 'praise be to Allah') about events good *and* bad.

We stayed as long as we dared, knowing that some guests had already arrived before we'd departed for our tea break. As we stood to leave he took Dan by the arm, and looking deep into his eyes, said, 'For a man to be himself, he must know himself.' Unnerved, Dan paid the outrageous bill (aphorisms do not come cheap), and sprinted over to our Norwegian friend Morten's house to post an invitation for the party.

Every car park and square in Marrakech was full of small, smoky bonfires, around which garlands of excited children danced, and over which were suspended the charred heads and feet of sacrificial sheep. Occasionally a gloomy man in a long dark djellaba would be scraping the worst of the singed fur from a sheep's head, prior presumably to sinking his teeth into some part of it. Apparently in Fez the eyes are indeed considered a delicacy, steamed and served with salt, pepper and cumin.

Unwilling to return home, we took the back route along the derbs to Jamal's music shop, where he was sitting in solitude. He greeted us with affection and an insistence that we take tea. 'I am at my shop because when I am at home with my family I fall asleep all the time,' he explained. It sounded very much like snoozing in front of the telly in the enforced family huddle at Christmas.

We crammed into his tiny cupboard of a shop, surrounded by stringed shoe-boxes and mother-of-pearl-inlaid lutes, corahs and rebecs, resist-dyed ebony-brown Tuareg cloths and silver dishes, while he discussed Arab music. There are three kinds, according to Jamal: Gnawa trance music from the Sudan, which he admired but whose wild

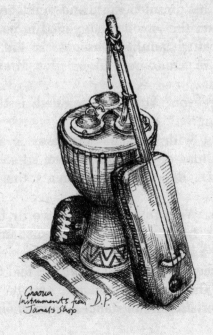

Gnaoua
instruments from D.P.
Jamal's shop

incantations of magic, religion and superstition he could not condone; Berber country dance music – just voices accompanied by clapping hands and stamping feet; and the urbane music of the city, classical Arabic, love songs warbled to a background of oud and tamtam. Eyes sparkling with pleasure, he told us of the festivals at Fez and Essaouira, in the El-Badi palace and the desert, while Tracy Chapman sang of love and pain as usual on his little CD player. He brewed sweet tea with a gas canister that appeared magically from inside a large ceramic drum. It did the heart good to look at him, with his dimpled smile and pink cheeks.

His friend the jeweller happened to be avoiding the suffocating familial closeness of Eid El Kabir too, so we wandered along the alley to his emporium.

'How are you? You look troubled; is there anything wrong?'

I replied with a small sour remark about the Moroccan idea of time, having waited so often for people who did not show, events that did not happen.

'Ah, yes. Well, in Europe you live by the clock, don't you?' he said with ineffable disdain. 'For us that is not a life. We live by Destiny.'

I muttered something about planes and trains not following the Destiny timetable, and he admitted that in certain circumstances and when dealing with Europeans he did find himself having to conform to our narrow-minded way of doing things.

At this point a moderately heated discussion took place between him and Jamal, as to whether by saying *In sha'allah* ('God willing') one was implying an open-ended possibility of discounting whatever arrangement had been made. This idea was a bit of a revelation to me: whereas *In sha'allah* had always implied to me a distrust of the vagaries of fate, so that whenever I said to Abdeltif, 'We'll be arriving on the midnight flight,' his automatic '*In sha'allah*' always filled me with foreboding about an imminent crash, in fact what he meant was that we might just not bother to catch the plane at all.

Once home I felt tired and scrappy, with a strong desire to *In sha'allah* my way out of the evening's festivities: there was a mountain of things still to do before our departure the following day, I had been moving furniture and running up and down stairs all day and I just wanted to *go to bed*.

But going to bed was not an option. Putting on lipstick or even brushing my hair were out of the question as well. I was shuffled past the twenty or so men who were sitting on the plastic chairs Khaled had assembled from somewhere, and was taken up to the gallery, where an alarming sight greeted me – eight women ranged in a forbidding row. After the first shock, their faces began to seem familiar, and I recognized the house-proud local ladies who had been so sweet and tolerant about the mess our building work had made in the derb.

First there was Fatima, young, dark and swathed in scarves; then Aisha, who had a wide face and a big smile; Madame Zakina, the manager of Rebecca's beautiful riad opposite and the most severe-looking woman I have ever seen since Miss Mulley who used to throw chalk at us in mathematics; Zahara, a wonderful, cuddly older woman with pebble-lensed glasses and a large smile, who gave me a purse called LUCKY 2002 and a small picture of flowers confected from shells on black velvet; Attica, a pretty young woman with an amazing smile who had brought her young son Eunis; Souad, a seventeen-year-old who could speak Spanish, and her friend Najwa who spoke French, and last but by no means least, the lovely, naughty-looking Zorah, who was ready to laugh at just about anything.

I was delighted to see them, honoured by their presence, hoping it meant that we had really been accepted in this backwater of the medina. We sat sedately upstairs, and Zahara threw up her hands and smiled a lot and Zorah rolled her eyes and smiled a lot and the others just sat there. I put myself at the end of the line and chatted to the two teenagers about school, feasts, the paucity of weddings in the area and whether or not they wanted to get married – of course, I cautioned against it, but they looked at me strangely, so I did not pursue favourite rant number forty-three – Ill Effects of Marriage on Women.

Dan's good friend Moulay Omar ambled up when music was mooted, and indicated to Zakina that she should ululate, which she did. In fact she, Zorah and Aisha all did, the others joining in the chorus of whatever familiar traditional song they were singing. I believe it was a wedding song.

Hassania took a break from her chicken-cooking to bring up a tray of mint tea and we ladies all politely drank. Then she brought up a tray of petits fours, which we all politely ate. Then we all politely waited for *two hours*, with the occasional burst of giggles from one or other of the women and the occasional ululation. A group of scarlet-clad musicians arrived, singing and playing loud and rhythmically. The ladies sang along – the whole routine was obviously familiar to them, and I recalled Maggie complaining about being invited to weddings and sitting for hours with the women, drinking sticky orange or brown soft drinks while nothing happened. However, at this party, Zorah of the ready smile was moved to dance, and indicated that I should partner her. She and Zakina boxed me in close and rolled their loins in a most suggestive way. Zorah had a belly-dancing move that I could not fathom at all – somehow she made her stomach move up and down. I tried, but mine stayed just where it was, thank you very much.

Zahara passed me a package – my fifteen minutes of nightmare was come. It contained a pale-green satin djellaba, with a transparent devoré nylon over-gown sprinkled with peach-coloured velvet leaves, and a ghastly gold metal belt encrusted with 'jewels'. She and Hassania frogmarched me to one of the bedrooms and indicated that I should put on these unflattering garments. Horrors. I have looked at them so often in the tiny shops in the souk, thanking God they are not obligatory. Every single detail is designed to make one look like nothing so much as a plump, satin-upholstered maggot. Worse still, I had to remove my clothes in front of the two innocent ladies and show them my fat tummy and Sumo wrestler's bra. There was no escape, and there were bound to be worse things to follow. So, trying gamely to look thrilled, I did myself up as a shiny bolster and endured much politeness.

A quartet of musicians filled the last remaining space in our gallery. Again I danced, in the tiny passageway left by the tables, mincing up to Zorah, flicking my scarf suggestively at Zakina and rolling my eyes at Zahara. This humiliation was com-pounded by someone putting a tiny skullcap on my head, making me look like a pinhead maggot just in case I didn't already qualify for the total nerd prize. For what seemed like hours I had to gyrate with my new lady friends, as the others pushed tiny-denomination notes into my hat. As a

money-making enterprise, you would do better selling used toothpicks. Finally, to my enormous relief,
the musicians retired downstairs to entertain the
men.

To my surprised gratification Morten did show
up, wafting around appreciatively like an aristo-
cratic ghost for a few minutes; Hassam the bank
manager dropped in for a few moments and Dan
gave him a guided tour, and Moulay Idrees the
policeman smiled his pixie smile and said that I
made a good Moroccan. I was honoured, but felt
very tired, and not like a good Moroccan at all.

The party continued. Down in the courtyard the
scarlet-clad musicians were playing their desert
music, looking and sounding passionate and
dramatic. Khaled and Abdeltif did a wild arm-and-
leg-throwing dance together, Abdeltif looking like
the devil in black from head to foot and wearing a
long black leather coat, and Khaled, in a white
djellaba and red tarboosh, playing the angel's part.
While Abdeltif chucked his solid kick-boxer's body
about, Khaled favoured a prim, rather Michael
Flatley kind of choreography. Abdeltif followed this
with a 'drunken' dance with a couple of pals, one of
whom looked like a young Paul Simon.

By this time, the ladies had gone home. It was
quite cold, and I was bundled up in a blanket,
sitting with Dan and his musical friends Jamal and
Abdul Latif, who occasionally strummed on a

three-stringed shoebox, warbling accompaniment in a strange falsetto. Jamal, with his round face, pink apple cheeks and Very Serious Demeanour, was the absolute opposite of cool. He had taught himself excellent English with the aid of the *Shorter Oxford Dictionary* and a translation of Saint-Exupéry's *The Little Prince*. These amazing feats are only possible if you do not drink, wench, smoke or play football.

'It is a good dictionary, I think,' he allowed. 'But it is not always correct. Take "violent", for example. It says that this should be pronounced vi'lent. That is not correct.'

He whizzed me through a tour of the Arabic alphabet, astonishing me by saying that there are no vowels in written Arabic, just modifications of the consonants. While Abdul Latif strummed and wailed, Jamal did an elegant calligraphic version of my name, and showed me how the vowel signs worked: a tiny mark like a shorthand blip which he said signified that the sound was a luawn. I was stumped, assuming this to be some kind of Arabic eccentricity. Over and over I asked him to explain what a luawn was. What followed was an audio glimpse that I cannot recall without embarrassment. Finally he wrote down '*alone*', and I said 'Oh, alone', sounding just like Joyce Grenfell. He repeated what I had said, and I blushed for the snotty fluted vowel that ricocheted back. I should never open my mouth.

Then, at this bleary drooping-eyelids hour, Abdeltif, Khaled and I had a tense money discussion. It seemed that if we could prevent Dan from doing anything too philanthropic in the next few hours – or buying any more rugs (out of the blue and quite unnecessarily he had just bought two) – we could just about pay everyone what we owed, leaving us penniless. These discussions always took place last thing at night, and were always wreckingly complex. I had to pay Khaled for the party, and send Abdeltif money for the completion of the building, a hefty float, and a month's salary for Khaled and the as-yet-undiscovered French-speaking cleaner. Somehow we sorted it, and finally, finally, after one of the longest days of my life, we abandoned the last few Fanta drinkers to their carousing and crept into bed.

This whirlwind visit, which had started on such a low, had somehow managed to end on a tenuous high. At least, with Khaled in charge, the riad was finally in good hands.

17

THREE MEN AND
A BELLY DANCER

This – the summer when we hoped at last to let the riad and make a small income, or at least to recoup our losses – was also the summer when George Bush decided to confirm American unpopularity and polarize the world by starting a war; when a short sharp epidemic, SARS, convinced people that it was better to stay at home; when the UK actually had a summer; and when a bomb shocked Casablanca. Our riad remained empty and unlet for the rest of the year.

And so it was that, when the Spanish campo was too hot for bare feet and the garden a depressing shade of brown, Dan decided to take his Dutch friend Frank and my boy Spigs to Marrakech. He was unusually determined – intending to take the thirty-six prints we had framed to deck the riad walls – and the thought of a week on my own had charms. He took the Jumpy to be checked over, filled it with works of art and three bottles of whisky for possible bribes, collected his passengers (turning a deaf ear to Frank's nervous monologue about delicate stomachs, avoiding tap water, never having ice in drinks, not eating salads, using foreign loos), prodded them into place, ignored their brief squabble about who should sit in front, and took off early one Monday morning.

For two days I heard nothing. I resolved not to worry, just to get on with my life. But despite myself I hoovered to a mental vision of their ferry sinking, cooked to a background of car smashes, walked the dogs picturing the Jumpy's latest life-threatening trick, and shopped to car-bomb freeze frames.

It was a curious thing, but when Dan finally rang I gave him hell. Hell in proportion to how much one loves, misses and worries seems to be the rule.

After a huffy beginning, sympathy won. The Jumpy had started being tricksy before Algeciras: odd noises, unpredictable behaviour, temperamental on long straight stretches of road, clutch slipping, that sort of thing. Like the good old-fashioned hero he is, Dan kept his worries to himself, decided not to turn back, and on the ferry when the others went on deck to smoke, he sat in a quiet corner and chanted, summoning up a positive, courageous attitude from the unexplored depths of his psyche. I was mightily impressed – the car was one problem, Dan's demons were another. At least he was tackling the more approachable, and succeeded in being the Jumpy's Svengali and keeping it under control until the military compound sixty-four kilometres outside Marrakech, where he passed a posse of traffic police. Immediately the gears went floppy and the clutch pedal fell off at his feet. A lesser being might have wept, from long-distance-chauffeur's fatigue if nothing else, since the others did not drive. The police showed perfunctory interest, before returning to the more important matter of extracting dirhams from passing lorry-drivers. Dan and Frank left Spigs to mind the van as they started the long trek along the melting tarmac to a phone. Dry of throat and itchy of eye, they plodded along, whipped by the gritty slipstream of passing cars. On all sides, flat, brown dust to the ambiguous shimmering distance. No garage, no perky little phone booth in sight, just dust. And after a few minutes, a tow truck. They watched it pass, waving feebly, until it became a dot on the road . . . and stopped next to the van. Marrakech in August is not ideal for sprinting, but they sped back in seconds, incredulous that even in this miraculous country a tow truck could materialize from nowhere. It was the police, they had phoned a friend, would doubtless get some kind of payback.

Well deserved, thought the intrepid trio sitting proud and elevated in the cab as the Koutoubia beckoned ever nearer.

So they arrived in style, to be greeted rapturously by Khaled, who had at last people to care for, willing recipients for his dreams and treats. *Carrossas* were summoned in an instant, stacked with prints and trundled back to the riad, where Latifa, the efficient new femme de ménage, welcomed them anew. The road-weary trio were allotted rooms – Frank had a bed moved into the north-facing pink salon for coolness, Spigs was down in the green room and Dan in the small blue room by the front door. This is the smallest and least splendid of all, but Khaled decided that it was ours and so it has remained.

That evening they ate an exotic dinner of the wonderful soup *harira*, traditionally eaten to break the Ramadan fast at sundown, a plethora of little salads, and couscous with seven vegetables cooked by Latifa, in the romantic new Berber tent on the roof, while curious droning music from the antiquated tapes we had brought, twenty years past its cool-by date, wafted up from below.

Khaled arranged a trip to a hammam for the following day, presenting them with individual blocks of argan soap (rather than the strange axle-grease soap sold by the scoop from plastic bowls in the spice shops) and counselling them to take towels and a change of clothes. Ever since Maggie had said indignantly that she was excoriated on her solitary visit, I had decided the hammam was a thing to avoid.

Bravely, though with a twinge of trepidation, the chaps followed Khaled through a small doorway of the derb, stripped to their underpants, and, each carrying a couple of unexplained plastic buckets taken from a pile by the reception desk, went through a door into a warm and steamy domed room with lots of tiny windows in the ceiling. The room was positioned above the boilers (which double as communal ovens), with a hot tiled floor and low platforms upon which they lay. After a few minutes steaming, a professional masseur appeared and scrubbed their exposed parts with something that initially felt like a scouring pad but, according to Dan, soon became strangely pleasurable. He then soaped and manipulated them as strongly as an osteopath – heaven for Dan and Spigs, but Frank did a fair amount of creaking and groaning. After this the plastic buckets came into their own as Khaled indicated that they should all slosh themselves with an extravagance of hot water. The four of them luxuriated for a while longer in the soporific heat, feeling wonderfully relaxed. And then, sloth-like, they dressed, paid, and wandered back out into the derb. Khaled stressed the importance of cooling down gently and taking things slowly, lest they catch a chill.

So, at a lethargic snail's pace, the trio ventured out into the wavering twilight for dinner – Dan braved the serried rows of tables in Djemaa El Fna and sat down to a butch repast of rams' testicles. The others, being more conventional in their tastes, wandered off to Chegrouni's, where they had the usual excellent tagines. Though not, unfortunately, without dire after-effects. Dan was fine, but his charges fell foul of some loud and cramping stomach complaint, for which Dan had to dispense pills and sympathy. The acoustics of the house meant that everyone else was also aware of the internal tribulations of Frank and Spigs. Latifa, who had taken an inexplicable shine to Frank, brought him soup and tenderly laid Chilali's teddy bear alongside him in bed.

For the next few days, in loco parentis responsibilities weighted Dan's every decision and he became increasingly apprehensive about the return journey in the vehicle from hell. The groaning Jumpy had been towed to the same garage that had tended to its prolapsed engine at Christmas, where they now took it to pieces and sorted its comparatively simple problems, requesting just twenty euros for replacement parts. Stunned, Dan gave them thirty and one of the bottles of whisky, which made him a whole bunch of new back-slapping, double-kissing best friends.

In between dosing his patients with Immodium

and lending an increasingly irritated ear to their complaints, Dan also accomplished his self-set task, adding the finishing touches to what was becoming a dream riad. He succeeded with the tricky placement of the prints – some found natural homes immediately; others just would not fit in, no matter what. They depicted Staten Island frumps and runners, Brighton pier by storm and sunrise, wooded Suffolk lanes. Where they succeeded, the effect was a magical transformation of spaces from aloof to friendly, achieved with some difficulty and a dangerously ancient Black and Decker drill.

Under Khaled's management everything worked: the plumbing no longer drew attention to itself by spectacular eruptions or the aura of warm sewage; the hob did not remove all your facial hair and more; the lights did not send fifteen volts humming through your arm when switched on. The decisions he had made were sensitive and stylish. The tent on the roof, for example, was simple white canvas, lined within by sunset-scarlet hangings, patch-worked with Berber rugs on the floor and strewn with scarlet and orange striped cushions – at night it glowed with promise of comfort, warmth, pampered ease. Wherever the eye rested within the riad, there was some small improvement he had made – the kitchen drawers no longer hurled cutlery at your feet, mirrors had been cut to fit the finicky spaces behind the washbasins, rugs had been laid in the courtyard at the entrance to the rooms, giving them a grand palatial air.

A slight setback to a growing glow of complacency occurred when Dan visited Rebecca's house across the derb. The interior, as Madame Zakina beckoned him over the threshold, took his breath away: it was sexy and modern, having been completely gutted and renewed in a sophisticated but simple style, owing much to a clever architect. Each of the rooms had an en-suite bathroom; the roof was fantastic with smooth sculptural domes and walls, sheltered by an enormous tent of undyed camel wool. Best of all – apart from a stunningly beautiful girl sunning herself in a bikini – was the swimming pool in the courtyard: a luscious cool contrast to the sticky heat of Marrakech in August.

Dan's charges were still having trouble with internal combustion on his return, despite medication. But Khaled had hinted that this, their final evening, was to be no ordinary occasion, that he had laid on a stupendous surprise. So as the sun went down, the three adventurers climbed the spiral staircase to our Marrakech-pink roof, clocked its bizarre Tardis splashed fetchingly with sunset, and strewed themselves upon the rugs. A long wait ensued while nothing much happened bar the odd complaint from the invalids.

However, when it arrived, the trio applied themselves with gusto to the multi-course feast that

Latifa had prepared. They were trying to diagnose what the little salads consisted of – delicious but mysterious – when an unknown young man joined them on the roof, bearing an antiquated CD player which he put in the corner of the tent, shuffling through a pile of Arab CDs. They watched languidly, working their way through the ten dishes on the table, but sprang to electrified attention on seeing the beautiful sunlover from Madame Rebecca's step on to the roof, clad only in a sequinned bra and gauzy harem pants. She danced in the spotlight of their mesmerized gaze for an hour with great seriousness and grace, halted from time to time by a glitch with the CD player which her boyfriend sorted. Madame Zakina – her mother, it turned out – watched with the approbatory air of one whose daughter has just passed her law finals.

I did not see it, had not met this vision, and astonished Dan with my ungenerous reaction when he returned and told the tale. 'She was the Most Beautiful Woman I have ever seen,' he whispered in awe. My lips tightened to a malevolent slit. 'She was like a creature from a different species.' Even he, armoured in unimpeachable innocence, felt the temperature drop to a hypothermic chill. Later I heard him murmur to Spigs, 'I don't think she likes us to talk about the belly dancer. Better not mention her again.'

The return journey was uneventful except for the two occasions when Frank almost killed them.

The first was on the complicated road network outside Casablanca, where as he sat in the front passenger seat peaceably smoking, a hot rock fell from his roll-up into his flowing djellaba. In a panic, Frank stood up and flapped his skirts, incidentally blinding and burning Dan as he did so. He was consigned to the back seat for the next hundred kilometres.

But shortly before they reached the mind-boggling bustle of Tangier, Frank succeeded in ousting Spigs from the front passenger seat. Things were going fine, though the heat was still melting the tarmac. Frank reached into the voluminous folds of his garment and produced a cologne spray. 'This is very cooling I think. Here.' And sprayed Dan full in the eyes.

The Jumpy grumbled its way back to Almogia, where it collapsed with a temperature. The other two invalids continued to complain for several days. Dan very generously bought me a Coca-Cola bottle of genuine argan oil, but since discovering what was involved in the gathering and processing of this delicious elixir of youth, I could not slosh it into salads with quite the same chutzpah. It all depends on how you feel about goats' innards.

18

FOUR GO MAD
IN MARRAKECH

Living in the hidden backwaters of rural Spain, I assumed that my fellow Brits would be a conservative and cautious bunch, their wildness confined to an extra glass of sherry at Christmas. I was wrong.

Beverly, Margaret and Julia were the loyal remains of Dan's painting classes, which had been brought to a premature stop by his decision to become a writer. Margaret and Julia are lovely women of a certain age – slightly less than my certain age – and Beverly is a slender blonde beauty a decade or two younger. The four of us continued our painting without Dan, doing pretty unsatisfactory watercolours of flowers or china figurines, teddy bears or hideous ceramics, accompanied by the hoots and cackles of laughter that characterize all girl assemblies.

As I turned up one Thursday, Beverly said out of the blue, 'Why don't we all go and stay in your house in Marrakech? Just the four of us? It'd be fun. No husbands; they'd spoil it. They'd always be complaining and wanting attention. What do you think?'

I thought quite a lot in the ensuing four seconds – like, I don't *really* know these people – we might hate each other in enforced intimacy. How will we get there? Will I have to be responsible for them? They may loathe it, be madly fastidious and ever ready with Dettox and J-cloth. Will they plague me with questions? Will they be afraid? Do they speak French? Will they all get belly problems or something worse?

'Great idea,' I said.

Their lives and mine were complicated at the time, so there were only five possible days for this jaunt. With a slight qualm I pencilled the five days in mid September into my diary, confident that something would happen to rescue us from the expedition. It did not. Each week their excitement grew. They would ask how much the ferry cost. Was there a quicker one? Was there food on the ferry? Could we drive to the desert from Marrakech? Or to the seaside? Was it going to be hot? What should they wear? Would they need special footwear? How many dirhams were there to the euro? How much did rugs cost? Could they get plain djellabas for their husbands? Would they have to order them? Were Moroccan men as big as British?

My spirits did not rise as the day approached, and the questions became ever more esoteric, requiring a knowledge of Arabic dietary habits and Muslim religion that might have taxed Mohammed himself. Any small comment I made would elicit a shoal of subqueries, so increasingly I kept my mouth shut. I was not an authority on Arabic anything, still less a tour leader with a crowd-pleasing spiel, did not want to be cast as Mummy, and my feeling grew that they should find out these things for themselves.

No major global event occurred to prevent our trip – apart from a very unsightly cold I collected in the UK – so at eight thirty one sunny Sunday morning we clambered into Beverly's car. My luggage consisted of a huge hideous hi-fi from Lidl, astonishing for its cheapness. We settled ourselves into the car with a deal of clucking like hens at roost, settled our feathers, then Bev announced that she had left her driving licence on the kitchen table. So we kicked off with a detour for the paperwork, and forty minutes later were on the road. Now the questions were of comparative petrol prices here and there, and should we fill up before we leave Spain? I hadn't a clue.

'Yes, absolutely,' I said with authority. My new

policy was to invent something to throw them off the tracks or stop them dead. Did the garages have loos? 'Always.' Bladder control was an unexpected problem, and I began to plot the journey bearing hourly loo stops in mind. I pictured the vast stretches of blank desert without a solitary cactus and wondered how we could improvise. As each swigged her litre bottle of water I mooted suggesting that they drink less, but decided against it.

We had instituted a kitty and there was a predictable debate about whether we should use it to pay for our ferry fare — which the ladies thought pretty exorbitant until several minutes after payment, when they completed the mental arithmetic and realized that we were talking about a return ticket divided by the four of us. The grinning pixie who sold us the ticket advised us about arriving in Tangier — no, he said emphatically, no one should ever have to pay baksheesh to get through Customs. The thing to do was to make for a uniformed official and deal only with him. He indicated that it was only Type A personalities, always in a tearing hurry, who resorted to bribery. I was interested to see how this radical new approach would work, but we had a long way to go before my curiosity would be satisfied.

We arrived at Algeciras around midday, and it took half an hour to find ourselves after Bev had asked me which way to go at the port and I advised her firmly to follow a lorry. We had to move a row of cones in a deeply illegal manoeuvre in order to get back on track after that detour, but eventually we drove across the heat-blistered tarmac, sorted papers and passports and watched the fast boat we might have caught steam grandly out of port. The one to which we were assigned – most definitely not a fast one – was nowhere to be seen, so we rolled down the windows, swigged water and lolled.

The boat – whose *Stranraer* had been painted over in white and replaced with something suggestive of *Titanic* – was crumbly. We loitered around the restaurant and meandered around the duty-free, giggling at the curious stock: dusty bottles of Cardhu whisky, gallon containers of honey, three very old-fashioned amplifiers without boxes, grubby jewellery on dog-eared cards, packets of sweets several decades past their sbd. We trailed back to the restaurant and ate some whiskery chicken cinders. Beverly had forty winks, while the chaperones shrieked with unseemly laughter at some aspect of manhood. It was a lengthy crossing.

At Tangier harbour we were given the usual contradictory instructions about where to go, but eventually made our way to the scene of many a rant. Bev spotted the uniformed official of her choice, handed him our papers, and we proceeded to wait for an hour while he sprinted back and forth from one booth to another, having this paper stamped, that one copied, the third matched against something on the computer. BUT it cost us nothing, bar the one dirham paid to a man who confirmed that indeed we were two hours behind Spanish time.

I sat in the back of Bev's little car and sniffled and sneezed and rubbed my itchy eyes while the others drove heroically without drama. As they said, 'It's all right, it doesn't matter if we get lost, we'll just find our way again. We're *women*, there won't be any temper tantrums, no slamming things, no shouting. We'll just sort it.' And they did. Peaceably, calmly, to a maddening whispered background of the Carpenters, they drove the entire 620 kilometres without a murmur of complaint.

Cautiously they asked, en route, was it true what their respective husbands had said, that it would be dangerous to wander alone? Should they always go in a posse in Marrakech? I laughed, said that I had never felt a moment's fear, not even when followed by the nocturnal glue-sniffer all the way back to the house. This did not seem entirely to reassure them.

We arrived at two a.m. Moroccan time, and rang Khaled from the Grand Hotel Tazi, ten minutes' walk from the house, where we had stayed all those centuries ago with Maggie. He was with us moments later on his motorbike, and led us on the most circuitous roundabout route to Ben Saleh Square that could possibly be devised – right out of the city in a great loop, and in through a different distant gate, along winding alleys where reluctant cats stretched and then ambled out of our way, under low arches, through narrow enfilades, all completely unrecognizable. Some town-planner had decided to institute a one-way system and to shut Djemaa El Fna to traffic. Finally we debouched into Ben Saleh by a hitherto unexplored road, and I could tell the girls that the driving was over. Khaled summoned *carrossas*, and within minutes we were standing outside the handsome new efficiently antiqued front door, holding our breath. The entry had been tidied up, there was no sign of the orange cat sifting through bags of rubbish – in its place there was a rather etiolated oleander in a tall pot, and a lamp casting sprinkles of light on our dishevelled selves. But it looked welcoming.

With a little skip of excitement, Khaled flung open the door, and we walked into a dream. There were roses everywhere; he had hung our Mexican mirror above a little glass-topped table; the ceiling of the entrance hall was cutely vaulted, and a brass lantern cast golden specks on a garnet and black Berber rug. The ladies all went 'Oooh' in satisfactory chorus, then again when we entered the courtyard, where low lights illuminated fountains and orange trees, candles flickered, the huge painted doors glinting with gold opened to inviting

The Courtyard at 95

D.P.

dimly lit rooms, and jasmine perfumed the air. It was a stage set for something more glorious than a quartet of tired ladies with aching backs, but we did our best and Margaret was just saying, 'Well, no question, you've got to have the best room' to me, when Khaled threw open the cupboard doors in the little blue room, and lo! There were all my peculiar shapeless Marakchi clothes.

Well, that was me sorted; no matter that I had rather a fancy to luxuriate in the privacy and opulence of the *doueria*. This was assigned to Beverly.

'Oh, all right, I'll sleep in the wonky room then,' she said, as a great favour to the others.

'Wonky?' I gasped. 'That room is a veritable palace.'

She looked at me coolly. 'I meant the stairs. The stairs are wonky.'

Somehow everyone found a room that suited, and very shortly afterwards the house sank into a trance of deep peace.

I was awoken early the following morning by Julia's litany of nocturnal 'trips for a wee' which she was recounting to Margaret, and incidentally to the rest of us. We had intended to sleep late, but had forgotten that the time change meant that eleven, when Khaled proposed breakfast, would actually be one p.m. Spanish time. We were very hungry by the time he laid pancakes, orange juice so whiskery you had to chew it, pain au chocolat and hard-boiled eggs before us.

Having put out the food, Khaled turned to Beverly. 'I have met you before,' he said. 'You have been here before.'

She was intrigued and asked when. He did not know. I suggested that perhaps it had been in a previous life.

'Perhaps,' he said, his gaze lingering on Beverly's face, and she surprised us all by announcing that, yes, the muezzin – the amplified wailing call to prayer that she had never knowingly heard before in her life – had a strange air of familiarity. It was just the mystic thrill we all wanted, and we sat back hoping for more. What we got was more tea.

A contented silence followed, which seemed like the right time to try out the new hi-fi. I set it up and put on the good ol' Pachelbel's Canon, only to be embroiled in some peculiar stilted monologue about traffic dramas. I snatched out the tape – *Teach Yourself English*, it said, no matter what the box promised. This was how Khaled was improving his English, by learning set conversations about car accidents and crowds. Weird, I thought, not much use for seeing to the needs of paying guests. I found the *Teach Yourself English* case. It contained the Pretenders. The Pretenders case contained a shameful Elton John tape.

Thus it was that I spent my first morning playing Pelmanism with tapes and boxes, playing ear-shattering snatches of the unlabelled home recordings that had strayed from their containers. Some malevolent sprite seemed to have thrown the whole lot up in the air and put them all in the wrong boxes. Hecham's last curse. Quite a few were missing, including one I was very sorry to lose – a recording made at dawn and dusk in the South American jungle by a gorgeous blond anthropologist whom I had interviewed for *Country Living*. For several years thereafter I had obliterated the office babble by working to the sounds of the rainforest – a tropical storm, deep growls of approaching thunder, big drops battering on huge glossy leaves, the hoots and cackles of birds and monkeys, bright chips of waking sound and cosy mutterings of approaching sleep.

Tapes sorted, I came across the girls, showered and shiny, lounging in the gallery.

Beverly was fretful, and bemoaned her lack of a dressing-gown. A brilliant thought occurred to me – I could give them the last vestige of the Dark Age of Hecham. A blue gandora he had given Dan suited Julia perfectly, a black one looked fine on Margaret and the shocking pink was just right for Bev. Wonderful.

We wandered out into the souks where, intrigued but apprehensive, the girls tried to tread a path as far as possible from the beseeching stall-holders who crooned 'gazelle' as they passed, and I tried to remember the route to Djemaa El Fna. I kept my orienteering ineptitude to myself and was relieved when we emerged in the familiar shimmering expanse of the great square, relatively quiet at this time, with only a few token snake and monkey men, water- and false-teeth vendors to widen their eyes with a whiff of the exotic.

We had lunch on the shaded balcony at Chegrouni's, alarming a small Frenchman by our cackling proximity, and then, emboldened by our keftas, we plunged back into the fray and looked at rugs. Dangerous.

'Don't have the mint tea,' I hissed.

The first emporium gave the girls an eyeful of Islam. Four well-fed rumps were raised in a west-ward direction to greet us, in the neatly choreographed exercise of prayer. It threw their concentration slightly, and Margaret kept glancing sideways, hoping that we were not disturbing them and apologizing for our presence to the non-praying assistant. He was serenely unbothered, and snapped his fingers for the mint-tea boy to do his thing, at which we all burst into a jabber of refusal. He shrugged, and the mint-tea boy was assigned instead to the rug show. Out they all came, one after another, starting with the astronomical and working down to the lees. Wearily I foresaw the inevitable wrangle with Khaled: 'You paid how much? We must take them back, that is too much. You must let me buy them for you. I will get Marakchi price.' But once started, there was no stopping the intrepid trio, and we dipped into every rug shop we passed – maybe ten – and went through the same routine.

Finally, the time came when exhaustion weakened our defences. We succumbed to mint tea. Thereafter, all resistance gone, Margaret bought two small but pretty flatweave rugs made of what they called agave silk – '*Very* good. Perfect for people with allergy to wool' – and Julia fell for a faded embroidered indigo. Beverly then bought a leather bag, having been introduced individually to the entire stock by the starstruck stall-holder, and Margaret decided that her husband Dave would like a leather hat. This involved hauling strangers with likely-looking heads from the derb to try them on.

Having found the ideal hat, Margaret decided that what Dave also needed was a plain salwar kameez. We felt the fabric ('No, it's polyester, feel'), and pondered the cut ('No, he'd look like Andy Pandy in that') of several dozen, until the choice narrowed down to a simple V-necked top and trousers in white cotton. Again passers-by were brought in and had garments of various sizes pressed to their fronts. The stall-holder held open various trousers, and we all gazed into the crotch obediently, none the wiser for staring into their depths. After quite a bit of this pantomime Margaret made her choice, deaf to our bemused wonderment – 'But Margaret, they're too short for *you*. They'll be like pedal-pushers on Dave' – and we bustled back to the riad, all chattering satisfaction and crackling paper bags.

Khaled made us proper tea and was politely positive about our purchases, congratulating the girls on getting good merchandise for a good price. He smelt the leather, felt the cotton, threw down the rugs appreciatively and a contented glow settled about our party as we sipped. Beverly fell asleep. Margaret had a shower and emerged wearing Dave's salwar kameez. 'It just fits me! Could have been made for me. And it's so comfortable. You're quite right, he'd never be able to get into it. I suppose I'll just have to keep it myself.' Julia had a shower, and made the interesting discovery that her gandora had slits at pocket level. 'Perfect if I want to play with myself.' Horrified groans from the non-sleeping ladies, a light snore from Bev.

After serious discussion we decided that we would like to eat in that night. We gave Khaled money for the shopping, asked for dinner at nine, and indignantly refused his offer of wine.

'I think we can probably get by for one night without wine. It'll do us good,' said Julia decisively.

Beverly found *The Alchemist* on the shelves – 'I've always wanted to read that, can I borrow it?' – and settled to a quiet sleep, the book open in her hand. The rest of us pottered around until eight o'clock, when we suddenly realized that we *needed* a glass of wine. I burst into the kitchen, where complicated chopping and pressure-cooking were taking place, and confronted Khaled with our unruly demand. He looked alarmed but undaunted. What name of wine did we want? How much? What would it cost? It dawned on me that he had never bought wine before, and I felt like a playground drugs-pusher. But he assured me that it did not trouble him to lose his alcoholic virginity in search of a tipple for three idle boozers – naturally I blamed the others for this sudden change of plan, pretending academic interest myself.

Two hours later he returned empty-handed, having been all the way out to Marjane only to find it, and all the other likely shops, closed. Dinner was an hour late by this time, and we were forced to acknowledge quite how powerful was our desire for a drink, and quite how tetchy this combined with a late dinner made us. But the couscous was wonderful, deeply comforting, and we mellowed with food, agreeing that though a glass of wine would have set it all off to perfection, it was very virtuous and healthy just to have a nice cup of tea instead.

Beverly had a mind to see the mountains at Imlil, where someone had told her you could gaze out into an infinity of drifting sand dunes. 'I want to see the desert,' she said. 'I like wide open spaces.' We found the map and the guidebook and they plotted their route, though nothing would persuade me voluntarily to spend another day in the back of that car. I just had a feeling that it would be a long, cramped, disappointing wild-goose chase. However, they alerted Khaled to their plan, asked for breakfast at eight, and shuffled off to bed early.

Khaled provided the usual excellent breakfast at nine, and laden with water, maps, guidebooks, mobile phones, sweets, loo paper, cameras, pens, notebooks bearing the name and number of the riad and the number of Khaled's mobile phone, they set off. He led them out of town on his Mobylette, and showed them the big, bustling taxi rank where they would meet him on their return.

I spent a happy day reading and listening to music. To justify my truancy I wandered briefly round the house making notes of the few remaining problems, and observing the many improvements that Khaled had effected – retiling the bath and sink so that they were smoothly finished and did not splatter water all over the floor; levelling the clanking manhole cover that used to wake Maizie every time we stepped on it; polishing the brass basins and taps so that they looked like Midas'; sanitary ware; sealing the *mizmat* with linseed oil to give it a rich sheen impervious to mess; applying logic to the kitchen and high style to the bedrooms; making

317

sweeping full curtains for the *doueria*. What a man!

It was after six when the phone rang and Khaled's assistant Buddr indicated that it was for me. Khaled had gone to the mosque. The tiny tinny voice of Margaret in a whirl of traffic.

'We're lost. We found the taxi rank, but Bev's phone's not working and there wasn't a phone box. So we went to find one, and the first didn't work. A man tried to help us but he got the wrong number, and then he wanted paying. We can't get through to Khaled's mobile at all. Then we got lost. We had to go for miles to find this phone; I don't know where we are. I think we must be inside the city walls.'

'Try to find your way to the Koutoubia, and ring again from there.'

'How do you spell that?'

'KOUTOUBIA. It's the tall mosque, the centre of Marrakech.' I had just put the phone down when Khaled returned, so I described the conversation and said that I had advised them to aim for the Koutoubia. He set off into the darkness and radio silence ensued for an hour or so. When the phone rang again it was Margaret.

'We couldn't remember where you said to meet. K something. All the people we asked told us different things. Most of them only spoke Arabic, and my French is almost non-existent. We asked for the big square, but they kept sending us in different directions.'

'Where are you now?'

'I don't know. Near a cinema, I think.'

'What's it called?'

'I don't know.'

'Well, try and aim for the Koutoubia. Khaled is looking for you somewhere round there. Don't panic, you'll be all right.'

'Yes. No. I hope so.'

Half an hour later they all tumbled through the front door, breathless with adventure.

M: We were just driving along –

J: We were following a taxi –

M: When Khaled drew up beside us –

J: He tapped on the window –

B: I nearly jumped out of my skin –

M: We had no idea where we were –

J: And we had to catch up and pay the taxi –

B: We had to point and pretend to pay –

M: He understood what we meant –

J: He caught him up and paid for us –

B: And then he brought us home. I'm dying for a cuppa.

Latifa was already there, carrying out a tray of perfectly brewed PG Tips, brought by Julia, which calmed and soothed and revived.

We had decided to eat out that evening, and Khaled had made a list of likely places, mostly in the French commercial area outside the medina known as the Guéliz. But I had dissuaded him from booking somewhere too far away, suspecting that the girls might not want to do any more driving, and suggested the Marakchi, overlooking Djemaa El Fna, within easy walking distance.

The Marakchi had been renovated since my last visit. The fountain awash with rose petals had been replaced by an extra table; the ancient oud player who endlessly and tediously mimicked the pouring of tea on his instrument had gone and there was no sign of the vest-clad belly dancer. But it was still heady with romance, the crisply calendered table-cloths were strewn with red rose petals, the lights of candles and the glitter from the square flickered in reflection on the fine *zellig fessi* walls, and they brought us wine immediately. As we settled deep into the velvet seats and clinked our glasses, a glorious sense of achievement enveloped us, such as Frank Kingdon-Ward must have felt on returning from the Himalayas. We debated the ingredients of the ten little salads that were spread before us, attacked our tagines with gusto, shared puddings and felt on top of the world.

Margaret refused to let me pay. 'It's the least we can do,' she said,

'In gratitude for sharing your wonderful house,' Julia added, and I was very touched.

So far it had all been fun, but I had to do penance the following day. The first excitement was the arrival of the masseuse that Khaled had arranged as a treat. As she set up her table in Julia's room we decided the order of massage – Julia, then Margaret, then Beverly and finally me – and assembled for breakfast in the courtyard. We had finished eating, Beverly had just trodden on my glasses and we had asked Latifa to put our white clothes through the washing machine. Khaled had asked casually what I thought of henna patterns on peoples' hands and feet and I had said they looked like a skin disease, and we had arranged to eat at home at nine o'clock *with wine*, when the doorbell rang, and a shy young man, Brahime Terrab, was ushered in, clutching a brown plastic briefcase.

To the accompaniment of many cups of coffee – in the hope of sharpening the intellect – I discovered that I was having breakfast with an *accountant*; that French was our only common language; and that he proposed to explain to me the intricacies of my tax position and describe to me the seven varieties of tax for which I would become liable if and when I finally managed to let the riad. All this revealed itself gradually, since I merely thought I was meeting a friend of Khaled's, who would help register the house, thereby making letting legal. The conversation was complicated by the fact that the French words for obvious financial terms, such as tax, limited company, VAT and accountant did not slide transparently from one language to another, so we

321

had to go back to very simple basics and work from there. My part was to let out intermittent shrieks every time Brahime Terrab named a new tax, and say things like, 'But we can't pay tax before we earn any money, can we?', 'We will end up with *some* money, won't we?' and so on.

He dismayed me further by saying that we could not, after all, call the house Riad Maresco (Dan's middle name), since that title was already taken, and could I please think of three alternatives for him to check. Blank of mind, I suggested Riad Miranda, and he went pink and wriggled with embarrassment. That was the first intimation I had that my name, along with innocuous words like 'Tina' and 'zip', might have obscene connotations in Arabic. (Other words to avoid if you do not wish to shock: balloon, blue, left and lift are similar to the names of men's parts; cosy, quiz, twenty and zucchini to women's.) What can Miranda mean, I wondered. How can Khaled look at me with a straight face if I insist on introducing myself to his friends as 'arsehole' or 'haemorrhoid'? Whatever his reason, Brahime Terrab would have none of Miranda, writhing each time I sprang it on him praising its mellifluousness. He favoured Marinnes, which made me writhe in turn. He left me at an impasse, promising to return at six thirty that evening with my house papers, which he needed to photocopy.

I had done my penance, and ambled gratefully into our massage parlour. This Amina, Khaled's masseuse friend, was a star. She did a bit of reflexology and a bit of shiatsu. She asked me about my life and told me about hers, so that the picture of my flobbly bottom and the humiliation of lacking brownness and muscle tone, the horror of not being totally hair-free receded, and the pure healing pleasure of being expertly kneaded took precedence.

'Do you have children?' she asked.

'Yes, do you?'

'No, I am not married. I am waiting for Prince Charming,' said with irony.

'Could be a long wait,' I answered in a dreamy trance. She did brilliant work on foot knobbles, back knots and head throbs, murmured that she was masseuse to the princesses and often at the palace, cooed that she did do men, but would probably stop if she did get married out of respect for her husband, and forty minutes later I drifted, as limp as dough, back into the courtyard.

More shopping was the obvious antidote to serene relaxation, and the girls were ready in minutes for another foray into the consumer jungle. As usual, the cash-dispensers were playing frisky – no, they concurred, there were not sufficient funds in my Spanish account for me to withdraw anything. No, they agreed, there was a problem with my English account and would I like to try later. But, yes – when I had broken out into a light sweat – I might have some money from my Moroccan account. So, with some money, but a grim sense of foreboding about why I was again poverty-stricken, I stood banker to the girls so that they could return to the handbag man and have a re-run of his stock. Shoes next. Gandoras too. I was successfully inching them in the general direction of home when Margaret and Beverly disappeared somewhere in the spice souk.

Julia and I were standing abandoned, not knowing where to start our search, when a good-looking young man stepped from a doorway cluttered with apothecary jars, caged tortoises and snake skins to ask, 'Mr Dan? Is Mr Dan here?' It was one of Dan's mates from his guitar-playing saunters into the souks. 'You have lost your friends? A tall and a short blonde in white clothes? They are over there.' And there they were, busy buying terracotta skin-buffers, oblivious to the panic they had caused.

Waylaid only by a sudden need to buy candle shades, we were making good progress homewards when the rosy-faced young man whom I remembered from our party accosted us. Jamal, who had written my name so beautifully in Arabic, who had not tittered at the prospect of writing 'haemorrhoid'. He invited us into his shop for tea, which sounded like a good idea to me. Unfortunately, Beverly had noticed that a small sign a few paces further on read 'jewellery souk', and was pawing the

ground in her eagerness to plunge into that Aladdin's cave.

Jamal suddenly looked at her more sharply, and then said, 'You have been here before. I know your face,' which made Beverly shriek in denial, and gave us all a bit of a frisson. But airily dismissing this mystic coincidence he took us in hand, and led us to 'The best shop. It belongs to the father of my good friend from school. You will get Marakchi prices. And he has the best jewellery — not fake — real Berber silver.'

This was an opportunity to be grabbed, so we shuffled into the jewellery souk and were led into the familiar tiny narrow shop whose every surface glittered with gems and whose owner observed Destiny time. Brass and silver lanterns hung in clotted stalactites from the ceiling, the walls were tapestried with pendants, necklaces, earrings, rings and bangles, brass-studded boxes spewed inlaid daggers and flintlocks, and carved mirrors multiplied the dazzle ad infinitum.

For a moment there was complete silence. Each woman immediately turned to the nearest cabinet and started a feverish search for the one gorgeous jewel that would change her life. Jamal dragged us from our quest to introduce us to Moulay Abdul, the owner, who looked hard at Beverly and said, 'You have been here before.' This was the third time, and it was getting a little creepy.

'In a previous life?' I asked.

'No. Two, maybe three years ago. American, maybe. I know your face.' It crossed my mind that this might be the Moroccan equivalent of 'Do you come here often?' and as a chat-up gambit infinitely superior, implying a wonderful, lasting memory of a passing but poignant encounter. Beverly, though briefly stunned, returned to the cabinet to rummage.

She found the earrings that would make her life complete and set about bargaining with admirable sang froid. The sad fact was that, like Leo, she really could just walk away, and that was why everything cost her a third of what the rest of us paid. Even more annoying was her ability to find the object that we then set our hearts upon, only to find that hers was the only one in the shop.

After much rootling, all three found earrings they wanted and Moulay Abdul put a brass bowl containing white powder on the counter and started rubbing the silver with it to a fine gleam.

'What is it?' we asked as one.

'Cocaine,' he replied, and snorted at our open-mouthed gullibility.

'Talc,' he relented, and we all made a mental note to clean our silver with talc in future.

Jamal led us back to his shop and started on the mint tea. I glanced at my watch and realized that I had ten minutes to get back before Abdel Jalil was due. So, ascertaining that the others knew their way home, I left.

The riad was balm to the harassed chaperone. I found the Pachelbel, made some ayurvedic reviving tea and collapsed in a torpor among the cushions on the banquette in the sitting-room. Vague sounds and smells of cooking drifted my way from the kitchen next door. But there was something troubling about the music. It seemed to have an intrusive percussion beat where I remembered none. On investigation it turned out to be the unfortunate accountant who, uniquely, observed European rules of punctuality and who had been banging on the door for ten minutes or so.

I ushered him in with copious apologies, and he smiled pinkly and said 'No matter.' I admitted that I had not been able to come up with three alternative names, but could he try Riad Maizie after my adorable granddaughter.

He beamed with relief. 'That is a good name. I'm sure that will be fine. I will check and let you know tomorrow.' And handing me my papers, he left. A few more precious minutes of Pachelbel and that cussed percussion started up again. This time it was the tea-drinking trio, whom Jamal had kindly accompanied home.

There followed the habitual flurry of showering and hair-washing and drying, and it was eight o'clock when we gathered in the gallery, some of us thinking how very nice a glass of Cabernet Sauvignon would be right now. I had already rescued the red wine from the freezer where Khaled had stashed it, noting that there were two full bottles of red but the white-wine drinkers – Beverly and Margaret – only had a half between them. However, Khaled was quite firm: no wine at all was to be drunk until we were all settled up on the roof.

To pass the shining hour he gave me a package – my glasses, crushed that morning by Bev, as good as new. Khaled had another trick up his sleeve – over one arm he bore a sheaf of beautifully washed and ironed white shirts and trousers, and from behind his back, with a smile, a wink and a ringmaster's flourish, he brandished a hanger upon which were tastefully displayed three large white bras and several pairs of big white knickers. Laughter all round.

And relief, as he finally conceded that we could go up to the roof. He had illuminated the tent with low lamps, and the new Lidl hi-fi was up there in the corner with a pile of Arab CDs. Wine, pistachios, salted almonds and olives; we lolled and luxuriated and I mentioned a successful experiment of Dan's with a hubble-bubble. Khaled was on to his mobile phone immediately. Conversation over, with a look of great relief, he ushered Latifa up. We hoped that meant supper, as we were beginning to feel a little peckish, but instead she brought with her what looked like a hypodermic syringe filled with spinach soup. She proceeded to draw the sort of design you find on crewel-work tapestries on my left hand and right foot in henna. I watched, marvelling at her skill and regretting my crass remark of the morning. One by one she did us all, causing a riffle of consternation when Julia discovered the difficulty of modest manoeuvring in a billowing gandora, having dispensed with underwear.

Beached, waiting for the exquisite black designs to dry, we wondered idly who was cooking supper, if Latifa was up here with us. But with our remaining usable hands we brought our glasses to our lips and put the thought out of our minds.

When Beverly, the last of us to be done, had fallen quietly asleep with her painted hand wafting vaguely in the air, Khaled emerged on to the roof bearing a blue glass pipe. Fastidiously he packed it with strongly scented apple and molasses tobacco. Apple tobacco, he said with reverence, could bend your brain. The hot coals were tenderly laid athwart the silver paper, and he passed the mouthpiece to me – I took a lungful and pronounced it brilliant. Mild, cool, no grief involved, it seemed to me the perfect way to smoke and I waited with interest for the bending of the brain. Awed by their daring, the others all took a drag, Beverly waking especially for the purpose and commenting how her husband

Jem would hate it – 'He can't drink out of my cup even, he couldn't cope with this mouthpiece being passed around.'

Perhaps it was the wine, perhaps the peculiar one-handed luxuriance, perhaps borderline starvation or perhaps it was apple tobacco, but we did giggle. Beverly had another short nap while we waited, wondering, for food. We had suggested nine o'clock. Dinner finally made it to the table at half past one, by which time we were past eating, though what we were offered looked wonderful. Latifa dabbed the henna with a pungent and sticky mixture of sugar, garlic and vinegar as a fixative and we were allowed to go to bed. Khaled, Latifa and Ibrahim asked to stay the night since it was too late for them to go home, we said of course, requested breakfast apologetically at seven thirty, since we hoped to leave for Spain at eight thirty, and finally, gratefully, we all shuffled off to our beds.

Breakfast was at nine as usual. We were grateful for the extra sleep and agreed that apart from minor aberrations in the time department, Khaled was a faultless manager. Our mood was slightly clouded on discovering that when we washed off the intricate black tracery on hand and foot we were left with what looked like a nasty orange skin disease.

'Age spots. That's what it looks like,' said Margaret, and we all had to agree.

* * *

As we left the riad we bumped into Spigs, who had decided to take advantage of the lack of paying guests and stay for a few days with a friend. They had taken the overnight sleeper and both looked as fresh as new lettuces, while we had a long day's drive ahead of us. We said a fond hello and goodbye, packed ourselves into the car and drove off, the girls talking with enthusiasm about their next visit. Beverly very generously said that they would do all the driving – possibly from a sense of self-preservation – and we settled into eighteen hours of desert and the whispering Carpenters.

There were no problems at Tangier, the boat looked seaworthy, the food was surprisingly good, Beverly slept on board and we arrived home at two a.m.

I was so glad the girls had sprung this trip on me. It was amazingly healing, expunged almost entirely the memories of nightmares past, replacing them with echoes of carefree uncomplicated laughter. I felt happily indebted to them. For the first time I could talk about the riad with pleasure, for the first time I could recommend it wholeheartedly to strangers without a sense of imminent disaster. It had finally become a wonderful, magical place to be.

19

LAST RIGHTS

On my return, it occurred to me for the first time that Dan and I could go to Marrakech for a *holiday*: it might be possible to have a good time in our riad. The idea was way too revolutionary to mention for a day or two, and I let it brood, trying to picture what having a good time there might be like. Our riad, which so recently had been a house of darkness, had been transformed by Khaled's loving touch into a warm and welcoming refuge.

It was Dan who actually came out with it. 'We should go to Marrakech to get it ready for the winter – we'll need thick curtains and some kind of heating. We could go by train and bus. We could have fun there, what do you think?' Sounded bold and good to me; we found a free week when we could run away, and warned Khaled.

His hands were full at the time with our first serious party of paying guests, and I was too apprehensive to ring and see how things were going. However, the woman we let the riad to sent me an email of such glowing rhapsody that I felt obliged to translate the whole thing very badly into French for Khaled's benefit: she was alive to his charm and excellence, he had arranged quite singular trips for her – taking her miles out of the city on the back of his moped to a *tadelakt* pottery, for example, where she had plunged her arms into the wet clay and tortured it along with the *tadelakt* masters, returning home dangerously balancing a huge box of beautiful bowls on the bike. She said he was wonderful, Latifa and Buddr were magnificent, and the house was a palace.

For the first time the weight of this aberrant investment began to lift from my shoulders. Gradually, doubting and testing every inch of the way, I began to wonder if perhaps the riad might really be a life-enhancing place, a place that I could sincerely recommend without my nose growing. If that were the case, it would be possible to advertise and do all the sensible things without feeling criminal; we might even finally make a bit of an income. I did not dare to look down that route. I needed to be certain that demons no longer lurked in the shadowed corners. We had to visit together just once more to be completely convinced.

Dan and I decided to travel light. Just our laptops and a spare pair of knickers, which for some reason weighed about a hundred kilos. Well, we brought some books too. Thus laden, we set off. First the dogs to their old friends at the kennels, then Spigs to his new home by the sea in a leafy, friendly quarter of Malaga old town. Parking the Jumpy outside his flat, we took a bus into town, walked the remaining half-mile to the bus station, and began a journey that was to take quite a bit longer than we had calculated and introduce us to some new aspects of Morocco. We had decided to do the entire journey by bus, boat and train, braving the overnight express to Marrakech.

I read Salman Rushdie non-stop on the coach all the way to Algeciras, stopped briefly while we bought boat tickets, and then continued while we sat on the boat.

We sat on that boat for two hours, without leaving port. The *Al Mansour* was suffering irreparable gut trouble, and reluctantly, late, but full of misleading assurances – that we would reach Tangier before we left Algeciras because of the two-hour time difference, that this was a *fast* boat and we would certainly catch our train at eleven o'clock – we were shuffled, along with a large party of tired but amazingly tolerant Chinese people, on to another, newer boat, where I continued, appropriately, with *Fury*. I finished the last page as we docked, in perfect time for a frenetic burst of entirely pointless anxiety about catching the overnight express to Marrakech.

We missed it.

A scrofulous taxi-driver loomed from the teeming darkness and offered to drive us to Marrakech for 230 euros, which we declined, electing instead to let him charge us ten euros for the twenty-yard drive up the hill to stay overnight in the spartan two-star Mamora, bang in the middle of the medina under the wing of the mosque. Three times the rasping – but we thought sincere – voice of the muezzin shattered our dreams. Three times we felt the consoling presence of each other in this grasping and, to me, still very threatening place, associated with nothing but panic and harassment.

By morning light the shifty cutpurse shadows had evaporated, the people and the sunlit streets were scruffy but no longer alarming, the shuffling glue-sniffers innocuous, and we wandered up to the main square to drink coffee overlooking gardens, traffic and the busy gossip of morning. We had the unexpected gift of a day to get acquainted with Tangier, having decided to take the Marrakech Express that night and dream our way to the pink city.

High above the crowds we sipped and speculated, decided this couple were English on account of their knees, that German because of their matching beige, those French due to her manicure and his crumpled pussywhipped walk. We finished our coffee and wandered into tattered, once-elegant small streets, past crumbling houses with magnificent carved mouldings and garden walls awash with bougainvillea and frangipani.

After an excellent lunch in a tiny cupboard called Brochettes Andaluz, given additional piquancy by the extraordinary antics of a topless, thong-bottomed female contortionist on the television, we ambled through the town towards the sea, finding amusements all the way – a gorgeous young girl strode past smiling, her skin-tight swirly top proclaiming 'I hate you' across her fine bosom in silver script; a shaggy boy's T-shirt told the world 'Evo-Stick builders do it perfectly'; a hamburger bar called Ray Charly; a dusty-shuttered shack bearing the legend 'Jimmy's world-famous perfumerie patronized by film stars and the international jet set.'

We wandered down to the vast empty beach and lay on the sculpted dunes in fast-disappearing afternoon sun. Tangier was all right. The people were hustlers, the city was a mess and becoming worse with the addition of every new building, the loss of every old garden, but there was a disconcerting friendliness to it, a jostling humour and warmth. I could finally and thankfully discard another little patch of fear and loathing.

Determined not to miss another overnight train, we took the cautious option of going to the station four hours early.

'There'll be loads of places to eat there. We'll just sit in a café, read our books and watch the world go by and wait.' A friendly Tangerine (person from Tangiers – we were not yet addressing fruit) at lunch had extolled the space-age beauty of the new railway station opened just the previous month, refulgent with light and animated by moving staircases, rising like a phoenix from the ashes of the shattered city, replacing the old station in the port from which the trains had run fatally parallel to the beach, occasionally mowing down inattentive beachbums.

We were, however, unprepared for the extraordinary apparition, like a glittering Hollywood mausoleum or an unaerodynamic spacecraft, landed incongruously in the middle of scarred and empty wasteland way out of town. Light blasted into the night from a building that looked like an overturned table, with tall glowing towers at each corner reflected in a platform of polished marble, a blinding beacon in empty darkness, surrounded by acres of lifeless taxi-ranks. Reluctantly we bid our taxi farewell; it sped into the darkness and left us alone, paused on the threshold. The automatic glass doors rolled silently back and our steps echoed in the vacant three-storey atrium whose heart was a pair of shiny but motionless escalators.

Above our heads were empty galleries, bristling with signs, portents of the busy commercial dramas that might one day be there enacted. But at seven thirty p.m. on that October night there was just one woman plying a broom, swaddled in the usual shapeless bundle of layered pyjamas and shawls, and us. Across the spotless expanse of slippery marble there was a ticket office in which sat two lonely railway employees waiting for life to begin. There were no passengers, no sign of anything so banal as a train; absolutely nothing in the nature of a bar, restaurant, coffee machine.

It took a while to get our tickets, due I think to the novelty of the computer system, but with tickets in hand we eventually stumbled out again into the wasteland with four hours to kill, hungry, tired, laden with amusingly solid laptops, and nowhere to go.

We returned after a foray for food to find that things had changed in our absence. Four knapsacked couples were propped against the marble: one had invented a game involving many postage-stamp-sized scraps of paper; another was practising bowling with a tennis ball. We selected a site close to the loos, with an electric socket into which we surreptitiously plugged Dan's laptop so that he could while away the time pursuing his current obsession with Spider while I read Rohinton Mistry's *Such a Long Journey*, appropriately enough. I can't say the remaining two hours sped by, but they did pass eventually, and we tottered, stiff and frozen about the nethers, to the waiting train. Thank God for books.

I had envisaged a British couchette – crisp clean cotton sheets and a thick blanket, reading lights, a cute little handbasin with boiling-hot water. For thirty euros overnight to Marrakech you get a narrow shelf, one grey sheet and a small piece of maroon cretonne that would keep straying, leaving patches of back and bottom exposed to the surprisingly cold night air.

I slept perfectly and awoke to a grey Dan, face like a bloodhound's, full of complaint. But we were in Marrakech, the sun was brilliant, taxis abundant, and the riad awaited.

Latifa and Buddr greeted us with dates and a mixture of milk and rosewater, a sweet Moroccan welcome. They looked magnificent in their new traditional garb, white salwar kameez embroidered with braid and worn with slippers. The riad was full of roses – the fountain splashed through a pink, red and white kaleidoscope of petals. The rooms were all ready, neat and orderly, the handsome brass basins and taps in the bathrooms gleamed, the floor had a polished patina like old leather, the terrace was awash with vinca, bignonia, jasmine, oleander and a couple of olive trees in pots, the tent was absurdly opulent with hangings and cushions:

everything looked loved and cared for, thanks to the ministrations of Khaled. The shock of pleasure gave me goose pimples – the house was a different place, welcoming, romantic, all the things I had hoped for. I wandered from room to room, noticing all Khaled's newest additions – low seats by the fire, small bougainvillea-bright flowerbeds in the courtyard, wafts of jasmine on the terrace, while Dan flung himself into the bath and then bed to make up for his insomniac journey.

We spent the next morning in the new soothing and civilized splendour of our riad, and ventured out for lunch at Chegrouni's, where we found ourselves sitting next to Morten and a photographer friend of his, a short round pixie-like man who may well have been Father Christmas taking an autumn break in the sun. We were delighted to see them, and Morten's Nordic froideur seemed to melt slightly. He was almost chatty. Having finished their lunch they left, Morten walking as always like a stringless puppet – very straight back, no connection between his upper torso and whatever his long rigid legs were doing. We watched them leave with a surge of strange affection.

Busying ourselves with our chips, we did not observe the approach of a bulky figure in black who suddenly clapped us on the back with a great roar of greeting – Abdeltif loomed over us, and we hugged him with unfeigned delight, reciprocated with many hugs and smiles.

'I am *very* hungry,' he acknowledged, tipping the entire contents of the salt cellar over my salad.

There was much catching up to do – he had a new baby boy, Ahmed; Layla had been very ill but was now recovered; he himself had had to spend three weeks in bed after a knee operation connected with his kick-boxing career; but the most important news he kept till last – he had a new car.

'Very smart, a Mercedes, very fast. Tangier to Marrakech in four and a half hours. Though I cannot always drive so fast – I have to be careful, what would my people do if anything happened to me?' He laughed a huge expansive royal laugh, picked at my salad and made a face, ordered another which he approached with more caution and less salt, and extolled as always the virtues of Coca-Cola.

'Delicious. American, but delicious.'

There is a curious time warp that afflicts the visitor to Marrakech. For a start there is the time difference. That is confusion enough to be going on with, but is further complicated by the shifting Muslim lunar year, which is eleven days shorter than the familiar solar Gregorian year, so that Ramadan is always creeping forward and calendars are apt to admit that in one sense it is 2003, but on the other hand it is also 1424. To confound things further, Muslims' calendars begin with the Hijra of Muhammad to Mecca in AD 622. The Muslim year = the Gregorian year − 622 + ((the Gregorian year − 622) 4 32). Simple. Khaled threw an extra complication on to the heap by referring to the months by their number − month four or eight. And asserting with absolute certainty that it was Wednesday when in fact it was Thursday. And on another occasion eleven o'clock when it was twelve. As yet we had not replaced Hecham's clock, and Khaled was too respectful to actually write anything in the diary I had given him, so I was in a perpetual fret as to when we should be where, and on what day we should be doing what.

Buoyed by optimism after our previous visits, we had invited our friends Candace and Andrew to stay, hoping that our tentative confidence in the place and Khaled was not premature. We invited Carl along too, though he couldn't come until later. But the house looked so splendid that we waited for Candace and Andrew at the airport that night around midnight with childish excitement.

Many hugs later, they were entranced by the palm trees, the warm night air and the high pinkish-brown ramparts of the city. Djemaa El Fna was closed to traffic so the taxi dropped us quite some distance away from the house, but they had travelled light, and the long walk through the darkened square and empty derbs heightened their anticipation. Unphased by grim reapers and scuffling cats, they were thrilled by every step of the route, and gasped satisfactorily on entering the house. For the first time I felt unqualified pride, and rushed about like a three-year-old at Christmas, pointing out the niceties of the *tadelakt*, the glories of the tilework, the seductive charm of the tent. Not to mention the dates and rose-scented milk Khaled had left as a welcome, and the plethora of deliciously complex salty sweet dishes Latifa had concocted to meet my request for a simple salad to revive the careworn travellers.

Andrew, as always, had brought some wonderful music, and it was to a soothingly sepulchral Johnny Cash lullaby that we fell into our beds.

My complacency was slightly dented the following morning by a visit to Rebecca's divine riad across the derb. It was a complete work of art, designed with such sophistication, attention to detail and ingenuity that for a moment ours seemed like the amateurish work of infant finger paints. Rebecca's colour scheme was subtle and harmonious, everything perfectly matching and toning. Carpets, balustrades, light fittings, vast wooden beds with arched bedheads, sumptuous throws in deep aubergine and black, curvaceous sculptural *tadelakt* baths, fireplaces, wrought-iron shelves, culminating in a vast romantic terrace where every self-indulgent whim was catered for – it was an astonishing achievement. Somehow one knew that everything would work, and at dusk it would be as gorgeous as an Arabian Nights dream. Rebecca admitted that, yes, to get everything so perfect had required a great deal of energy, she had thought of nothing else for an entire year and had lived on site without the comforting company of her husband for four months, exercising exacting quality control over every tiny detail.

'Sometimes I was so tired and lonely that I would just sit 'ere and weep.'

I offered to introduce her to Carl in the hope that someone somewhere would want to do justice to the perfectionist riad in a glossy feature.

My private consolation was that if I lived in a house of such grandeur, I would feel like the mistake – the chipped *tadelakt* or the stained tile. Perhaps, I hoped wanly, our dolly-mixture exuberance was more relaxing, more homely. And we did, after all, charge our non-existent visitors per week more or less what she charged per night. On the other hand, she deserved every dirham.

We plodded back across the derb in a state of advanced disgruntlement, so to cheer ourselves I suggested doing the full tourist thing and taking a calèche to the Majorelle Gardens. We skipped out to the square, found a man whose horses were glossy and well fed, and whose bright-green carriage sported rather fetching brocade upholstery and plastic-flower garlands, and scrambled in. Once you get used to the idea of ambling through the eye of the motor hurricane in a vehicle both slow and vulnerable, once you reconcile yourself to a short life and stop worrying, this becomes a pleasant way to travel, especially away from the busy epicentre, where the roads are quiet, flanked by high whispering trees and bordered by 1930s villas with lush gardens. The whole of Marrakech is a garden city.

Yves St Laurent took over the painter Jacques Majorelle's garden with Pierre Bergé after Majorelle's death in 1962 and filled it with colour. There is a kaleidoscope fountain of *zellig fessi*, cool pergola'd walks are thatched with pink bignonia and punctuated by scarlet hibiscus, bold architectural cacti and succulents grow from Ali Baba pots painted powder blue, turquoise and yellow, the winding concrete paths are cinnabar red with a lattice of black shadow. Shaded tanks of water – painted vibrant cobalt like all the constructions – overgrown with dramatic *monstera deliciosa* reflect patches of forget-me-not-blue sky. Rainbows arc from assiduous sprinklers at the corners of ponds, whose water drops rattle on to lily leaves. Here, in contrast to the enclosed courtyards of the city, there is a wonderful feeling of space, with woodpigeons cooing among the palms, whispering thickets of huge striped bamboos, and always the sound of water. There are beds of mammoth cacti sitting among stones looking like things at the bottom of the sea, and succulents in chic metal colours – bronze, verdigris, iron oxide and pewter.

And, if this were not magic enough, there is a little museum, filled with a magpie collection of beautiful bits – clothes, jewels, intricate carpets, carved doors and furniture of the nomads, rich with symbols and arcane details. Practical and lovely things made by the workmen of the Sahara from a repertoire of leather, goats' hair, wood, metal and vegetable fibres. We sat for a delicious moment on a bench in the dense shade of a fiddle-leafed fig, and sighed happily at the way this strange, sophisticated garden seemed to soothe and refresh, calming all the petty frets caused by the demanding city. Then we trotted home through the leafy grandeur of the Hivernage, entering the old city at Bab Jdid, where palm trees were silhouetted against the snow-topped mountains.

Khaled had chosen El Baraka restaurant for us that evening, for its quality and authenticity. Candace was a picture in shocking pink and plastic, Andrew had managed to find a purple silk shirt whose sleeves were several inches too short and whose front sported a great rip, Dan was as full sailed as a quinquereme in his djellaba and I was looking distinctly odd in a dark-red Indian salwar kameez appliquéd with black blobs. We scurried across Djemaa El Fna where, in addition to the usual dramas – drummers, story-tellers, ostrich-egg vendors, snakes, monkeys, curls of smoke rising from the food stalls – an airy metal dome was being erected for a circus, with great tightrope wires stretched away over the crowd to the post office, the bank and the police station.

We were greeted at the restaurant by a phalanx of figures in long black hooded robes, bearing flaming brands. Most were in Nike footwear; one or two tenderly placed their glowing cigarettes in the crevices of a palm trunk while they did their brandishing.

Having negotiated the entrance we found ourselves in a grand riad whose broad courtyard was filled with plants and rich with ornamentation. We were easily outnumbered by the waiters, a situation that always makes me nervous; however, we bravely requested a table in the garden, and sat expectantly among the frangipani. The excellent first course was enlivened by a short, dumpy middle-aged woman, clad in multiple spangles with a fringed belt of beads that whirled like water droplets around her solid hips, balancing a tray of glasses and lit candles upon her head. She gyrated in such a manner as to reassure large-hipped women that they have something pretty damned special, while the candles burned and the glasses did not flinch. Maybe Blu-Tak was a secret element in the choreography.

Her saucy roving eye clocked Dan, and before the candles burned much further she grabbed him by both hands and compelled him to gyrate with her, which he did, looking like an ungainly flapping heron thanks to his voluminous djellaba. She then invited Andrew to join in, and the three of them plodded solemnly in a slow motion ring-a-roses, the men curiously stately and the candle dancer exuding musky motherliness.

The chaps' feathers had barely settled after this excitement, they had hardly finished their tagines, when two gob-stoppingly gorgeous women sashayed past our table, wearing six-inch spikes and sprayed-on jeans, swinging their long black hair and making Dan quite forget what he'd been going to say.

The very polite waiter in the grey suit bent over to us with his hands clasped behind his back. 'Those are the belly dancers. They are going to dance in the tent – perhaps you would like to take your coffee there?'

Curiously Candace and I were more interested than the men, who watched for a minute and then wandered off. But we stayed, mesmerized by the fluidity of the women's bodies, and the eroticism of the dance blended with its curious innocence. Green Sequins had large, mostly exposed bosoms that got a good shaking, and I decided that she was just in it for the money. Red Sequins definitely lost the battle of the bosoms, but danced with a beautiful smile and a touch of unhinged passion that kept me transfixed. There was a pattern – the girls danced alone to start with, and then each drew some protesting, blushing man from the audience to accompany her in a dance that was more athletic than sexual. When the blokes lumbered back to their seats, sweating and mightily relieved, the dancers picked a couple of women with whom they danced in a far more overtly saucy way. At this point, maybe out of a sense of self-preservation, Candace and I joined the men and we all went home.

Candace and Andrew trawled the glories of the souk for the few days of their stay, and we wandered the empty roofless halls of the once incomparable El-Badi palace, plundered by Ismael the Blood-thirsty, where delicate ghosts of fine *zellig fessi* on the floor attested to the glories of the 360 rooms long gone, and where the only other visitors that day were the storks stomping about the walls from one high-stacked nest to another, clattering their beaks. To build it, Al Mansour the Golden had used gold from Guinea, onyx from France, Irish granite, precious stones, ivory from Africa and India, as well as the Carrara marble swapped for sugar. The Heliotrope Room, where his favourite black concubine would hang out, appeared to have been restored but was locked.

Frustrated by this glorious ruin, we visited the Bahia palace in the medina, whose great empty courtyards retained their *zellig fessi* and their *jibs* frieze, and whose rooms had their original cedar ceilings plus a few tiny fireplaces for those long cold winters. The old Grand Vizier Ba Ahmed Ben Moussa built it at the end of the nineteenth century for his four wives, twenty-four concubines and swarms of children. His favourite concubine had a pretty desirable private apartment, but the best things were the gardens, cool and shaded by tall spreading trees, and at twilight a deafening cacophony of roosting birds.

That night we ate at Riad Tamsna, where Candace's signature Schiaparelli pink made a startling contrast to the prevalent cool beige. Throwing teetotal caution to the winds we sipped pina coladas and admired the breathtaking stylishness of it all – hundreds of candles revealed a grand interior with *blanc cassé* walls, low dark wood and metal furniture designed by the awesome owner Meryanne Loum-Martin, paintings, objets, and beautiful French people in tiny Prada garments. The food was one gorgeous sweet-sour ginger-spiked treat after another, culminating in a kif au chocolat that only Dan ordered but we all fell on like gannets – we had to order three more. No one could call it cheap, but we had everything, including a brilliant Moroccan Cabernet. In London they would not have let us through the door, but one wonderful thing about Marrakech is that scruffs can masquerade as toffs for an evening here and there, and still afford the fare home.

We had invited Khaled, Abdeltif and Layla to join us for a meal on Candace and Andrew's last evening; Carl was due to arrive later on. Latifa started cooking the previous morning, and spent a good solid eighteen hours chopping, steaming, frying and arranging, so there was enough food to satisfy a rugby team. Khaled cautioned us that we should not drink, since Layla – his sister and Abdeltif's wife – is a seriously religious woman, to whom the very sight of a glass of rioja is abhorrent. I have to admit that I was disappointed and muttered one or two rather uncharitable things along the lines of whose house was it anyway? But we had nicely chilled non-vintage Coke and plenty of water, and Layla gave me such a powerful hug (she had been one of Morocco's top women footballers until she married) that it fair knocked the whinge out of me.

To begin we had *harira*, a truly wonderful soup: thick, rich and irresistible. After three bowls of this we were confronted with the usual array of salads. Abdeltif muttered sotto voce, 'This is just the starter,' and the gluttons paused thoughtfully. Eight salads, each more delicious than the last. A small berg of couscous followed, embedded with lamb and vegetables and anointed with *smen*, which we tackled rather half-heartedly, groaning the while. The *smen* still smelled like a wet yak jacket, but mixed with couscous it tasted like mature parmesan. Finally our long-stemmed Coke glasses were taken away to return brimming with fruit salad.

Soon we'd eaten ourselves into a state of terminal torpor and the non-Muslims felt like stretching out in the tent with a glass of something other than Coke.

As if to a prearranged signal, Abdeltif and family rose, thanked us gravely and thoroughly, and having hugged and squeezed us like people of putty, they went home, inviting us to return for dinner with them a couple of days later. Five minutes after their departure, when we were happily sipping our wine and lounging to our bellies' content on the rugs, Carl stepped on to the roof looking like a Bollywood film star, and beaming from ear to ear. Hugs and kisses all round, everyone was thrilled to see him, and we toasted each other with an unreasonable number of glasses of wine to compensate for an evening of Coke. We talked fast and loud and long, competing with the songs of Natacha Atlas, Rachid Taha, Khaled and Jah Wobble's Invaders of the Heart to extract the last drop of excitement from the one evening when we would all be at the riad together.

* * *

The next day, after Candace and Andrew's much-regretted departure, Carl and I shopped – no more need be said. And then we had more fun. We started with drinks at Rebecca's, greedily eating the home-made crisps and bitter home-cured olives, lounging on soft sofas opposite the pool which reflected fifty shivering candles, the pink *tadelakt* walls freckled with light from delicate pierced-tin lanterns. As we sipped our wine, someone in six-inch spikes and studded jeans was seen to flit from the kitchen to the sitting-room, Madame Zakira following to supervise the placement of a large ghetto-blaster to the side of the glowing swimming pool.

Rebecca smiled like Merlin's accomplice, and suddenly a blast of Arabic music ricocheted around the courtyard. Much fiddling with the CD player ensued, and after a particularly impassioned yodel, out stepped the Most Beautiful Woman in the World, barefoot, and clad in as many sequins and wafty bits as could be attached to a pair of very tiny garments. She was an unqualified stunner. Tall, slender, with long black hair and enormous dark eyes, she moved like mercury, with liquid, floating undulations, her eyes almost permanently fixed on Carl.

Having completed a sinuous Arabic dance, she followed with a Bollywood spectacular, singing along to the words and miming the inevitable plot of love frustrated but in the end triumphant.

Caught in the beam of her sultry megawatt gaze, Carl was becoming ever more silent. Depressed, one might have thought. Rarely have I seen such despair as when the Most Beautiful Woman in the World indicated that he should get up off the cushions and dance with her. Carl is shy, not a dancer, and immune to the lures of seductive women. But he cannot but be polite, so, paralysed with embarrassment, he complied, shifting his body maybe one centimetre to the right, and then another to the left, wafting his hands around like a pair of unexpected bedroom slippers. He had all the grace and fluency of a Meccano man, and had to do the full errant-daughter, indignant-father, passionate-paramour scenario, which went on for quite a while. Finally, to everyone's relief, he was allowed to resume his protected roost among the cushions while the dancer changed for her grand finale.

She re-emerged in white high heels and tight pale-blue jeans with many applied spangly bits to do a disco-diva version of a song by Shakira. She was still a beauty, but there was something inescapably chav about the costume, the choice of music and the stomp and shake. It was a bit of a disillusionment.

I have to make an admission here – Marrakech is extremely foreign to me, and while that has its charm, I occasionally long for a bit of cosmopolitan

sophistication, for candlelight, wine and calendered napery. And Khaled had found us the very place for dinner that night, called the Fondouk: we could have been in London, New York or Paris. The architecture was slick, food cheeky modern, the place awash with what looked like members of an angry Liverpudlian pop group, the men wearing tea-cosy hats, and we did not feel like pariahs for drinking wine. Bliss. Pathetic, I know, but it was so comforting momentarily to feel familiar with the rules, not to worry lest we inadvertently cause some terrible infringement. The charm of Marrakech lies, of course, in its foreignness, but a touch of comforting familiarity can add enchantment to the view. Anyway, we had a great dinner (including my pretentious favourite, that old rocket and parmesan salad) and found our way home without mishap.

Home. I realized that at last I could use the word and not shiver with apprehension. I did not have to touch wood fearing baroque and unpredictable dramas. The riad was peaceful, beautiful, welcoming, and Khaled had lit constellations of candles to greet our return, whose reflections flickered prettily on the smooth *tadelakt*. We sat on the roof looking at the stars, and for the first time, sitting there with my wonderful Mr Dan, the place radiated a sense of benediction.

At last, that evening, I knew that thanks to Khaled's devoted care I could with confidence encourage my good photographer friend to let loose with his Nikon, could allow the riad to appear in the guides, could recommend it wholeheartedly as a place to soothe away the troubles of work and getting by. For the first time I did not wince when people asked me what our house and Marrakech were like, knowing at last that whatever adventures they might have there, they would be benignly life-changing.

GLOSSARY

These are all phonetic, and you will find hundreds of spelling variations for each word.

Riad: Largish house around a garden, which can just be a couple of trees in pots though a Koranic paradise garden should have a fountain – the source of life – at its heart, shaded by bird-filled trees and surrounded by four parterres overflowing with frangipani and jasmine, surrounded by high walls.
Dar: Small house with a courtyard.
B'hou: Large shady alcove overlooking the garden.
Doueria: Self-contained separate granny flat, overlooking the courtyard.
Pise: Reinforced packed mud – the building

material that gives Marrakech its characteristic colour.

Bab: Gate.

Hammam: Bathhouse, sometimes communal.

Muqarna: Moorish ceiling decoration like carved plaster stalactites.

Tadelakt: Waterproof surface, traditionally used for the walls and horizontals of hammams and now used by beady-eyed decorators everywhere. It is made of marble dust mixed with pigment and buffed by hand with olive-oil soap and a smooth stone to a polished, subtly coloured marble-like finish.

Jibs frieze: Five-inch-wide bands of decorative carved plaster following traditional designs as complex as Fair Isle knitting, used to outline doors and windows. The design is drawn straight on to the wall with carbon paper and a template.

Mizmat: Floor surface made of small cut tiles, natural terracotta banded and patterned with glazed tiles, usually from Fez.

Zellig fessi: Similar to Mizmat but finer, using postage-stamp-sized pieces cut from six-inch tiles arranged in intricate patterns and used for pillar bases, walls, table tops, window sills, etc. Astonishing skill and wastage. All these amazing ancient techniques are to do with a passion to pattern and a prohibition against naturalism. *Fessi* because the brilliant glazed tiles come from Fez.

There are around 360 different traditional shapes cut to make infinite permutations of kaleidoscope designs.

Tazouakt: Carved and painted wood in the Berber style.

Mousharabi: Perforated wooden lattice screens made from turned bobbins, used to protect women from being seen, while giving them a tantalizing glimpse of the world outside.

Marakchi: Someone from Marrakech.

Amazigh: 'Free men'. What the Berbers prefer to be called, rather than 'Barbarian'.

Marabout: Holy man or saint.

Muezzin: Mosque official who intones the *idhan* – call to prayer – five times daily.

Gnawa: Musicians descended from slaves taken from the Sudan.

Sidi: Saint or person of high rank, occasionally used with irony.

Moulay: Title of honour.

Qadi: Judge.

Hijab: Headscarf worn by devout Muslim women.

Haik: Cloak.

Kameez: Fine cotton tunic worn with trousers, like the Indian Salwar Kameez.

Carrossa: Two-wheeled metal cart usually pulled by a very old man, though occasionally by a donkey.

Smen: Rancid butter used in Moroccan cooking; an acquired taste for visitors.

Djellaba: Long-sleeved, floor-length, hooded cover-all for men.

Kaftan: Lightweight and coloured or striped version of the above without hood.

Gandora: Sleeveless summer version of the same.

Babouches: Soft pointed slippers, usually bright yellow, easy to remove when entering a room.

Baraka: Blessings.

Baksheesh: Politely, a tip, otherwise a bribe.

Souk: Market, usually out of doors.

Kissaria: Covered market.

Bled: Countryside.

Derb: Street.

Medina: The old town, the heart of the city.

Mellah: The Jewish quarter.

Bismillah: Said before eating; means 'in the name of God'.

Hamdullah: 'Thanks be to God', in gratitude for anything good.

In sha'allah: 'If God wills.' Opinion is divided as to whether this ties the participants into an agreement or lets them off the hook altogether.

La: 'No.'

Nam: 'Yes.'

Salaam alaikum: 'Peace on you. Hello.'

La bas: A greeting meaning 'no harm', to which the polite response is just to say it back.

Bislemah: 'Goodbye.'

GLOSSARY

Shukran: 'Thank-you.'
Wakha: 'OK.'
Meckee mushkeel: 'No problem.'
Shoof, shoof: 'I'm just looking.'
Ismee Miranda: 'My name is Miranda.'
Metsharfin: 'Pleased to meet you.'
Zween: 'Pretty.'
Bzaf: 'Many, a lot, very, too much.'
Shwia: 'Few, a little.'

FURTHER READING

Culture Shock: A Guide to Customs and Etiquette, Orin Hargreaves, Kuperard, 2003. Essential reading for anyone going to stay in Morocco for longer than two days, and who would like to understand rather then skim the surface.

Marrakech, Justin McGuinness, Footprint Handbooks, 2003.

Marrakesh, Everyman CityMap Guides, 2003.

Marrakech and the Best of Morocco, Andrew Humphreys, Time Out Penguin Books, 2003. The best and brightest of the guidebooks.

Marrakech, Michelin Travel Publications, 2002.

Things Seen in Morocco, L. E. Bickerstaffe, Seeley, Service & Co. Ltd, 1929.

Marrakech, the Red City, edited by Barnaby Rogerson and Stephen Lavington, Sickle Moon Books, 2003. The city through writers' eyes.

Morocco That Was, Walter Harris, Eland, reissued 2002.

Majorelle: A Moroccan Oasis, Pierre Bergé and Madison Cox, Thames and Hudson.

The Voices of Marrakesh, Elias Canetti, Marion Boyars Publishers Ltd, reprinted 2003.

Eat Smart in Morocco, Joan Peterson, Ginkgo Press, Inc., 2002.

The Golden Book of Marrakesh, Ennio Macconi, Casa Editrice Bonechi.

The Golden Book of Morocco, team work, Casa Editrice Bonechi.

The Koran, translated by N. J. Dawood, Penguin Books, 2003.

Introducing Islam, Ziauddin Sardar and Zafar Abbas Malik, Icon Books, 2001.

Islam for Dummies, Malcolm Clark, Wiley Publishing, 2003.

Arabic Verbs and Essentials of Grammar, Jane Wightwick and Mahmoud Gaafar, Passport Books, 1998.

ACKNOWLEDGEMENTS

I would like to thank Maggie, without whose enthusiasm we would never have embarked on this adventure. Also Noureddine, who is unquestionably the most important person in Morocco as far as we are concerned, and every one of the twenty-six craftsmen who made Riad Maizie into an extraordinary work of art. I have to mention Illiass the demon fixer and thank Khadija for being kindness personified. Thank you to Araminta, my agent, and to Selina at Transworld, who has continued to grapple serenely with my irredeemable beastliness to fashion something more silk-purse-like from a bristling manuscript.

GETTING TO MAÑANA
Miranda Innes

'AN INSPIRING READ'
Glasgow Herald

In January 1997 Miranda Innes's life did an
unexpected somersault.

Tired of London, becalmed in her career, disenchanted
with her long-standing partner, she decided that she
wanted to start afresh. She took her younger son to
Andalucia, found a romantic ruin and fell in love with
it. She made an offer – all that remained to do was
sell her London home, rearrange her work and slip
away to the sun.

But she had not anticipated either the appearance of
a new man in her life, nor the struggle involved
in rebuilding a house and creating a garden in the
hostile terrain of southern Spain – even with
the kindly guidance of Juan, their builder, and an
array of local eccentrics.

'A TRUE LOVE STORY, AND A WHOLLY ENJOYABLE
ACCOUNT OF A LIFE CHANGING MOVE FROM
ENGLAND TO ANDALUCIA'
Joanna Lumley

'A TERRIFIC READ, LYRICALLY DESCRIPTIVE AND
DOWN TO EARTH'
Choice

'A BEAUTIFUL BOOK, A TREAT IN STORE'
Susan Hampshire

0 552 77098 1

BLACK SWAN